D0933845

L. H. M. Ling
POSTCOLONIAL INTERNATIONAL RELATIONS
Conquest and Desire between Asia and the West

Pierre P. Lizée
PEACE, POWER AND RESISTANCE IN CAMBODIA
Global Governance and the Failure of International Conflict Resolution

S. Javed Maswood
JAPAN IN CRISIS

Ananya Mukherjee Reed
PERSPECTIVES ON THE INDIAN CORPORATE ECONOMY
Exploring the Paradox of Profits
CORPORATE CAPITALISM IN CONTEMPORARY SOUTH ASIA (*editor*)
Conventional Wisdoms and South Asian Realities

Cecilia Ng
POSITIONING WOMEN IN MALAYSIA
Class and Gender in an Industrializing State

Fahimul Quadir and Jayant Lele (*editors*)
DEMOCRACY AND CIVIL SOCIETY IN ASIA: VOLUME 1
Globalization, Democracy and Civil Society in Asia
DEMOCRACY AND CIVIL SOCIETY IN ASIA: VOLUME 2
Democratic Transitions and Social Movements in Asia

Ian Scott (*editor*)
INSTITUTIONAL CHANGE AND THE POLITICAL TRANSITION IN HONG KONG

Mark Turner (*editor*)
CENTRAL–LOCAL RELATIONS IN ASIA–PACIFIC
Convergence or Divergence?

Ritu Vij
JAPANESE MODERNITY AND WELFARE
State, Civil Society and Self in Contemporary Japan

Fei-Ling Wang
INSTITUTIONS AND INSTITUTIONAL CHANGE IN CHINA
Premodernity and Modernization

International Political Economy Series
Series Standing Order ISBN 0–333–71708–2 hardcover
Series Standing Order ISBN 0–333–71110–6 paperback
(*outside North America only*)

You can receive future titles in this series as they are published by placing a standing order. Please contact your bookseller or, in case of difficulty, write to us at the address below with your name and address, the title of the series and one of the ISBNs quoted above.

Customer Services Department, Macmillan Distribution Ltd, Houndmills, Basingstoke, Hampshire RG21 6XS, England

The Political Economy of East Asia

Regional and National Dimensions

Kevin G. Cai

Associate Professor, Director of East Asian Studies, Renison College, University of Waterloo

© Kevin G. Cai 2008

All rights reserved. No reproduction, copy or transmission of this
publication may be made without written permission.

No paragraph of this publication may be reproduced, copied or transmitted
save with written permission or in accordance with the provisions of the
Copyright, Designs and Patents Act 1988, or under the terms of any licence
permitting limited copying issued by the Copyright Licensing Agency,
90 Tottenham Court Road, London W1T 4LP.

Any person who does any unauthorized act in relation to this publication
may be liable to criminal prosecution and civil claims for damages.

The author has asserted his right to be identified
as the author of this work in accordance with the Copyright,
Designs and Patents Act 1988.

First published 2008 by
PALGRAVE MACMILLAN
Houndmills, Basingstoke, Hampshire RG21 6XS and
175 Fifth Avenue, New York, N.Y. 10010
Companies and representatives throughout the world

PALGRAVE MACMILLAN is the global academic imprint of the Palgrave
Macmillan division of St. Martin's Press, LLC and of Palgrave Macmillan Ltd.
Macmillan® is a registered trademark in the United States, United Kingdom
and other countries. Palgrave is a registered trademark in the European
Union and other countries.

ISBN-13: 978–0–230–20589–5 hardback
ISBN-10: 0–230–20589–5 hardback

This book is printed on paper suitable for recycling and made from fully
managed and sustained forest sources. Logging, pulping and manufacturing
processes are expected to conform to the environmental regulations of the
country of origin.

A catalogue record for this book is available from the British Library.

Library of Congress Cataloging-in-Publication Data
Cai, Kevin G., 1956–
    The political economy of East Asia : regional and national
    dimensions / Kevin G. Cai.
        p.   cm. — (International political economy)
    Includes bibliographical references and index.
    ISBN 0–230–20589–5 (alk. paper)
    1. East Asia—Economic conditions.   I. Title.
    HC460.5.C24 2008
    330.95—dc22   2008015866

10   9   8   7   6   5   4   3   2   1
17   16   15   14   13   12   11   10   09   08

Printed and bound in Great Britain by
CPI Antony Rowe, Chippenham and Eastbourne

For my parents, wife and son

Contents

List of Figure and Tables

Figure

Tables

Abbreviations

ADB	Asian Development Bank
AMF	Asian Monetary Fund
APEC	Asia-Pacific Economic Cooperation
APO	ASEAN Plus One
APROC	Asia-Pacific Regional Operations Center (Taiwan)
APT	ASEAN Plus Three
ASEAN	Association of Southeast Asian Nations
ASEM	Asia–Europe Meeting
BIS	Bank for International Settlements
CCP	Chinese Communist Party
CEFP	Council on Economic and Fiscal Policy (Japan)
CEPA	(China-Hong Kong) Closer Economic Partnership Arrangement
CEPD	Council for Economic Planning and Development (Taiwan)
CETRA	China External Trade Development Council (Taiwan)
CIECD	Council for International Economic Cooperation and Development (Taiwan)
CITC	Committee of International Technical Cooperation (Taiwan)
CNOOC	China National Offshore Oil Corporation (China)
DAC	Development Assistance Committee
EAEG	East Asian Economic Group
EASG	East Asian Study Group (APT)
EAVG	East Asian Vision Group (APT)
EC	European Community
EEC	European Economic Community
EFTA	European Free Trade Association
EPA	Economic Planning Agency (Japan)
EPB	Economic Planning Board (South Korea)
EPC	Economic Planning Council (Taiwan)
EPZ	Export-processing zone (Taiwan)
EROA	Economic Recovery in Occupied Areas
ERSO	Electronic Research and Service Organization (Taiwan)
EU	European Union
FDI	Foreign direct investment

FKI	Federation of Korean Industries (South Korea)
FTA	Free trade agreement
GATT	General Agreement on Tariffs and Trade
GDP	Gross domestic product
GNP	Gross national product
GSP	Generalized system of preferences
ICDF	International Cooperation and Development Fund (Taiwan)
IECDF	International Economic Cooperation Development Fund (Taiwan)
IMF	International Monetary Fund
ITRI	Industrial Technology Research Institute (Taiwan)
JCIPO	Japan–China Investment Promotion Organization
JCRR	(US–Taiwan) Joint Commission for Rural Reconstruction
JETRO	Japan External Trade Organization
KDI	Korea Development Institute (South Korea)
KIST	Korean Institute of Science and Technology (South Korea)
KITA	Korea International Trade Association (South Korea)
LDP	Liberal Democratic Party (Japan)
MAC	Mainland Affairs Council (Taiwan)
METI	Ministry of Economy, Trade and Industry (Japan)
MFN	Most-favored-nation
MITI	Ministry of International Trade and Industry (Japan)
MOEA	Ministry of Economic Affairs (Taiwan)
NAFTA	North American Free Trade Agreement
NIE	Newly industrializing economy
NPL	Nonperforming loan
NSC	National Security Council (US)
ODA	Official development assistance
ODM	Original design manufacture
OECD	Organization for Economic Cooperation and Development
PBEC	Pacific Basin Economic Council
PECC	Pacific Economic Cooperation Council
PPP	Purchasing-power-parity
R&D	Research and development
SCAP	Supreme Commander of the Allied Powers
SEATO	Southeast Asian Treaty Organization
SEZ	Special economic zone (China)
SMEs	Small- and medium-sized enterprises

TNCs	Transnational corporations
TRA	Taiwan Relations Act (US)
UN	United Nations
UNCTAD	United Nations Conference on Trade and Development
VER	Voluntary export restraint
WTO	World Trade Organization

Acknowledgement

The author would like to thank OECD Publishing for their kindly helping update the statistical data on Japan's ODA used in this book. Thanks are also given to the Department of Overall Planning, Council for Economic Planning and Development of Taiwan for allowing me to directly cite their statistical data free.

1
Introduction

This work is a systematic study of the political economy of East Asia. A central theme that runs throughout the book is that the political economy of East Asia has been consistently defined by the interactions of regional and national dynamics, and in this process Japan has been playing a pivotal role in not only organizing the regional economy around the Japanese economic power but also influencing the development path of national economies in the region through its developmental state structure. In the post-World War II years, the political economy of East Asia was substantially defined by Cold War politics and American hegemony. Since the 1980s, however, there has also been a rising influence of the Chinese power on the political economy of East Asia. As a result, the regional political economy is now jointly influenced by American, Japanese, Chinese, and other national powers, and the region is moving toward increasing economic integration in the early 21st century.

The subject is important primarily because the rise of East Asia is probably one of the most phenomenal events in the global political economy in the postwar years, an event that has had substantial impact on global politics and economics over the past several decades and will likely continue to influence the trajectory of global politics and economics in the coming decades.

Indeed, over the past five decades East Asia has witnessed sustained fast economic growth that has no parallel in world history. Actually, the rapid economic growth of East Asian economies has experienced three major waves since the 1950s. From the 1950s through the 1980s, Japan represented the first wave with its quick recovery from the devastation of World War II and subsequent high economic growth rate. Then, during the 1970s–90s, South Korea, Taiwan, Hong Kong, and Singapore experienced a second wave of rapid economic growth in the region. Since the 1980s,

1

China, together with the Southeast Asian nations of Vietnam, Malaysia, Thailand, and Indonesia, has been bringing a third wave of rapid economic growth in the region. More importantly, the rapid economic growth in East Asia over the past five decades has been accompanied by a process of steady transformation of the traditional economic structure of agriculture-oriented economy to that of industrial economy. Currently, Japan, South Korea, Taiwan, and Hong Kong are moving toward a post-industrial economic structure in which high-tech and services are becoming the most important economic sectors, while China is rapidly industrializing. Even though the East Asian economies have achieved sustained rapid growth, they have kept inflation low. Consequently, there has been a steady reduction in poverty, a continuous increase in real wages, and steady improvement in living standards. As a result of these remarkable achievements, frequently dubbed "the Asian miracle," East Asia has been accumulating increasing wealth and economic power and has moved from the "periphery" of the capitalist world economy toward its "core," creating a new center of the world economy alongside the two existing centers of North America and Western Europe. In this process, Japan has obtained an economic superpower status, second only to the United States, while South Korea, Taiwan, Hong Kong, and Singapore have become newly industrializing economies (NIEs). More recently, with its rapid economic growth since the 1980s as a result of the economic reform, China is emerging as a new economic power, exerting an ever-growing influence on the global political economy. The rise of East Asia in the world economy has fundamentally transformed the global balance of economic power and has led many politicians and scholars even to claim that the 21st century will be a Pacific century.

This study covers four major East Asian economies that are central to this subject, namely Japan, South Korea, Taiwan, and China. Where relevant, the discussion also involves Hong Kong. More importantly, these economies under discussion share some most significant attributes that group them into an international region. According to Bruce Russett, an international region may be defined by a set of criteria, either individually or collectively. These criteria include the following: (1) social and cultural homogeneity, that is, a region is composed of states that are similar with respect to several kinds of internal attributes; (2) similar political attitudes or external behavior that are shared by the states in a region; (3) political interdependence, that is, the countries in a region are joined together by a network of supranational or intergovernmental political institutions; (4) economic interdependence, as identified by intraregional trade as a proportion of the country's national income;

and (5) geographical proximity.[1] According to these criteria defined by Russett, the economies studied in this book are grouped as a region by at least three of the above five conditions, that is social and cultural homogeneity, economic interdependence, and geographical proximity. Although political interdependence as defined by Russett is nonexistent in East Asia today, common interests in maintaining a region-wide stable political environment do exist among the states in the region. Added to these conditions is regional consciousness and mutual identification of the populace in East Asia. Furthermore, it is also important to point out that certain features of state–society relations are unique to the East Asian region. Indeed, these shared attributes of East Asian states clearly distinguish them from other international regions.

As a matter of fact, the use of the geographical term "East Asia" is quite confusing in the existing literature. In various documents of the United Nations, "East Asia" is seen as an area that consists of China, Japan, the Korean peninsula, and Mongolia. For John Fairbank *et al.*, "East Asia" refers to "the Chinese culture area," which involves China, Korea, Japan, and Vietnam.[2] For many other scholars, especially those of social sciences, however, what is identified as "East Asia" by the United Nations is called "Northeast Asia." So according to these scholars, "East Asia" actually consists of two sub-regions: "Northeast Asia" and "Southeast Asia." "Northeast Asia" is comprised of China, Japan, the Korean peninsula, Mongolia, Taiwan, and Hong Kong (as part of Greater China), whereas "Southeast Asia" refers to the area from Vietnam down to Indonesia, which today involves all the ten members of the Association of Southeast Asian Nations (ASEAN). The concept of "East Asia" used in this book may be identified by some scholars as "Northeast Asia."[3]

The origin of the modern political economy of East Asia was associated with the rise of the Japanese imperialist power in the late 19th century and its subsequent empire-building in the Far East. In the course of imperialist expansion, Japan first grabbed Taiwan in 1895 and then annexed Korea in 1910 and absorbed these two colonies into the Japanese empire in the subsequent years. In building this empire, Japan developed Taiwan and Korea first into its agricultural appendages and markets and later into industrial supporting bases that manufactured some labor-intensive goods and provided raw materials and industrial supplies for the heavy industry on the home islands of Japan. Moreover, Japan's imperial policy was designed not only to incorporate but also to assimilate these two colonies politically, economically, culturally, and socially into the Japanese empire. This colonial policy of Japan, together with the influence of the Japanese political economy, had substantial impact not only on the economic development of both Taiwan and Korea, but also on the regional political economy of East Asia in the first half of the 20th century and beyond.

In the post-World War II years, the political economy of East Asia was dramatically transformed by a completely new global setting of the Cold War and US hegemony.[4] Because of the strategic needs of Cold War politics against communist threat in the Far East, Washington adopted an Asia policy that substantially influenced the trajectory of the East Asian political economy in the postwar years. Through a series of security arrangements, huge economic and military aid to its protégés, the opening of its huge market to its allies, and other supportive measures, the United States not only provided the crucial external environment for the rapid economic development of East Asian capitalist economies, but also had the regional economies grouped once again around Japan.

It is within such a favorable external environment provided by the US hegemony in the context of the Cold War that the capitalist countries of East Asia have taken a unique capitalist development path, dubbed the "Asian model," a development approach that is very different from that of developed countries in the West. Particularly, the political economy of East Asia is characterized by a strong development-oriented state that is actively involved in economic development and that deliberately pursues an export-driven economic growth strategy. This model was first developed by Japan, and then followed by South Korea and Taiwan, although the degree and mechanism of state involvement varies among these economies due to different national conditions. In general, the capitalist states in East Asia provided administrative guidance for economic development, adopted an industrial policy of channeling resources into desired sectors, protected domestic newly emerging industries from foreign competition, and provided subsidies and assistance for leading companies. Moreover, in pursuing economic development, the East Asian states also promoted technology imports, adopted a high domestic saving and investment policy, maintained strong connection and cooperation with the business community, and emphasized the importance of education and equitable distribution of income. Consequently, this unique development model, supported by the favorable postwar international setting, led to the economic miracles first in Japan and later in South Korea and Taiwan.

By the end of the 1960s, the global political and economic environment had undergone a major transformation as a result of the breakup of the Sino-Soviet alliance, the relative decline of US hegemonic power, and the rise of Japan and Western Europe in the world economy. In the course of the 1970s–80s, Cold War politics was gradually weakening and eventually came to an end following the collapse of communist regimes in Eastern Europe at the end of the 1980s and the disintegration of the Soviet Union in the early 1990s. In the meantime, South Korea and Taiwan were rapidly industrializing. Consequently, Japan, followed by South Korea and Taiwan, evolved from being political, economic, and military dependents of the United States in the early postwar years to effective economic rivals from the 1970s onwards. As a result, US relations with its allies in East Asia were increasingly troubled by disputes over economic issues.

The political economy of communist China has taken a very different path from that of Japan, South Korea, and Taiwan since the founding of the People's Republic in 1949. During Mao's era, China adopted a socialist approach to development that was based on the orthodox Stalinist model of command economy. Under this development model, while private ownership of the means of production was effectively transformed into public ownership, the Chinese state controlled almost all economic activities and ran the economy through central planning and administrative directives with the role of market minimized. In the meantime, Mao's China effectively isolated itself from the capitalist world economy through a self-reliance policy. While the adoption of the Soviet model of economic development seemed politically, ideologically, and economically logical for a new communist state created in a hostile world of the Cold War in the late 1940s and early 1950s, it became increasingly clear over time that this development approach was highly inefficient. As a result, the post-Mao Chinese leadership initiated economic reform in the late 1970s, moving away from the socialist command economy to embrace the capitalist market economy. Through three decades of reform, the Chinese economic system has been substantially transformed from the previous command economy of Mao's era into a rudimentary market economy, which in many ways is quite similar to the type of capitalism in other East Asian economies. While the reform is still in process, its final objective, according to the Chinese communist leadership, is to establish a so-called "socialist market economy," in which market forces play a decisive role in guiding economic activities while at the same time the state undertakes macroguidance of the economy through purely economic measures. As a result of this economic reform, China has achieved remarkable and sustained rapid economic growth over the past three decades and is now emerging as an economic superpower.

It is in the context of the transformed international setting and the rise of East Asia in the world economy that, since the mid-1980s, there has been increasing economic ties and deepening economic interdependence among East Asian economies characterized by rising intraregional trade and investment flows, while on the other hand the importance of the United States both as a market and as a source of investment for East Asian economies has been declining. This process of growing regional economic integration in East Asia is the result of changing comparative advantages between economies in the region and is closely associated with economic restructuring in both capital-exporting and capital-importing economies. Through regionalization of manufacturing production, a network of division of labor and commodity chains has been established in East Asia. While Japanese multinational corporations are a central driving force behind this regional division of labor, East Asian NIEs (Hong Kong, Taiwan, and South Korea) are also promoting the process of regional integration through foreign direct investment (FDI) outflows. On the other hand, China is the primary recipient of FDI in the region. It is important to note that rapidly increasing economic ties in East Asia are primarily driven by market forces and far from institutionalized. Due to existing political constraints in the region, regional economic integration in East Asia falls short of a formal regional grouping similar to the European Union (EU) or the North American Free Trade Agreement (NAFTA). Despite the continuing existence of political constraints, however, the Asian financial crisis of 1997–98 has stimulated rethinking of the issue of institutionalized regional economic cooperation among political leaders, businesses, and academics in the region. Particularly significant, in the wake of the Asian financial crisis, the governments in the region seem to have taken concrete moves toward bilateral and regional free trade arrangements.

More significantly, while there has been accelerating globalization since the 1980s, there has also been concurrent rise of economic regionalism and protectionism in the world economy, exerting mounting pressure on East Asia – the only major region that has not yet been organized into an economic grouping of any form. Under such circumstances, East Asian governments have been searching for cross-Pacific economic cooperation in the framework of the Asia-Pacific Economic Cooperation (APEC) forum since the late 1980s. In the wake of the Asian financial crisis, East Asia has also moved toward institutionalized regional cooperation with Southeast Asia through the ASEAN Plus Three (APT) forum with an intention of eventually creating a regional grouping for all nations of East and Southeast Asia. Obviously, these moves on the part of East Asian governments will inevitably bring significant impact on the East Asian region and beyond.

To pursue the development of the East Asian political economy, this book is organized into the following chapters.

Chapter 2 explores the historical origin of the East Asian political economy. It argues that the regional political economy in East Asia was originally brought into being by imperialist Japan in its pursuing a Japanese empire in East Asia from the late 19th century through World War II. Japanese colonial policy not only substantially transformed the economy of Taiwan and Korea but also helped create a regional economic relationship that subordinated Taiwan and Korea to Japan through a pattern of vertical regional economic integration (which is referred to as the "flying-geese model" by many scholars) in East Asia with implications going far beyond the Japanese colonial era. In the meantime, the developmental state structure that was planted by the Japanese in their two colonies was in many ways inherited by the postcolonial South Korean and Taiwanese states, which substantially influenced the economic development of South Korea and Taiwan in the postwar years.

Chapter 3 provides an account of the external setting and domestic dynamics of the political economy in East Asia in the postwar years. The major argument of this chapter is that the postwar political economy of East Asia was substantially influenced and defined by the postwar external setting of the Cold War and US hegemony and their transformation, as well as by the region's internal dynamics in the form of the Asian model.

Chapters 4–6 apply the major themes developed in Chapters 2 and 3 to the analysis of the postwar political economy of Japan, South Korea, and Taiwan respectively. Organized in a similar fashion, these chapters start with a discussion of the influence of the Cold War and US hegemony on the evolution of the political economy in the three states, followed by a section that addresses the role of the state in national economic development in the postwar years. The three chapters then look at the economic development and rising economic power of the three states in Section 3 and their regional economic ties in Section 4. The last section discusses the recent economic performance and prospect for these three economies.

As a rising economic power, China is exerting increasing influence on the political economy of East Asia. Chapter 7 is devoted to the analysis of the Chinese political economy since 1949. However, as China under the communist rule has taken a very different path of economic development as compared with capitalist economies in the region, the chapter follows a different line of discussion. After a discussion of the command economy during Mao's era in 1949–76 in Section 7.1, Section 7.2 addresses the economic reform that has been pursued by post-Mao Chinese leadership since the late 1970s. Sections 7.3 and 7.4 look at the rising Chinese economic power and China's regional economic ties respectively. The last section addresses the problems and prospects of the Chinese economy in the 21st century. The major theme of the chapter is that China is increasingly becoming a driving force behind the political economy of East Asia.

Following the major themes developed in Chapters 2 and 3, Chapter 8 moves to examine the rising regional economic integration in East Asia over the past two decades. The chapter first provides an account of increasing regional economic ties in East Asia since the mid-1980s and then explains why the process of regional economic integration in East Asia differs from those in Western Europe and North America. This chapter also addresses the implications of the Asian financial crisis of 1997–98 on the regional institution-building in East Asia. The major argument of the chapter is that driven by market forces rather than government initiatives, regional integration in East Asia since the mid-1980s is primarily reflected in the rising flows of capital, goods, and people among regional economies but short of a formal regional grouping like EU or NAFTA.

The concluding chapter succinctly revisits the major theme developed in the book.

2
The Historical Origin of the East Asian Political Economy, 1895–1945

2.1 Introduction

The modern political economy of East Asia can be traced back to the rise of the Japanese imperialist power in the late 19th century and its subsequent building of a Japanese empire in the Far East. In the course of imperialist expansion, Japan annexed Taiwan and Korea and pursued a colonial policy that was designed to incorporate and assimilate these two colonies into the Japanese empire. This colonial policy of Japan not only substantially transformed the economy of Taiwan and Korea but also helped create a regional economic relationship that subordinated Taiwan and Korea to Japan through a pattern of vertical regional economic integration in East Asia with implications going far beyond the Japanese colonial era. In the meantime, the developmental state structure that was planted by the Japanese in their two colonies was in many ways inherited by the postcolonial South Korean and Taiwanese states, which substantially influenced the economic development of South Korea and Taiwan in the postwar years.

2.2 Japanese quest for a colonial empire in East Asia

In order to overcome humiliating diplomatic inferiority imposed by Western imperialist powers under the unequal treaty system, Japan, starting with the Meiji Restoration of 1868, was undergoing a process of modernization, which involved three major tasks: consolidation of military and political power at the center; establishment of economic self-sufficiency through the expansion and exploitation of an agricultural base; and the transformation of society through basic education and a variety of innovations in social engineering in order to develop new skills and attitudes among the people and to shape their loyalty and obedience to the new state.[1] As a result of these efforts, Japan had transformed from a weak, feudal, and agrarian country into a modern industrial power within a period of about three decades, economically and militarily capable of resisting foreign domination.

The achievements of Japan's modernization were most illustratively reflected in Japan's victories over China in the Sino-Japanese War of 1894–95 and over Russia in the Russo-Japanese War of 1904–05. Japan's victories of these two wars indicated that an economically underdeveloped and militarily vulnerable semi-feudal nation had been transformed into an imperial power. On the other hand, however, the victories of these two wars set Japan on a course of expansion and empire-building in East Asia. Japan forcefully annexed Taiwan from China in 1895 as a result defeating China in the Sino-Japanese War and then formally annexed Korea in 1910 following a decade and half of consolidation of its control over the peninsula.

The Japanese quest for a colonial empire in East Asia was supported by various domestic interest groups and clearly impelled by its economic concerns, notably, markets for surplus production and secure sources of raw materials.[2] In addition, a variety of noneconomic motives were also behind Tokyo's efforts to establish a Japanese empire in East Asia, including Japan's overriding concern for its insular security, a sense of mission to bring about development in Asia, a sense of excitement and adventure, a sense of pride and prestige, and expansion of living space.[3]

The industrialization of Japan was achieved primarily through the mobilization of agricultural resources of land and labor. The rural sector was therefore made to bear the financial burden of modernization during the initial stage of an emerging industrial sector in Japan. On the other hand, the rapid industrialization not only transformed the Japanese economic structure but also brought about a series of problems that inhibited continuing rapid industrialization. By the late 19th century and early 20th century, there had been changing economic conditions that confronted industrialized Japan. It was within this context that Japan attempted to establish a Japanese empire in East Asia and transform its two newly acquired major colonies, Taiwan and Korea, into an economic base that would support the continuing development of Japanese economy in the home islands.

On the other hand, compared to Western colonial powers, colonial Japan enjoyed many unique advantages in the development of its empire. The geographical proximity of Japan to its colonies provided Japan with lower transportation costs and more rapid communication between the imperial metropolis and the colonies. In the meantime, both Japanese and colonial peoples shared rice as a basic and traditional agricultural commodity. This made it possible for Japan to aim toward the integration of the colonial economies with that of Japan proper, in contrast to most tropical European colonies that could evolve only as export-oriented enclaves. The indigenous populations of Taiwan and Korea were also racially akin to their Japanese masters and shared with the Japanese a common cultural heritage of Confucianism and Buddhism. This sense of racial and cultural affinity with its subject peoples made Japan unique among the colonial powers of modern times and profoundly shaped Japanese attitudes toward colonial governance once the empire was established.[4] Moreover, unlike many Western colonial powers that created an artificial state entity out of a political vacuum in their colonies, Japan forcefully established their control over an ancient state and society with a long historical experience and high degree of racial, ethnic, cultural, and linguistic homogeneity. As a matter of fact, responding to external pressures, Korea and Taiwan under the rule of Qing dynasty had already started the process of transforming their traditional institutions. As a consequence, Japan's annexation of these two well-established societies disrupted the indigenous political movement to create a modern nation-state.

Like the European colonial powers, Japan pursued its colonial policy in its newly acquired territories for its own interest. Japan's empire-building underwent two major phases from its emergence in 1895 through its demise in 1945, reflecting evolving imperialist objectives that the Japanese leaders attempted to pursue under changing domestic and external conditions. The first phase, which started with Japan's annexation of Taiwan in 1895 throughout the 1920s, was characterized by Japanese efforts to turn Taiwan and Korea into Japan's agricultural appendages. Japan's empire-building entered the second phase in the 1930s and ran throughout World War II, during which the Japanese attempted to transform Taiwan and Korea into Japan's strategic bases in the nation's war effort in the context of rising militarism in Japan and the Great Depression.

As a result of industrialization, urbanization, and trade expansion, Japan's economic structure had been transformed by the late 19th century and the early 20th century. Particularly, starting in the late 19th century, Japan experienced a persistent balance of payments deficit, which worried the Japanese leaders about the loss of national power. Especially, from 1896 to 1904 Japan spent an annual average of 22 million yen on sugar imports, which accounted for about 50%

of Japan's total trade deficit. In the meantime, in the course of the 1910s there were rising food prices in Japan as a result of the exhaustion of traditional means of improving agricultural productivity through extending best farming practice, which finally led to the "rice riots" in 1918. While the government could have imported food from abroad or shifted resources from industry to agriculture, this would inevitably have further worsened the balance of payments deficit and hampered the nation's drive for further industrialization. Furthermore, continuing industrialization required secure sources of raw materials and export markets. Consequently, colonies were viewed increasingly important as a way to resolve Japan's balance-of-payments difficulties, as a new base for supply of agricultural products to the homeland, as a source of fuels and industrial raw materials for Japanese industries, and as a secure market for Japanese manufactured goods.

It was under such circumstances that Japan started its first phase of colonial development in an attempt to turn Taiwan and Korea into its agricultural appendages, which were to supply inexpensive rice to prevent Japan's industrial wages from rising rapidly and to serve as markets for Japanese manufactures. Particularly, sugar production in Taiwan would help ease Japan's balance-of-payments problem. This decision of the Japanese leaders brought far-reaching implications for all parties involved in the following decades. It is important to point out that different from most Western colonial powers at the time, Japan, in transforming Taiwan and Korea into its agricultural appendages, intended to eventually assimilate these two colonies politically, economically, socially, and culturally. The Japanese colonial policy was precisely designed along this line of strategic thinking in the following years.

Japanese colonialism began with bloody conquest. After annexing Taiwan and Korea, Japan took it as its first priority to eradicate opposition resistance and consolidate its colonial military and political power. In the process of consolidating its political control, Japan created a highly efficient central administrative system in both the colonies to promptly and effectively carry out reforms and insure the compliance of the colonial peoples with its colonial policy. Semi-autonomous and highly authoritarian, the Japanese colonial government in Taiwan and Korea possessed enormous executive, judicial, and even legislative powers.[5] The colonial state so created was even more centralized and authoritarian than that in Japan. It was within such a highly controlled state structure that the Japanese colonial government began to pursue the colonial objectives set for Taiwan and Korea through various important policy measures.

The first and foremost policy measure that the Japanese colonial authorities adopted was the launching of land reforms to establish a rationalized agricultural tax base that could provide a stable source of revenue in both the colonies. With the new land tenure system and agriculture-based tax system established, the Japanese began to take policy measures to promote the development of the sugar and rice sectors in line with the colonial objective of turning Taiwan and Korea into major suppliers of sugar and rice for Japan proper. In the meantime, special tax revenues were used to influence the behavior of farmers, disseminate modern agricultural technology, and establish monopolies in certain agriculturally based industries that would provide substantial revenue.[6]

On the other hand, during the first phase of colonial development, nonagricultural industries were restricted by the Japanese colonial government to prevent the emergence of competition in the colonies with industrial enterprises in Japan. Whereas the colonial government encouraged agricultural processing industries of sugar, vegetable, and soybean oil, the manufacturing sectors that would compete with the home industries were discouraged. As such, the Japanese leaders were quite cautious in formulating their industrial programs in the colonies. By the same token, the Japanese colonial government discouraged *zaibatsu* from extending their activities to the colonies. As a consequence, the industrial development in the colonies before 1930 was primarily related to agriculture.

As a result of this pattern of colonial development, an economic relationship had developed between Japan and its two colonies by which Taiwan and Korea were made agricultural appendages, which primarily functioned to solve Japan's domestic food problems, to improve the balance of payments situation of the metropolis through provision of sugar for the home islands and to absorb Japanese manufactures as markets. By the end of the 1920s, both Taiwan and Korea had been effectively transformed into colonial economies that were linked to the Japanese home economy by a trade cycle of the flow of raw materials and foodstuffs from the colonies to Japan proper and the flow of manufactured goods the other way round.

The early 1930s, however, marked a watershed for Japan's colonial policy. Thereafter, Japan entered the second phase of colonial development in Taiwan and Korea, which lasted until the collapse of the Japanese empire at the end of World War II. This new phase of empire-building emerged in the context of rising militarism in Japan, which increasingly pushed Tokyo toward military adventure and expansion in the region and preparation for war. In the meantime, as a consequence of the Great Depression of the early 1930s, there was growing protectionism in the West against Japanese products. Under such circumstances, Japan began to move toward a semi-war economy by diversifying its economic structure, expanding strategic heavy industries and creating a self-sufficient industrial base within its empire. This new strategy required shifting more resources from agriculture to industries. Accordingly, Japan's colonial policy was also modified to support this new industrialization drive. Under the new strategy, the Japanese leaders promoted not only self-sufficiency of the entire empire and increased self-sufficiency of all colonies but also transformation of Taiwan and Korea into Japan's strategic bases. Particularly, preparation for war played an increasingly important role in determining the pattern of development in the colonies. This new vision led to a push to the development of strategic industries in both the colonies. While agricultural products continued to be shipped to the home islands, agriculture in the colonies was sharply downgraded as an economic priority. On the other hand, the Japanese now saw industrial development in the colonies as complementing, rather than competing with, industrial development in the home islands. While keeping Japan proper as a manufacturing center for the entire empire, the Japanese leaders began to encourage the colonies to develop those industries that would provide raw materials and industrial supplies for the heavy industry on the home islands and to relieve Japan's hard-pressed manufacturing sector. In designing this new strategy, the Japanese planners cautiously kept a balance between preventing competition from colonial industries and reducing the pressure on Japanese industries. Reflecting this new colonial policy, the colonial government encouraged big Japanese businesses to launch mining and large-scale manufacturing projects in the colonies. Under this new pattern of colonial development, the Japanese leaders promoted an industrialization drive in Taiwan and Korea in the 1930s, which was primarily based upon energy, mineral resources, hydroelectric power, and chemicals. In the meantime, in order to mobilize more resources for development of heavy industry at home, the Japanese also moved some labor-intensive light manufacturing industries, such as textiles, to the colonies. This Japanese newly directed colonial development, in sharp contrast to the previous agriculture-based industrial development, was to influence the pace and pattern of industrial growth in Taiwan and Korea. In addition, in the context of the Great Depression of the early 1930s, the role of both the colonies as markets for Japanese products also increased substantially.

More importantly, strategic considerations were highly behind Japan's new colonial policy of the 1930s and the first half of the 1940s. Whereas Taiwan was turned into a strategic base for Japan in its expansion of influence in South China and Southeast Asia, Korea was made to play a strategically important role in supporting Japan's military presence and adventure in Manchuria and North China. This role was particularly crucial following the outbreak of Japan's war in China in 1937, as Taiwan and Korea functioned as important logistical bases for Japanese military operation in China. Especially, the industrial plants in the Korean peninsula were converted to produce war materials that were needed by Japanese armies operating in China.

2.3 Japan's colonial transformation of Taiwan

Taiwan was under brief control of the Dutch East India Company during 1624–62. In 1662, the fleeing military forces of the Ming dynasty came to control the island after being defeated by the Manchus, who founded the Qing dynasty. In 1683, the remnants of the Ming dynasty finally surrendered and the island came under the jurisdiction of the Chinese Qing government. In 1885, Taiwan was made a separate province of China. After the island was taken over by the Japanese under the Treaty of Shimonoseki in 1895, the Taiwanese resisted Japanese annexation and the armed resistance continued for 2 years before it was finally put down by the Japanese forces.

After annexing Taiwan from China, Japan soon forcefully established an unprecedented degree of order and stability on the island by resorting to harsh means and constant police surveillance. Moreover, the *bao-jia* system enabled the Japanese colonial authorities to establish effective community control down to the lowest levels of Chinese Taiwanese society.[7] The Japanese colonial government enjoyed supreme legislative power with its decrees as effective as law. Tribunals and capital punishment were frequently used to keep order and to preclude independence movements.

After internal order was established, the Japanese colonial government began to undertake measures to promote economic development in Taiwan in line with Japan's objective of transforming the island into an agricultural appendage that would serve the homeland's need for agricultural products, sugar in particular. In accordance with this objective, the colonial government launched a land reform on the island in 1898–1906. On the eve of Japanese colonial rule, Taiwan had a traditional subsistence-oriented agrarian economy centered on rice and sugarcane and based on a weakening dual land tenure system of absentee land-lords as legal landowners and perpetual tenants as actual land possessors, a land system that could hardly provide a stable source of tax for the colonial government.[8] The primary aim of the Japanese-directed land reform was to establish a solid base for land tax extraction and improve agricultural productivity. Under the land reform, the colonial govern-ment conducted a comprehensive land survey that identified owners, classified land use, and assessed the land value. On the basis of the land survey, a modern tenure system of land ownership was created, under which absentee landlords were bought off with government bonds and land titles were given to the perpetual tenants who had been tilling the land. The established owner–farmer land system more than tripled land tax revenues. In the meantime, through the land reform the colonial government took and sold large amounts of untitled land to Japanese companies that were engaged in agricultural or forestry activities and to Japanese settlers and colonial officials, who were financed by the gov-ernment with small land grants. As a result, much of the land in Taiwan came under the control of large Japanese companies and Japanese farm-ers. According to Ho, the Japanese land holdings probably accounted for between 20% and 25% of the total cultivated area in Taiwan before World War II.[9]

In addition to the land reform, the Japanese colonial government also took measures to modernize the island's subsistence agriculture. Better farming practices, fertilizers, and new high-yielding varieties of sugar-cane and rice were introduced to boost productivity. Irrigation and flood control projects were undertaken, at first with government funding, later becoming the responsibility of farmers' association. Railways and roads were built and harbor facilities developed. Moreover, the Japanese adop-ted policies to encourage small farmers to produce for market rather than self-consumption. As a result of all these measures, Taiwan experienced steady agricultural growth until World War II.

While the Japanese encouraged rice growing in the northern part of the island and sugar in the south, their initial interest in Taiwan's agricul-ture was to get low-cost sugar for Japan. So arrangements were made to insure Japanese control of sugar production in Taiwan. While the sugar-cane was produced by a large number of small-scale Taiwanese farmers, Japanese capital concentrated on the milling phase of sugar production. The colonial government provided Japanese companies with subsidies to build large, modern sugar mills. In the meantime, the Japanese sugar milling companies were also given monopoly rights to contract with

Taiwanese farmers for the purchase of their sugarcane. As a result, smaller Taiwanese-owned mills were driven out of business. While Taiwan's sugar production rose from 50,000 tons in 1905 to over 1.1 million tons in 1940, over 90% of the island's sugar output was exported to Japan annually. Providing nearly 75% of the sugar consumed in Japan in the 1930s, Taiwan was Japan's major supplier of sugar.[10]

By the mid-1920s, Japan's growing industrialization led to a rising demand for rice imports to feed its expanding urban industrial workforce. This helped boost rice production in Taiwan too. The rising rice production was further aided by the introduction of better quality strains of rice that were more palatable to Japanese tastes and of modern farming techniques that increased productivity. Consequently, rice yields increased rapidly. By the 1930s, Taiwan produced a rice output that was twice as much as the population consumed, of which about 45% was exported to Japan annually, accounting for over 30% of Japan's rice imports.[11]

For the first three decades of its colonial rule, Japan treated Taiwan as an agricultural appendage of the metropolitan home islands and therefore emphasized only sugar and rice production on the island. Accordingly, industrial development was confined by the Japanese mainly to food processing. By the mid-1920s, only a few large, modern industrial firms existed, most of which were Japanese sugar companies. On the other hand, numerous small enterprises (mainly food processing, handicraft, and other local industries) were owned and operated by the Taiwanese. As a result, the island remained largely an agriculture-based economy.

It was only in the 1930s that the colonial government began to promote the development of industries and broaden the industrial base on the island, thanks to the strategic position of Taiwan in the context of Japanese war preparation. In preparation for war, the official planning for the industrialization of Taiwan commenced in 1935 and a commission responsible for the island's industrialization was created. Under the drive for industrialization, the Japanese selectively established some industries in Taiwan by moving to the island the Japanese-used machineries for production of manufactured goods, previously imported from Japan, and industrial raw materials, needed by Japan's heavy industry. Japanese investments were involved in such industrial sectors as metals, chemicals, ceramics, and machine tools. After Japan entered war first with China in 1937 and later with the Allied powers in 1941, Japan intensified the industrialization of Taiwan in support of its military needs. New industries were established on the island to process vital raw materials (such as bauxite, iron ore, crude oil, and rubber) that were transported from Malaya and the East Indies. After being processed in Taiwan, they were then shipped to industrial centers in metropolitan Japan. In the meantime, in the context of war more seaports and electrical generating facilities were developed and the island's prime industries (including mining) were upgraded in support of the industrialization drive.

The Japanese-directed wartime industrialization led to a number of notable accomplishments. Most significantly, heavy industry was introduced into Taiwan and industrial production in both manufacturing and mining sectors expanded rapidly. Equally important, industrial technology also improved substantially, which came with large Japanese companies. Massive hydroelectric installations were constructed, new harbors were created, and modern industrial complexes were established. Consequently, a rudimentary modern industrial economy emerged on the island. This Japanese-directed industrialization in the 1930s and in the first half of the 1940s paved the way for future industrialization in Taiwan in later years.

On the other hand, however, Taiwan's wartime industrialization was primarily driven by the Japanese capital. The emerging modern industries were controlled almost entirely by the Japanese (such as Japan Aluminum Company plants that began operating in 1940), while Taiwanese enterprises were kept weak and small in scale, largely involved in traditional sectors. Consequently, industrial power was dominated by the Japanese, while the emergence of indigenous industrial class was never encouraged.

The Japanese-engineered industrialization brought about a growingly large workforce in Taiwan's nonagricultural sector. In 1935, somewhat over 68,000 workers were employed in 7,000 factories (mostly of small size). By mid-1943, the number of skilled workers in manufacturing plants increased to around 147,000, while the total workers employed in the nonagricultural sector (which also included mining, transportation, communications, and services) rose to some 214,000. An additional civilian workforce of this magnitude became engaged in construction and military-related employment.[12] In the meantime, with the increase of specialized openings in many fields, more and more Taiwanese were hired for the position of lower-level managers that had previously been filled only by the Japanese.[13] In addition to the regular nonagricultural employment, the colonial government also mobilized the Taiwanese for productive services in support of Japan's war effort. Sizable segments of the population were mobilized for the construction of new plants, industrial sites, roads, bridges, military airports, and defense installations. As a consequence, the industrialization led to a change in occupational composition with a movement of workers from the agricultural sector to the nonagricultural sector. As statistics show, the male employment in the agricultural sector dropped from 69.9% in 1905 to 61.5% in 1940, while the male employment in the nonagricultural sector increased from 30.1% to 38.5% during the same period. Within the nonagricultural sector, the male employment in the mining sector rose from 0.5% of the island's total male employment to 2.5%, that in the manufacturing sector from 5.0% to 7.4%, and that in the construction sector from 0.6% to 2.4% during the period in question.[14]

It is important to point out that in the process of colonial development the authoritarian colonial state was heavily involved in the economic management to mobilize resources to promote the development of the island. The government's heavy involvement in colonial development is well illustrated by the huge government expenditures, which after 1920 stood at 11–16% of Taiwan's total product. Realizing that economic infrastructure was essential for economic development, the colonial government invested heavily in building and upgrading railways, roads, harbors, and communication facilities. The colonial government also helped standardize the monetary system, establish banks, and promote uniform commercial practices. All these measures helped build a modern economy in Taiwan.

In the meantime, the colonial government also invested in social infrastructure on the island. Medical services were improved and various hygienic measures were introduced to improve public health, including waste removal, compulsory testing, quarantine, and vaccination programs. As a result of these measures, public health improved dramatically in Taiwan during the colonial period with infectious diseases reduced, the death rate dropped, and the population doubled. Likewise, the Japanese also promoted elementary education in Taiwan, which helped increase the literacy rate of Taiwanese from 1% in 1905 to 27% in 1940. By 1944, nearly three out of every four children were enrolled in primary schools.[15] A healthy and literate population in turn helped improve the productivity of the human capital, which indirectly facilitated economic development in colonial Taiwan.

In essence, the colonial development of Taiwan was pursued by the Japanese to benefit Japanese interests. In the course of colonial development, the colonial government, through its various policy instruments and preferential treatment of Japanese investors, insured that economic power in Taiwan was kept under Japanese control. As the Japanese monopolized the agricultural power in Taiwan, the prices paid for sugarcane and rice were kept low, which in turn enabled the Japanese to keep the real wage low so that maximum profits could be obtained by the Japanese from agricultural and industrial growth. Part of the profits was reinvested in Taiwan, but a large part of them was transferred to Japan. Consequently, the living standards of the Taiwanese remained low. But on the other hand, as the colonial economic development required Taiwanese participation, Japanese colonialism did help improve Taiwanese general economic conditions modestly over time. In few areas, such as education and health, the conditions of the Taiwanese improved even significantly. The benefits that the Taiwanese enjoyed from colonial development are illustratively reflected in the rise of the real wage over time, though it was still kept relatively low. Despite the slow improving economic conditions of Taiwanese, however, the growth in real wage was significantly slower than that of labor productivity. As the relevant statistics indicate, from 1910 to 1939 agricultural labor productivity increased by 3% a year on average, while agricultural real wage increased only by 1.3% a year. Similarly, in the 1920s and the 1930s labor productivity in manufacturing rose by 3.3% a year on average, while the average annual increase in real wage was only about 1.5%. By comparison, the economic conditions of agricultural workers improved less consistently than those of nonagricultural workers. This is important because the agricultural employment accounted for almost 70% of the male Taiwanese workers.[16]

In a further analysis, the colonial development of Taiwan was pursued in a way that satisfied Japan's economic needs. Japan had imposed on Taiwan a pattern of economic development that was heavily dependent on the export of primary products to Japan. This connection of the Taiwanese economy with the Japanese economy was particularly reflected in Taiwan's distorted trade pattern. As two major export commodities, rice and sugar accounted for 50–70% of Taiwan's total exports. Nearly all of Taiwan's rice and sugar exports went to Japan, which comprised approximately 15% of Japan's total imports.[17] It was within this structure of colonial development that Taiwan achieved rapid economic growth during the Japanese colonial period through substantial inflows of material, human capital, and technology combined with the domestic resources such as land and labor.

Furthermore, the Japanese also resorted to forceful social changes to achieve the declared objective of assimilation of Taiwan. In accordance with this objective, the Taiwanese were forced not only to learn the Japanese language but also to adopt the Japanese state religion, Shintoism, so that the Taiwanese would give up their own culture and customs as well as their Chinese heritage. This policy of assimilation of the Taiwanese was intensified in the late 1930s. The colonial government made sustained efforts to completely Japanize the colonial population, the Han Taiwanese in particular. The Chinese-language newspapers were abolished, classical Chinese was removed from the elementary school curriculum, and a large campaign was launched to discourage the use of Chinese and increase the percentage of Japanese speakers among the Taiwanese population. In the meantime, a name-change campaign was initiated to replace Chinese names with Japanese ones as a means to detach the Han Taiwanese from their descent groups and ancestral areas in China. Finally, through a movement of imperialization (*kominka*), the Taiwanese were to be transformed into imperial subjects (*komin*) fully loyal to the Japanese emperor and devoted to Japan's national cause. It was the belief of the Japanese that only after being assimilated would the Taiwanese become fully committed in both mind and spirit to Japan's war effort.[18]

Within five decades, the Japanese substantially transformed Taiwan from a backward and economically fragmented society into a modern, economically self-sufficient colony through the massive restructuring of the political, social, and economic order, which would bring significant impact on the political economy of Taiwan in the postcolonial era.

2.4 Japan's colonial transformation of Korea

Japan formally annexed Korea on 22 August 1910, which ended the Yi dynasty that had ruled the peninsula since 1392. Japan's annexation of the peninsula brought an end to Korea's more than a thousand years of history as an independent political entity. Japanese colonialism faced antagonism and strong resistance in Korea, where a sense of Korean national identity had emerged and developed. But the Korean resistance was forcefully suppressed by the Japanese. To consolidate their colonial rule, the Japanese established a legal basis for full-scale repression, suspended publication of all Korean newspapers, disbanded political organizations, and prohibited public gatherings of all types. With the whole peninsula being pacified, the Japanese moved to construct a powerful colonial state with a highly authoritarian, centralized government structure. The governor of the colonial government, who was always a Japanese military leader, relied heavily on police powers to rule and enjoyed total control of Korea through issuing legislative directives, overseeing the judicial system and police, having fiscal independence, exercising total control of appointments within his bureaucracy, and administrating the economy.

At the time of its annexation, Korea possessed a largely subsistence-oriented agricultural economy, in which land was controlled by traditional elite, commercial infrastructure was underdeveloped, up-to-date and accurate land survey data was lacking, and the tax revenue base was unstable and deeply corrupted. Thus, Japan's first major task was to rationalize and codify the land system to serve as a stable, self-sustaining tax revenue base, as was the case in Taiwan. From 1910 to 1918, the colonial government carried out a comprehensive land survey to determine the type, quantity, productivity, and ownership of land. Land without properly documented titles was taken over by the colonial government from Koreans together with the land formerly owned by the Yi state. The result of this land reform was the outright transfer of a large quantity of land to the Japanese. A similar procedure transferred all formerly state-owned forest land to the colonial state as well. As a result, the colonial government became the largest landowner in Korea. Statistics from 1930 show that the colonial state owned approximately 40% of Korea's agricultural and forest lands combined.[19] Many of these lands were later sold at greatly reduced prices to Japanese land development companies, such as the semi-official Oriental Development Company, as well as to individual Japanese farmers who immigrated to Korea. In the meantime, Japanese policy also deliberately supported the development of a highly dependent but wealthy Korean landlord class as its supporting base in Korean society. This land reform thereafter became the basis of a land tax system that began to be implemented in 1914. By 1930, the land tax was responsible for 45% of annual revenue of the colonial government.[20]

But Japanese land policies led to the impoverishment of Korean farming population, the great majority of which were forced into tenant farming. In the south, for example, approximately 90% of farmers worked as tenants. Most of them paid rents that were equal to 80–90% of their harvest.[21] In addition to heavy rents, tenants also had to pay for tools, seeds, water rights, and fertilizer, which few tenants could finance without borrowing. This, compounded by widespread usury, led to increased indebtedness of tenants. As a result, there was widening economic gap between land owners and tenants, which created tremendous tensions in Korean society.

More importantly, Japanese colonial agricultural policy was designed to improve agricultural productivity and promote agricultural growth so as to insure massive export of foodstuffs to Japan. Accordingly, Japan increased its investment in Korean agriculture, especially starting in 1920. The colonial government supervised and coordinated application of new inputs, improvement of irrigation and drainage works, adoption of crop rotation principles, and expanded use of agricultural machinery. These measures led to rise in agricultural output in Korea, rice output in particular. However, rice exports to Japan increased even faster than production. While Korean rice production grew only 38% from 1912 to 1936, exports grew by over 700%. From 1932 to 1936, Korea was exporting more than half of its total rice output. This massive flow of rice to Japan enormously contributed to the stabilization of food consumption and wages in Japan proper. This was what Adrian Buzo calls Korea's "famine export,"[22] under which Korean farmers were forced to export rice to Japan while they themselves had to consume cheaper grains such as barley, sorghum, and millet. Consequently, Koreans' rice consumption was reduced in both absolute and per capital terms under Japanese agricultural policy.[23]

Korea was transformed into not only a cheap, reliable producer of agricultural goods, but also an important source of raw materials for Japanese industries. Shortly after the annexation of Korea, the colonial government surveyed the mineral holdings on the Korean peninsula and, in coordination with a selected few giant Japanese conglomerates, undertook the exploration and mining of raw materials such as gold, silver, iron, lead, tungsten, and coal. Such mining activities greatly increased during World War I, allowing Japan to earn considerable foreign exchange through sales to the Allies.[24]

While agricultural production continued to be the focus of the colonial government's economic policy in the 1920s, the Japanese began in 1920 to promote the expansion of industry in Korea, particularly in light manufacturing sectors, such as textiles. But this early industrialization in Korea was still quite small in scale. It was in the context of Japanese military expansion in the early 1930s that the role of Korea was formally transformed from a colonial supplier of agricultural products and raw materials for metropolitan Japan into a vital military rear supporting base of the Japanese empire. Given the geographical location of the peninsula, the mobilization of Korean resources was seen as uniquely important in support of Japan's war effort. On the other hand, the Great Depression also convinced the Japanese leadership of the need to insure control over the raw materials and markets in the colonies for sustaining the homeland's economic growth. Under such circumstances, the Japanese greatly accelerated industrial investment in Korea, although food and agricultural production still dominated the economy in the peninsula. *Zaibatsu* led the way in new investments, especially in mining and related extractive industries, but also in munitions and related heavy and chemical industries such as oil, rubber, fertilizer, drugs, and medicine. As a result, an agrarian economy of Korea was gradually transformed into a rudimentary industrial economy, heavily dependent on Japanese capital and technologies. By the late 1930s, the structure of the Korean economy had been significantly altered. The share of the manufacturing sector rose from 17.7% in 1925 to 39% in 1939. Within the manufacturing sector itself, the share of heavy and chemical industries rose from 16.5% in 1930 to 47% in 1939.[25]

The breakout of the Pacific War in 1941 further stimulated the industrialization of the peninsula. The chemical industry in the north was made a primary source of munitions for the Japanese army, the textile industry was promoted by inexhaustible demand of the Japanese armed forces, and the steel industry and sophisticated tool and machinery industry emerged to manufacture a range of war-related parts. As Korea and Manchuria were largely spared from Allied bombing during the war, the Japanese shifted many of their manufacturing facilities to these Japanese-controlled territories.

Financed by land taxes, mineral royalties, and traditional government monopoly sales of rice, ginseng, tobacco, salt, and opium, the colonial government also pursued a vigorous investment program of constructing economic infrastructure, which helped extend the railway, road, coastal navigation, and port facilities. In the meantime, the colonial authorities established a modern monetary and banking system in Korea, closely linked to the parent Japanese system. More significantly, in the process of colonial development, the government's administration of economy became increasingly intense, detailed, and comprehensive. Through allocation of raw materials, production quotas, sale and distribution at fixed prices, the colonial government allocated human and material resources to designated priority industries and turned the whole industrial sector into an arm of military procurement. To perform all these governmental functions, the colonial state created a massive colonial administration employing 246,000 Japanese and additional 63,000 Koreans, which controlled approximately 21 million Koreans. Consequently, nearly 42% of all Japanese in Korea in 1937 were in government service.[26]

As Korea was geographically so close to Japan, Japanese colonial economic policy was particularly designed to integrate the Korean economy into the Japanese economy. The Japanese-directed industrialization tied the Korean economy even more closely to the Japanese economy in a division of labor organized and dominated by the Japanese. This close economic integration was particularly reflected in the Japanese–Korean trade pattern. By 1931, 95% of all Korean exports went to Japan, while 80% of all Korean imports came from Japan. In turn, Korea was Japan's main export market, accounting for approximately 34% of all Japanese exports in 1939.[27] More significantly, the composition of Korea's trade with Japan was dramatically transformed by Japanese investment activities in Korea. While raw materials accounted for over 80% of Korean exports to Japan in 1929, this fell to less than 50% by 1939. Over the same period, manufactures as a percentage of Korean exports to Japan rose from approximately 13% to approximately 46%.[28]

However, the Japanese-directed industrialization neither responded to Korean needs nor was driven by the Koreans. According to 1938 data, Japanese companies owned almost 90% of all manufacturing capital in Korea. The same was true for mining. In 1945, Japanese companies accounted for almost 95% of all investments in coal mining and their share of investment and facilities in other mining industries was even higher.[29] On the other hand, the Japanese-directed industrialization was achieved with very little regard for the well-being of Korean wage workers. Wages in 1935 were 50% less than they had been in 1927. The normal industrial work day was lengthened over the same period from 12 to 16 hours. Moreover, health and safety conditions were nonexistent, resulting in a very high rate of industrial accidents, diseases, and deaths.[30]

As industrialization deepened and rural conditions deteriorated, large numbers of peasants were forced off the land into mines, factories, and service sectors, which led to the emergence of an industrial workforce that eventually rose to 2 million by 1944.[31] With the breakout of the Pacific War in 1941, the Japanese made further efforts to mobilize the labor of the entire peninsula for their war effort. Koreans were recruited to work in the mines and factories in Korea, Japan, and Manchuria, guard prison camps, build military facilities, and serve Japanese troops in a variety of ways on all fronts. By 1945, nearly four million Koreans, roughly 16% of the total population, were working abroad within the Japanese empire.[32]

While Japan's initial colonial objective in Korea was to transform the colony into a base that would provide the home islands with foodstuffs and raw materials, its long-term aim was the eventual assimilation of Korean society and extinction of Korea as an independent, identifiable, autonomous culture. In the late 1930s, Japan's assimilation policy reached its apex through the slogans of "Japan and Korea as one body"

(*Nai-Sen ittai*) and "harmony between Japan and Korea" (*Nissen yuwa*), under which the colonial authorities adopted a comprehensive and diverse array of social and cultural policies, all designed to "Japanize" the Koreans. Tokyo's intention was to have Korea cease to be a colony and be ruled as an integral part of Japan itself. In preparation, the colonial government forced the Koreans to participate in Japanese Shintoist ceremonies and rituals associated with the cult of the Emperor, forcibly inculcated Japanese spirit and values among the Koreans, forced the use of Japanese in schools and public offices and imposed wide-ranging restrictions on the use of the Korean language and script, forced the Koreans to adopt Japanese names, and Japanized Korean history. The forceful assimilation of Korea was even seen only as a part of the grand plan to bring all of East Asia under the benevolent blanket of Japanese rule. According to Japanese logic, the "fortunate" Koreans were to be a special part of the inner empire within the vast area of the Greater East Asia Co-Prosperity Sphere.[33]

Japanese colonial policy brought enormous impact on the political economy of Korea. Because economic growth in Korea was primarily directed by the colonial state and economic power was dominated by a few large Japanese firms, the Japanese-initiated industrialization did little to strengthen the power or position of Korean capitalists. Japanese colonialism thus left Korea with a strong centralized state apparatus and a weak capitalist class. This experience provides a historical background for the later dominance of the state in South Korea. Moreover, Japanese colonialism not only created the conditions for a dominant state to arise in Korea, it also directly transmitted a development model based on military power, state direction of economic activity, production by large family-owned conglomerates, extreme exploitation of workers, and suppression of labor movement. Consequently, Japan's 35-year colonial rule had profound consequences for the manner in which modern Korea took shape.

2.5   The impact of Japanese colonialism for the political economy of East Asia

When turned into Japanese colonies, both Taiwan and Korea were largely in a traditional society dominated by traditional elite who not only possessed social privilege but also controlled social wealth. The state was poorly managed by a gradually weakened, corrupt, and inefficient agrarian bureaucracy. The emergence of a modern state was further hampered by a Confucian-oriented educational structure. In the mean-time, both Taiwan and Korea had a predominantly agrarian economy, which was underdeveloped, relatively stagnant, and based on a land tenure system that could hardly provide a solid base for taxes.[34]

After annexing Taiwan and Korea, Japan pursued a colonial policy that was designed to incorporate and assimilate these two colonies into the Japanese empire. This imperial policy of Japan substantially transformed the economy of both Taiwan and Korea in the years to come. Partic-ularly, the Japanese colonial government adopted the policy measures that insured Japanese predominant control of the colonial economy and transformation of the two colonies into a subordinate part of the Japan-ese economy. Consequently, Japan's colonial policy brought substantial impact for not only the economic development of both Taiwan and Korea but also the political economy of East Asia in the first half of the 20th century and beyond.

The impact of Japanese colonial policy was mixed, reflected in the dualistic characteristics of Japanese-directed colonial development. On the one hand, Japanese colonial policy helped establish a modern eco-nomic structure and promote economic development in Taiwan and Korea with both agricultural and industrial production dramatically increased. On the other hand, however, the colonial economic devel-opment was exploitative in nature and the emerging colonial modern economy was subordinate in essence. This exploitative development was essentially discriminatory and predatory, which was particularly reflec-ted in Japan's harsh demands upon its colonies, the economic inequities between the Japanese and the colonial peoples, and the distortions and imbalances in the economic structure of the colonies brought about by Japanese colonial policy.[35] As Japanese colonists owned and operated much of the modern sector, owned considerable land, possessed great market power, and firmly controlled agriculture, this colonial develop-ment brought Japan huge benefits in the form of transferring substantial material resources and surplus produced in the colonies to Japan in sup-port of Japanese development and war effort. Particularly, the remarkable agricultural growth in Taiwan and Korea in the first phase of the empire-building provided the Japanese home islands with sufficient foodstuffs and helped improve Japan's balance of payments. In the second phase of the empire-building, Taiwan and Korea became important sources of industrial raw materials for Japan's industry. Moreover, the colonies also functioned as a market to absorb Japanese manufacturing products and provided increased white-collar employment opportunities for the Japanese from the home islands. As such, this was a mixed pattern of exploitation and development with development intended for more effective exploitation and subordination of the colonies to serve the economy of Japan proper.

The exploitive development was first and foremost illustrated in the colonial agriculture of Taiwan and Korea, which had been fundamentally transformed under Japanese colonial rule. To turn both the colonies into Japan's agricultural appendages, the Japanese colonial government introduced institutional transformations and technological measures in both the colonies, which led to what Myers and Yamada called a "biological revolution."[36] The Japanese-directed land reforms clarified and legitimized private property rights, which helped bring farmers incentives to use their resources productively and encourage large, long-term investments in land. In the meantime, the colonial government also systematically introduced and distributed new technology and modern inputs such as high-yield seeds and chemical fertilizers, promoted the construction of irrigation through loans, capital grants, and direct investments, and supported rural institutions (e.g., farmers' associations) that served agriculture. On the other hand, Japan's colonial policy of turning its colonies into its agricultural appendages brought the effect of providing a secure market for agricultural products from Taiwan and Korea. Likewise, the improved transportation and communication infrastructure during the Japanese colonial period helped reduce transport costs for marketing agricultural products for both internal and external markets. All this helped create an efficient and productive agricultural system and provide a favorable economic and technical environment for agricultural development, which helped stimulate agricultural growth during the Japanese colonial period, although by comparison agricultural growth was more steady and continuous throughout the colonial period in Taiwan than in Korea.[37]

Despite the rapid agricultural growth as a result of Japanese colonial policy, however, the colonial agricultural development in Taiwan and Korea was achieved through Japanese domination of rural economic power and wealth. Japanese domination in colonial agriculture was illustrated by Japanese disproportionate control of not only land but also the export market. The result of this Japanese domination was that the indigenous share of the increase in agricultural output was far smaller than that of the Japanese. In the meantime, the land reforms helped establish a stable land-tax system that allowed the Japanese colonial authorities to generate more tax revenue than ever before. Furthermore, Japanese policy was also designed to shape the colonial economy to meet the needs of the home islands, which frequently worked against the interests of the colonial peoples. Consequently, for example, despite the remarkable increase in rice production in both Taiwan and Korea, there were substantial shipments of rice to Japan, and consumption of rice by Taiwanese and Koreans actually dropped so that the colonial peoples were forced to consume less desirable cereals instead.[38]

The colonial exploitive development was similarly reflected in the Japanese-promoted industrialization in Taiwan and Korea, which took distinctly dualistic characteristics as well. Primarily entering the 1930s, Japan began to promote industrial development in its colonies. However, Japanese colonial industrial policy, which discouraged general industrial development in Taiwan and Korea, was highly selective with only those industrial sectors that would complement and support the industries in the homeland being encouraged to develop, while those industries that would compete with Japanese industries being suppressed. Accordingly, the Japanese colonial authorities promoted the development of such industrial sectors as mining, mineral processing, and certain manufacturing industries like sugar and other light industries in its colonies. As a result, a limited industrial base was created out of the Japanese colonial policy.

Moreover, various industrial programs were designed in a way that those modern industrial sectors in the colonies were dominated by a small number of large, modern, and heavily capitalized Japanese companies, especially *zaibatsu*, which were supported by the colonial government through various preferential policies, including favorable regulations, low taxes, guaranteed dividends, subsidies, and most importantly, a cordial and cooperative officialdom. Likewise, the modern transportation and communication sectors were directly owned and operated by the colonial government. Although there also existed side by side a large number of very small native enterprises producing for the domestic market, the industrialization in Taiwan and Korea was primarily driven by these large Japanese companies with their products being predominantly exported to Japan.[39] With the control of the modern industry, the Japanese managed to capture a preponderant share of non-wage income from the industrial sectors in the colonies. Consequently, although both Taiwan and Korea experienced industrial expansion under Japanese colonial rule, a modern indigenous entrepreneurial class failed to develop in Korea and grew only marginally in Taiwan during the colonial period, and Japanese industrial policy failed to provide the necessary elements for sustained industrial growth in both the colonies.[40]

To create a favorable environment for colonial economic development, the Japanese colonial authorities made continuous investments in economic infrastructure at a high level throughout the colonial period. Consequently, a modern economic infrastructure was established in Taiwan and Korea under Japanese colonial rule, including modern transportation and communication networks, harbors, warehousing, banking and monetary systems, and education and health facilities. Particularly, transportation and communication projects absorbed the largest share of the investments from the colonial government in both the colonies, because an inexpensive and efficient transportation and communication system was seen essential by the Japanese for their effective control of the colonies and for integration of the economy of Taiwan and Korea with that of Japan. As a result, the well-developed economic infrastructure not only lowered transportation and transaction costs but also helped transform previously isolated local economies into integrated market systems, thus increasing the profitability of private investments in agriculture, commerce, and industry.[41] On the other hand, however, the Japanese-constructed economic infrastructure in Taiwan and Korea was used to promote colonial exploitative development, which, in the end, functioned to serve Japan's economic needs and strategic interests in East Asia.

Similarly, the Japanese colonial authorities also made great efforts to increase investment in health and education to produce a literate, skilled, and healthy labor force to raise productivity. Japanese investment in public health care in the colonies brought remarkable decreases in mortality and a general increase in the health of the colonial peoples. On the other hand, the human capital investment in education helped improve education and labor skills in both Taiwan and Korea. However, as part of the colonial policy of Japanese domination in both the colonies, the Japanese colonial education system was designed in a way that natives were confined to certain types, quality, and levels of education rather than have unlimited access to all education opportunities as a ladder of upward social mobility, for the educational advancement of native population was seen as a threat to Japanese control of the colonies. This very nature of Japanese colonial education policy was well illustrated in a two-track education system that was adopted in both Taiwan and Korea – an upper track for Japanese colonists alongside with a lower track for natives. Under this dual system, the education that the Japanese colonists received, which consumed the bulk of the government's education budget, was far superior to that provided to the natives, while the education for the natives was intended to train a literate and skilled labor force and to educate them to acquire Japanese customs, culture, and language. More importantly, this colonial education system was designed to provide a mechanism for broad transmission of Japanese cultural and political values in order to legitimize Japanese rule and to perpetuate the subordinate position of the Taiwanese and Koreans to the Japanese. As such, the natives were basically confined to the elementary education and strictly kept from going beyond. It is in this sense that Japan failed to provide its colonial peoples with true modern education. This colonial education system brought a profound long-term effect on Taiwanese and Korean society.

While the Japanese colonial government was harsh on the colonial populations, it did develop the economy in both the colonies. Unlike other colonial powers, Japan did not establish enclave plantation agriculture, and it did reinvest profits from industrial development in its colonies. It is in this sense that Taiwan and Korea benefited from Japanese colonialism in spite of its populations being very poorly treated by Japanese colonialists. More importantly, Taiwan and Korea emerged from its colonial period with a relatively healthy and modernized agricultural sector, an industrial base, good infrastructure, a well-educated labor force, and a relatively efficient government administration. Few other former colonies were left with such a favorable heritage by their colonial masters.

In a further analysis, through its colonial policy, Japan managed to establish an economic relationship in East Asia that had closely integrated the economy of Taiwan and Korea with the economy of the Japanese homelands. This economic relationship in East Asia was a division of labor engineered and dominated by the Japanese in which the colonies were made to play a mere role in supplying primary products (food, minerals, and energy-intensive intermediate goods) to Japan and serving as markets for Japan's manufactures. Industrial development in the colonies was only used to provide important complement and support for Japan's industrial growth. Especially, the metal and chemical industries located in the colonies to use their energy and mineral resources were developed in the 1930s as important extensions of Japan's heavy industry, which helped satisfy specific Japanese needs in Japan's industrial growth and war effort.

The close integration was most illustratively reflected in colonial trade, which became important to both Japan and its colonies. But again, the Japanese dominated the colonial trade and controlled the export sector, which colonial agriculture heavily relied on. Throughout the entire colonial period, 80–90% of Korea's trade was with Japan, and 70% of Taiwan's trade was with Japan in 1910, which later rose to 90%.[42] Over 90% of Taiwan's sugar in the 1920s–30s and between one-quarter and one-half of the rice produced in Taiwan and Korea were exported to Japan. On the

Japanese side, in the interwar period one-quarter of Japan's total imports consisted of food (including beverages and tobacco), the largest component being rice followed by sugar. In the late 1930s, over 90% of the sugar and 98% of the rice imported by Japan were from Taiwan and Korea. The development of colonial agriculture substantially contributed to Japan's achievement of self-sufficiency in food.[43]

Most significantly, Japan's colonial exploitative development of Taiwan and Korea brought long-term impact on the regional political economy of East Asia through the formation of a pattern of vertical economic integration in East Asia with Japan as a leading economy while Taiwan and Korea as follower economies in the process of regional economic development. This pattern of economic relationship in East Asia was theorized into a model by Japanese economist Kaname Akamatsu in the 1930s, called "flying geese."[44] According to the flying geese model, there is a cycle of emergence, rise, apogee, and decline of given industries in the process of a country's economic development. Accordingly, there is a corresponding cycle of import, import-substitution for the domestic market, subsequent export, export decline, and re-import of a given product. At a certain point in an industrial life cycle, it pays for a leading country to opt out of the production and transfer it to the follower countries of the "geese formation" where production cost is lower. According to the logic of the flying geese model, Japan follows the United States and Western Europe and tries to catch up, in stages, in the production first of simple consumer goods, then consumer durables and eventually capital goods. At each stage, Japan first imports foreign products for its domestic market, and then starts domestic production to increasingly replace these imports and eventually penetrate foreign markets. Each stage thus creates new imports of raw materials (from neighboring economies) and more advanced capital goods (from the United States and Europe), as well as new exports of the goods that are now being produced domestically. Finally, there comes a time when the increasing domestic cost of production and competition from new entrants in the region force Japan to move gradually out of the product in question, reducing exports and starting to import again.

The economic relationship in East Asia is said to represent its own dynamics of a flying geese format with Japan as a leading economy while Taiwan and Korea as follower economies. In their upward mobile process of industrialization, colonized Taiwan and Korea were significantly connected with the Japanese product-cycle phases in this flying geese mechanism, although this connection was forcefully imposed by Japanese imperialism. With diverse stages of economic development, a vertical division of labor between Japan and its colonies was formed over time with declining industries being moved from the former to the latter in the process of economic development. Both Taiwan and Korea, from very early on, were made to take over economic activities that were no longer found profitable in Japan. This transfer of production proceeded during the whole colonial era. It started with agriculture through Japanese-directed modernization of rice and sugar production destined for the colonial metropolis. In the 1930s, Japan initiated a new stage of this process by transferring such industries as iron, steel, chemical and electric generation production to its colonies within the Japanese empire.

This Japanese-coerced process of flying geese integration was interrupted as a result of Japan's defeat at the end of World War II, when Japan was forced to dismember its empire completely. However, the division of labor of flying geese nature resumed between Japan on the one hand and Taiwan and South Korea on the other in the postwar years in the context of Cold War politics, although it was then under the auspices of US hegemony rather than coerced by Japan as was during the Japanese imperialist period. So by the 1960s throughout the 1970s, South Korea and Taiwan had received declining textile and consumer-electronic industries from Japan. In the 1980s, Japanese companies were transferring cars and steel production to South Korea and Taiwan.[45] Through this process, the capitalist economies in East Asia became increasingly interdependent with Japan at the core of this regional economic relationship in the postwar years.

Equally significant, the basic structure of the modern Japanese political economy, which had finally been formed in Japan in the 1930s, was in many ways planted by the Japanese in their two colonies during the colonial period. The major features of this structure included national industrial planning that covered most major industries in Japan, the state's management of the purchase and use of foreign technology, government control of market entry through a licensing system, allocation of foreign exchange according to state planning priorities, development and integration of big banks and large family-owned conglomerates known as *zaibatsu*, militarization, and harsh repression of labor.[46] While Japanese colonialism was gone, the structure of the Japanese political economy was well mimicked in many important respects by Taiwan and South Korea in the postcolonial period, significantly affecting the course of their economic development in the postwar years.

3
The External Setting and Internal Dynamics in the Post-1945 Era

3.1   The external setting: Cold War politics and US Asia policy

World War II brought profound political consequences in post-1945 international relations. In the first instance, the military outcome of the war brought a politically and economically alienated great power, the Soviet Union, into the heart of Europe. Because of different war objectives, political suspicion, and ideological conflict of the Allied powers, the temporary occupation line in Central Europe between the Allied forces as a result of military victory over the Axis powers soon turned into a demarcation line of Cold War politics, dividing the former allies into two conflicting blocs – the US-led capitalist West and the Soviet-headed socialist East. The Cold War soon extended from Europe to the Far East as a result of the communist victory in China in 1949 and the Korean War of 1950–53, thus dragging East Asian countries into the two conflicting blocs of the Cold War.[1] On the other hand, the outcome of World War II had considerably reshaped the political map of global powers. As a result of the war, former major powers in world politics were either defeated or considerably weakened with unprecedented physical and human destruction. In contrast, the United States had emerged from the war with its power not only intact but actually enhanced. Having the monopoly over atomic weapons, holding almost half of the world's monetary reserves and two-thirds of the world's gold supply, and possessing half of the world's manufacturing capacity, the United States had acquired an unchallenged predominant position in world politics and economics, bringing a new age of US hegemony. While the United States remained the only Western power that was capable of providing capital and military protection that were desperately needed by other Western countries for their economic reconstruction and national security, what was more significant was the US leadership's political will of discarding isolationism that had characterized US foreign policy after World War I and clear ideological conception of the kind of international society they wished to construct.

It was against this historical background of Cold War politics and US hegemony that the political economy of East Asia was dramatically transformed in the postwar years. Particularly, within the Cold War context the United States substantially influenced the way that the postwar political economy of East Asia would evolve through a series of Washington-designed and -led security arrangements, US huge economic and military aid to its protégés, and its wide-range involvement in regional affairs.

After Japan was defeated by the Allied powers in August 1945, the Japanese Empire collapsed and Japan proper was occupied by the Allied forces, which were mainly the US forces. During the early years of US occupation, Washington's policy was to punish Japan as a former enemy and competitor and to eliminate Japanese militarism and ultra-nationalism through a range of demilitarization and democratization measures. This objective was clearly reflected in Washington's document entitled "The United States Initial Surrender Policy for Japan," which was publicly announced by Supreme Commander of the Allied Powers (SCAP) General Douglas MacArthur on 10 September 1945.[2] Under the guidance of this general policy objective, the US occupation authorities adopted a series of important measures, including dismantling of the Japanese military establishment, demilitarization of the economy, breakup of *zaibatsu*, liberalization of the economic system, legalization of labor unions, agricultural associations and other social organizations, reform of education, land reform, and imposition of a new democratic constitution that established a representative democracy and at the same time deprived Japan of the national right to conduct war.

However, with the Cold War between Washington and Moscow emerging and intensifying in 1947, particularly with the communist victory in China in 1949 and the outbreak of the Korean War in 1950, the United States adjusted its strategy and began to adopt containment policy in the Far East. In so doing, Washington paid particular attention to Japan, which in US view was a key in the new strategy. Washington's new policy was to make Japan a bulwark against communism, the new communist China in particular. As a result, US policy switched from that of punishing to that of revitalizing Japan. This shift of US Japan policy was formally endorsed in the US National Security Council's Resolution

13/2 of October 1948. Under this resolution, Washington was to remove many restrictions that had been previously imposed on Japan and to expedite Japanese economic recovery. This policy adjustment was also partly derived from Washington's assumption that the primary goals of the occupation had largely been accomplished. It meant that Japan had been sufficiently punished and that it could now be restored as a power and ally in US overall Cold War strategy.

To achieve this new strategic objective, the United States first concluded a peace treaty with Japan in San Francisco in 1951, thus formally terminating the US occupation of Japan and restoring Japanese sovereignty and independence, and immediately thereafter established a military alliance with Japan through the US–Japanese Security Treaty, which committed the United States to the defense of Japan and at the same time enabled the US forces to be stationed on Japanese soil more or less indefinitely. This arrangement therefore tied Japan to the United States and was aimed at responding to the rising power of the Soviet Union and China in the East Asian region. Consequently, Japan was formally identified as an important member of the US-led security system in the Far East.

In the meantime, soon after the outbreak of the Korean War, Washington decided to dispatch the Seventh Fleet to the Taiwan Straits to prevent a possible invasion of Taiwan from mainland China. Thereafter, the United States established a regional security network in the Far East through a series of bilateral and multilateral security treaties. Specifically, after signing a bilateral security treaty with Japan in 1951, the United States signed similar treaties with the Philippines, Australia, and New Zealand in 1952, with South Korea in 1953, and with Taiwan in 1954. The Southeast Asian Treaty Organization (SEATO) was also established in 1954, with the United States, Australia, New Zealand, the Philippines, and Thailand joining together in the alliance. With these arrangements, the United States had therefore created a security system for the Far East. The anti-communist orientations of Japan, South Korea, and Taiwan were thus considered the best guarantee of the systemic equilibrium in East Asia. This Cold War structure of power relations came to entail equilibrium between the two blocs into which East Asia had become divided. The United States, Japan, South Korea, and Taiwan were pitted against the Soviet Union, China, and North Korea. In terms of ideology, such a structure corresponded to the Cold War perception of world affairs. This bifurcated world of East Asia continued to be divided and maintained some sort of balance between the two blocs until the late 1960s.

On the other hand, economic concerns also justified US policy adjustment in East Asia at the time. In addition to Cold War politics, the revival of the world economy was another key consideration in US foreign policy in the immediate postwar years, which was seen as crucial in winning the Cold War. As the only prosperous and productive power following the end of World War II, the United States held the implicit responsibility for sustaining the global capitalist system and helping revival of the capitalist economies in the postwar years. It is therefore the political and strategic necessity combined with economic concerns that prompted the shift of Washington's Asia policy. In the Far East, the United States identified the revival of the Japanese economy as essential for creating a viable regional economy. As such, Washington vigorously pursued a policy of revitalizing the regional economy centered on Japan. To pursue this objective, the United States provided economic assistance for Japan under the Economic Recovery in Occupied Areas (EROA). Like the Marshall Plan for Western Europe, this program was designed to rebuild Japanese industry and promote its export-oriented production through financing the import of industrial technology and raw materials. In the meantime, the United States also encouraged regional integration around Japan, through which all other East and Southeast Asian allies were to provide raw materials for Japan while at the same time absorb Japanese manufactured goods. Particularly, Washington promoted the construction of a triangular structure that would involve the United States, Japan, and other allies in the region, under which the United States served as the leading unit, Japan as the intermediate, and other East and Southeast Asian allies as markets, sources of raw materials, and a hinterland for Japan. More importantly, according to Washington, such an economic structure would lead to the creation of a regional political–economic grouping comprising the United States, Japan, and other East and Southeast Asian countries. This scheme fitted in well with Washington's intention of creating economic interdependence in the region, while providing a political counterweight against communism and encouraging "the rollback of Soviet control and influence in the area." This setup was conceived in deliberations of the National Security Council leading to the document NSC 48 and became a cornerstone of US Asia policy in the 1950s–60s.[3]

While Japan was seen as a potential political and economic partner of the United States in the region, it was surely not Washington's intention to transform Japan into a competitor once again, as was the case in the interwar period.[4] During a Round Table Conference in fall 1949, George Kennan elaborated on the necessity to devise a formula that would, on the one hand, stimulate Japan's economic growth while, on the other hand, keeping the former enemy subordinated to US interests. The key to making Japan prosperous economically and dependent politically lay in maintaining US control of that nation's economic lifeline – that is, vital imports such as food, oil, and so on – in order to be able to apply pressure when and if necessary. By means of such an economic leash, "we could have veto power over what she does."[5]

Whereas Japan was seen as the key to the US new geopolitical strategy in the Far East, South Korea and Taiwan were seen as integral part of this strategy. As Jon Halliday points out, "Just as Japan's restoration and re-insertion into the world economy were precipitated by the fight against socialism, so South Korea and Taiwan were reshaped not only to 'contain' the Korean and Chinese Revolutions, but also as Japan's periphery."[6] As such, Washington's policy was to keep both South Korea and Taiwan within the capitalist framework by providing these two peripheral states with huge military and economic assistance. Except for the US aid to South Vietnam during the Vietnam War, South Korea and Taiwan were the two major East Asian beneficiaries of Washington's largesse. Though its significance was not much beyond the mid-1960s, US economic aid was critical for both allies to make up for the deficits in the balance of payments and the budget in the 1950s and to promote their economic recovery and early industrialization.

Moreover, with the economic and military aid as leverage, the United States deeply influenced economic programs and the societies of both South Korea and Taiwan through encouraging or even forcing various economic and social reforms. These reforms helped to lay the basis for the subsequent rapid development of these two economies, as was in Japan. Particularly important, the United States directed and supervised the reorganization of the economic structures of South Korea and Taiwan along the line of export-oriented development strategy and encouraged the gradual integration of these economies with the global and regional economy. To make this strategy work effectively, the United States allowed these two allies, together with Japan, to have virtually unrestricted access to the huge US market, while at the same time tolerating their highly protective policies and practices. The huge US open market and relatively liberal markets in other industrial countries paved the way for East Asian allies to pursue successfully the export-driven industrialization.

Clearly, it was the US geopolitical strategy and its political, military, and economic policies toward its East Asian allies that fundamentally defined the evolution of the regional political economy of East Asia and substantially influenced the trajectory of their economic development in the postwar years. The postwar foreign policies and development strategies of these countries can all be traced to this US-designed and -led system and US influence. As a result, a vigorous regional economy in East Asia emerged and became fully integrated with the world economy. In the process, while these economies became especially dependent on the United States for capital, technology, and market for their products, they were also increasingly interdependent as a region with the Japanese investment playing an important role in promoting the process of regional interdependence. Consequently, a trade pattern evolved between the United States and the East Asian economies. In addition to Japan's huge exports to the United States, Japan supplied capital, intermediate products, and technology to South Korea and Taiwan, which then exported their products to the United States. This was the revival of the "flying geese" or "product cycle" mechanism in East Asia as promoted by the United States.

In the meantime, endorsed by the United States, East Asian states also substantially benefited from the liberal international economic regime established in the postwar period, known as multilateralism. This liberal international regime was primarily embodied in such important organizations as International Monetary Fund (IMF), the World Bank, the General Agreement on Tariffs and Trade (GATT) – which was transformed into World Trade Organization (WTO) in 1995 – and Organization for Economic Co-operation and Development (OECD).

In a further analysis, East Asian allies enjoyed US security umbrella, which not only provided a secure external environment for economic development but also helped save these countries from the burden of high defense spending. As a result, the relatively low defense spending allowed these countries to be less burdened by nonproductive investments and allocate more resources for economic development.

Finally, it is also important to note that while the US war effort in Korea contributed to the economic recovery of Japan, the conflict in Indochina had a similar significant impact on all its allies in East Asia. As Cumings notes in his study of this period:

> The Vietnam War played for the ROK the role that the Korean War played for Japan; labeled Korea's 'El Dorado' it accounted for as much as 20 percent of foreign exchange earnings in the late 1960s. Procurements for the war were also important for Taiwan, and, by the 1970s Taiwan was exporting capital goods, technicians, and foreign aid to several Southeast Asian nations.[7]

In brief, it is the American factor in the context of the Cold War that provided the crucial external environment for the rapid economic development of East Asia. Japan, South Korea, and Taiwan were the "chosen few" in a Wallerstein's system of "development by invitation," whose principle of upward mobility is "many called, few chosen."[8]

3.2   The internal dynamics: the Asian model

Within the external setting of Cold War politics and US hegemony in the postwar years, domestic political, military, and technocratic modernizing elites in East Asian capitalist states were pursuing economic development through a so-called "Asian model," that is, a unique development path that is different from the one that the Western developed countries had previously taken. This was originally a Japanese model of economic development but later imitated by other East Asian states. While the Asian model might be presented in slightly different forms from one state to the other in East Asia, two crucial features of this model are well shared across the region, that is, a strong developmental state and an export-oriented development strategy.

In the first place, East Asian economies all had a strong development-oriented state that was actively involved in economic development. In Japan, followed by South Korea and Taiwan, the state provided a disciplined form of administrative guidance to pave the way for economic development. In doing so, the state, through direct state intervention and guided market mechanism, adopted industrial policy of channeling resources into desired sectors, protected domestic and newly emergent industries from foreign competition, and provided subsidies and assistance for leading firms. The crucial role of the state was particularly evident in the initial stages of development. The state's involvement in economic development was first seen in the land reform that was undertaken in these countries in the early years of their postwar development. The resultant rapid increase of agricultural output enabled surpluses to be transferred from agriculture to industry. In the 1950s–60s, state intervention was also thought as necessary to break the so-called "vicious cycle" of poverty, low income, low savings, low investment, and low productivity, as this vicious cycle could hardly be broken by market forces alone. In the later years, state intervention in economic development was further embodied in the government's promotion of technology imports and high rates of domestic savings and investment; emphasis on education, skilled, and cheap labor; strong connection and cooperation between the government and the business; emphasis on the equitable distribution of income; and rapid improvement of people's living standards. It is also important to point out that a competent and relatively autonomous bureaucracy constituted a crucial part of the strong developmental state in East Asia.

As national conditions vary from one state to the other, nevertheless, the developmental state shows some variations across the East Asian region. Most notably, while adopting a capitalist economic system, East Asian states clearly pursue different forms of the capitalist economy. On the whole, two different types of capitalist economy can be identified in East Asia, that is, the authoritarian capitalist economy and the negotiated capitalist economy. Under the authoritarian capitalist economy, which is represented by South Korea, there is strong state involvement either directly in organizing economic activities or indirectly in regulating them. In the meantime, autonomous economic actors such as organized labor are often suppressed, while economic elites are a small group of people involving family members and wealthy corporate interests. More recently, China has moved away from the socialist command economy to embrace the capitalist market economy, which is very close to this authoritarian capitalist economy despite Beijing's continuing official rhetoric of sticking to the communist ideology. On the other hand, under the negotiated capitalist economy, which is seen in Japan and to a less extent in Taiwan as well, informal compromise is stressed between the major parties involved in economic decision-making, specifically between government agencies and business, while overt state intervention in the economy is avoided.[9] Whichever form, however, East Asian capitalism is quite different from Western capitalism, US capitalism in particular, which is based more on a *laissez faire* principle and liberal market economy with individual economic actors free to conduct business activities and with only moderate state intervention in the economy through macroeconomic management rather than industrial policy.

Moreover, while East Asian capitalism is generally characterized by frequent state intervention in the economy, the degree and mechanism of state intervention varies from one state to the other. Some important economic policies are also different between East Asian states. For example, whereas foreign investment was encouraged in Taiwan, there was explicit bias against foreign investment in Japan and South Korea until very recently in favor of their domestic large business firms. Besides, while Japan and South Korea promoted the development of huge business conglomerates, *keiretsu* in Japan and *chaebol* in South Korea, the size of Taiwanese companies is much smaller. However, Taiwan has a higher level of public ownership of crucial industries, as compared to Japan and South Korea.

It is important to point out, however, that since the 1980s the global trend of liberalization and privatization has been affecting East Asia as well. In order to acquire efficiency and to be competitive in the world economy, East Asian states have been gradually liberalizing their economic system and policies. This trend is particularly strengthened by globalization and regionalism.[10]

A second key element of the Asian model, which is actually related to the developmental state in East Asia, is the adoption of an export-oriented development strategy that is deliberately designed by all East Asian governments on the basis of their respective comparative advantages to promote economic growth through exporting manufactures. In the 1950s, East Asian capitalist states primarily adopted an import-substitution strategy, a strategy that encouraged the development of domestic industry and protected domestic industry from foreign competition by creating tariff and non-tariff walls. But in the 1960s, these states departed from the inward-looking strategy of import-substitution and switched to a strategy that promoted economic development through export of manufacturing products. This export-oriented development strategy played a particularly important role in the rapid economic growth of East Asia. As Staffan Linder notes when referring to newly industrializing economies (NIEs), no observer of these economies could possibly doubt the critical role played by the rapid growth of exports, that is, the adoption of export-oriented strategies to sustain the steady growth between 1965 and 1985.[11] Linder's remarks are also applicable to Japan. Ian Little expresses a similar view when discussing the rapid economic growth of Taiwan and South Korea. According to Little, the major reason for their success is their labor-intensive, export-oriented policies.

> Nothing else can account for it. Taiwan and Korea do not have very good capital markets. Their tax systems are not very good... Planning...has not played a key role. Moreover, the nonhuman resources of Taiwan and Korea are not notably favorable to high income or growth...Luck has played little part in their development. Aid was...not important during the high growth period. Borrowing has remained very important for Korea but not for the others.[12]

Undoubtedly, East Asian states, in pursuing the export-oriented development strategy, substantially benefited from the unique conditions of the postwar international political economy that provided a favorable external environment for its successful implementation. In this respect, the US market played a particularly crucial role in absorbing the bulk of East Asia's exports, which made the export-driven rapid economic growth of East Asian economies possible. In the meantime, the liberal international economic system that was established and maintained by the United States in the postwar years also contributed to the success of the export-oriented development strategy of East Asia states.

In a further analysis, the export-oriented industrialization of South Korea and Taiwan also benefited from the restructuring of the world economy. South Korea and Taiwan began to adopt export-oriented development strategy at a time when Europe and Japan had completed their economic recoveries. The timing of adopting this strategy was particularly favorable when the United States and Europe, confronted with the competitive Japanese export challenge and declining profitability, encouraged multinational corporations to transfer some of their activities to third world countries. The effort to gain competitive advantages by exporting parts of production processes to countries with lower wage levels, lesser concern for environmental considerations and, not least, lenient taxation became a component part of the strategy of the companies in the Western developed countries. This is also the case with Japanese companies. Speaking of South Korea, but also applicable to Taiwan, Tony Michell notes,

> For a country located close to Japan there can have been no more favorable time to enter the world economy than in the early 1960s. Japan had passed the "turning point" in the labor market and companies were seeking to export labor-intensive manufacturing processes. In 1960 the various indirect barriers to trade with Japan were removed.[13]

This development in the international division of labor also coincided with technological changes in the industrial production process. The new conditions permitted an increased fragmentation of work and made possible the transfer to third world countries of the more labor-intensive production inputs that could be performed by largely unskilled labor. The prospect of gaining access to large pools of unorganized, cheap labor in the third world at a time of near full employment and pressure for higher wages in the industrial countries was attractive to investors. In addition, progress in the field of transportation and communications reduced the logistical costs of such operations.[14] As a consequence of this development, Taiwan and South Korea became suppliers of labor to an increasingly far-flung division of production.[15]

While the Asian model was widely admired for the economic dynamism of East Asia, it is important to point out that this model developed in a specific East Asian cultural and social setting, which is heavily influenced by a shared cultural tradition of Confucianism. This cultural tradition especially emphasizes such social values and ethics as the acceptance of authoritarianism and respect for seniors, paternalistic government, collectivism, social order and harmony, consensus, saving and frugality, education, discipline, hard work, and merit-based bureaucracy. Much of the Asian model may be explained by referring to these social values and ethics of Confucian societies. For example, the acceptance of paternalistic authority and respect for superiors made the strong authoritarian developmental state possible; the paternalistic government assumed the responsibility to achieve social and economic equity and well-being for all its citizens; the prevailing norm of collectivism assured the subordination of the individual interests to the interests of collective so that the government was able to mobilize its citizens for the achievement of national objective of industrialization, even though people's living standards had been kept low for a quite long period of time; emphasis on social harmony, national coherence and consensus helped avoid social disturbance and conflict, thus creating a favorable, peaceful domestic environment for economic development; the high savings as a result of the virtue of frugality and thrifty made high rate of investment possible in East Asia; strong belief in the virtues of education, discipline, and hard work produced a capable and cheap labor force; and merit-based bureaucracy made the East Asian bureaucracy quite competent and reasonably honest, which then played an important role in effectively promoting economic development.

3.3   The transformation of the external setting and internal dynamics

By the end of the 1960s, the global political and economic setting had undergone dramatic transformation as a result of a series of developments, most notably, the breakup of the Sino-Soviet alliance, the relative decline of US hegemonic power, and the rise of Japan and Western Europe in the world economy.

In the first place, the global power structure had been transformed by the end of the 1960s as a result of the breakup of the Sino-Soviet alliance and relative decline of US hegemonic power. The open split of China and the Soviet Union during the 1960s was a most significant event in the Cold War period. After the establishment of the Sino-Soviet alliance in 1950, the two communist giants enjoyed a period of honeymoon for about 5 years. Starting in the mid-1950s, however, disputes emerged and developed between Beijing and Moscow over a number of issues, including the evaluation of Stalin, Moscow's policy toward the United States, Soviet economic and nuclear aids to China, and China's lost territories that Tsar Russia took from Qing China at the time when the nation was weak. Behind these disputes were the two powers' conflicting national interests and competition for leadership in the communist world. In the course of the 1960s, these disputes escalated and finally culminated in a number of armed border clashes between the two countries in 1969, leading to the open breakup of the Sino-Soviet unity. As a result, China emerged as an independent power center in global power politics and began to adjust its foreign policy in the face of Soviet threat.

The breakup of the Sino-Soviet alliance coincided with the Soviet achievement of strategic parity with the United States by the end of the 1960s and US diminishing power in pursuing its containment policy, as illustrated in its unsuccessful war effort in Vietnam. President Nixon's 1969 speech at Guam, which was later dubbed "Nixon Doctrine," was the open acknowledgment of the limits of US power. In that speech, President Nixon urged its allies to undertake principal combat roles in defending themselves while the Americans would only play a supportive role of providing them with economic and military aid. This was a most important signal that indicated Washington's intention to limit its commitment under the containment policy.

It was against this background that the United States and China, for their respective strategic needs, reached rapprochement and established a *de facto* US–Chinese strategic alignment against the Soviet threat in the early 1970s. As a result, while the Cold War continued, the basic structure of bipolarity in global power politics that had existed during the 1950s–60s had been fundamentally transformed into that of tripolarity. Accordingly, Washington's Asia policy was also substantially modified. Particularly, the containment policy, which proved no longer feasible, was formally abandoned, as illustrated by US withdrawal of all its forces from Vietnam in 1973. By 1979, Washington formally established diplomatic relations with China at the expense of Taiwan. As a result, the security environment in the Far East had been substantially transformed.

In addition to its relative decline of military power, the United States had also experienced relative decline of economic power by the end of the 1960s as a result of uneven development in the capitalist world economy and redistribution of economic power among capitalist countries. The relative decline of US economic power was most evidently shown in Washington's drop of the fixed-exchange-rate system in 1971 by devaluing the dollar for the first time in the postwar period. The decline of US economic power inevitably undermined its ability and willingness to continue its commitment to the maintenance of the postwar liberal economic order. On the other hand, after two decades of economic recovery and rapid growth, Japan and Western Europe regained economic strength. Particularly, by the end of the 1960s Japan had obtained an economic superpower status in the capitalist world economy, next only to the United States. Thereafter, Japan continued its rapid economic growth, increasingly challenging the US economic power. In the meantime, starting in the 1960s, other East Asian capitalist economies also experienced rapid economic growth. By the 1980s, South Korea and Taiwan, together with Hong Kong and Singapore, had become NIEs. As a result, the East Asian capitalist economies substantially improved their relative positions in the world economy and vis-à-vis the United States. Consequently, US relations with its allies in general and its East Asian allies in particular were growingly overshadowed by disputes over economic issues and defense burden-sharing.

It was within this context that by the end of the 1980s and early 1990s, fundamental changes took place again in international politics. The Cold War, which emerged from the ruins of World War II, came to a final end after the collapse of the communist regimes in Eastern Europe and the disintegration of the Soviet Union. With the end of the Cold War and the demise of geopolitical imperatives, geostrategic considerations no longer assumed priority in US relationships with its allies in general and its allies in East Asia in particular and concerns over economic costs increased. Under such circumstances, the relationship between the United States and its East Asian allies was substantially transformed. While continuing to maintain explicit or implicit alliance with its allies in East Asia, Washington de-emphasized its patron role in the region and, instead, paid growing attention to the economic competition from its East Asian allies. Particularly, facing continuous huge trade deficits with East Asia, Washington found itself frequently dragged into disputes over economic issues with its former protégés.

It was under such circumstances that there was rising protectionism in major Western economies, the United States in particular. Concurrent with growing protectionism was the emergence of economic regionalism in Western Europe and North America, as respectively embodied in the creation of a single European market in 1992 and the conclusion of the North American Free Trade Agreement (NAFTA) in 1993. Unlike protectionism that is largely sporadic and sector-effected, the emergence of trade blocs was posing a structural threat to the trade-based dynamism of the East Asian economies. As the economies in East Asia were highly outward-oriented, the growing protectionism and regionalism in Western Europe and North America – two major markets for East Asian exports – portended to stifle the growth potential of East Asian economies. These developments in the world economy brought significant implications on the political economy of East Asia. As a consequence, regional cooperation was gaining growing popularity in East Asia.

In a separate development, starting in the late 1970s, the post-Mao Chinese leadership discarded Mao's command economy and policy of self-reliance and began to introduce the market economy and participate in the global and regional economy by initiating economic reform and opening the country to the outside world. Beijing's new policy orientation, together with China's rapidly rising economic strength as a result of the economic reform, substantially transformed the political economy of East Asia even further. With its rapid economic growth, China not only served as a huge market for other East Asian economies but also played an increasingly key role in the economic dynamism of the region. Consequently, the rise of the Chinese economic power has been helping to reconfigure the political economy of East Asia with implications going far beyond.

Thus, by the turn of the century, the changed international environment has created new external imperatives for East Asian economies. Facing the changed nature of US–East Asian relationship, growing importance of economic affairs in international relations, and rising protectionism and regionalism in the world economy, the East Asian economies are obliged to reorient their foreign economic policies and regional policies. Moreover, the rise of the Chinese economic power and its participation in the regional economy has been further transforming the East Asian political economy and even the global political economy.

On the other hand, the Asian model, which had played so important a role in helping capitalist states in East Asia achieve their economic miracle in the 1950s through the 1980s, has been gradually transformed since the mid-1980s in the course of global economic liberalization. Particularly, the Asian financial crisis of 1997–98 has brought the Asian model into sharp question. The developmental state intervention in the economy is criticized by neoclassical economists for market distortions, which is said to have been the very cause of the Asian financial crisis.[16] Moreover, "crony capitalism" of the Asian model, a type of capitalism that is based on personal ties and political favors rather than economic rationality, is also blamed for causing the Asian financial crisis. According to S. Javed Maswood, "developmental states (in East Asia) were able to both generate rapid economic growth and prosperity, and alleviate poverty,... but in a period of increased economic and capital market globalisation, developmental states are relatively powerless to implement strategies that had hitherto been the hallmark of their success."[17]

As such, there has been transformed regional geopolitical setting and declining efficacy of the state intervention in national economic management in the post-Cold War era. Consequently, regional economic development in East Asia has been growingly driven by market forces at both regional and national levels in the context of globalization and of the new regional setting of competing influences of American, Japanese, and Chinese powers.

4
The Japanese Political Economy Since 1945

4.1   The Cold War, US hegemony, and the Japanese political economy

The postwar Japanese political economy was substantially defined by Cold War politics and US hegemony. Following its defeat in World War II, Japan was occupied by Allied forces, primarily US forces, while the Japanese economy had been completely devastated as a result of the war. The immediate objective of the postwar Japanese government was therefore to seek Japan's political independence and economic recovery. As such, Washington's policy of revitalizing Japan and incorporating Japan into its security framework of the Cold War in the Far East was in line with Japan's strategy of the time.

According to the postwar Japanese leaders, since the country was confined by the "peace clause" in its US-imposed postwar constitution, Japan's future would lie in economic expansion through peaceful means. But in order to do so, Japan must regain political independence by concluding a peace treaty with its former enemies. Given the fact that the United States was the hegemonic power, the main occupier of Japan and the economic giant in the world, it would make sense for Japan to pursue its national objective through establishing close ties with the United States and making special arrangements with Washington. This economy-oriented and pro-Anglo/US foreign policy was also based on the fact that for its economic recovery and development Japan would have to rely on raw materials, capital, technology, and markets of the United States, Britain, and the territories under their control. Most importantly, it was the belief of the postwar Japanese leaders that the Cold War could provide an opportunity for inducing the United States to restore Japanese independence through a peace treaty, while at the same time having US forces stationed in Japan for security purposes of both the countries. Obviously, such an idea fitted the "peace clause" of the constitution, reflected the notion of peaceful economic expansion, and rationalized the strategy of maintaining close economic, political, and military ties with the United States. By adopting this strategy, Japan decided to incorporate itself into the US-led security framework of Cold War politics. This strategy was to remain a guiding principle of Japanese diplomacy for more than 20 years.

Despite the efforts of the Japanese politicians and US occupation authorities to put the country back on its feet, however, it was only after the outbreak of the Korean War in 1950 that the Japanese economy really got going again. Politically, the outbreak of the Korean War eventually paved the way for the conclusion of a peace treaty with the United States in 1951, hence officially ending the US occupation of the country. Economically, the Korean War greatly stimulated the Japanese economy, which benefited substantially not only from a big jump in its total export earnings resulting from a 23% rise of the unit prices of world exports caused by the Korean War, but also from the country's position as a supplier *par excellence* of military provisions to the US war effort due to its geographical proximity to the Korean peninsula. In the period of 4 years between 1950 and 1953, while Japan's combined export earnings reached $4.6 billion (as compared to $0.5 billion in 1949), US war procurement orders brought the country additional $2.4 billion. Moreover, the use of Japan as a staging area as well as a rest and recreation area by UN troops brought the country additional income from the spending of hundreds of thousands by foreign troops that passed through the country. Consequently, this huge amount of foreign exchange earnings had not only effectively diminished Japan's dollar shortage and improved its balance of payments, but also enabled the country to import $2 billion per year of equipment and raw materials for expansion of its industrial production, as compared to less than $1 billion of imports before the Korean War. In the meantime, US war procurement orders together with technological transfer and assistance had directly helped revive Japan's heavy industry and brought Japan new techniques and procedures that eventually found application in nonmilitary production. According to Takafusa Nakamura, the Korean War helped boost Japan's industrial production index from 22.3 in 1950 to 40.3 in 1953, with the year 1960 as 100.[1] Obviously, the injection of US money and technology together with the market created by the Korean War made significant contribution to the recovery of Japan's economy and paved the way for the subsequent rapid economic growth.[2]

In the years following the Korean War, the United States continued to play an extremely important role in Japan's economic growth by providing a favorable external environment. The positive effects of this "America factor" were multi-dimensional. First of all, US security protection under the US–Japanese Security Treaty saved Japan from the burden of defense and enabled the country to confine its military spending within 1% of GNP. The low defense spending therefore allowed Japan to be less burdened by nonproductive investments as compared to other industrial countries. According to the estimate of Hugh Patrick and Henry Rosovsky, if Japan, like the United States, had used 6–7% of GNP on defense from 1954 to 1974, the size of its 1974 economy would have been 30% smaller.[3]

Secondly, in order to prevent Japan from turning to communist China for market, Washington granted Japan a Most-Favored-Nation (MFN) status as early as 2 April 1953, which allowed Japanese products to have virtually unrestricted access to the huge US market. According to William Nester, opening the US market for Japanese goods was perhaps the most important reason for Japan's economic success. Until the 1970s, the United States was importing more than twice as much from Japan as would be expected on the basis of Japan's share of world exports; and the European Economic Community (EEC) less than half as much in comparison.[4] Since the 1950s, around one-fifth to one-third of total Japanese exports was absorbed by the US market, although the specific export items differed over time with textiles representative of the 1960s, color TV sets of the 1970s, automobiles of the 1980s, and semi-conductors of the 1990s. Obviously, Japan's postwar economic development would have been very different had not the United States played a central role as an absorber of Japanese exports. Equally important, while the United States allowed Japan to enjoy its huge market and the benefits of a liberal international economic system, it had also tolerated Japanese discriminatory institutional arrangements and policies in the 1950s through the 1960s. All this led to Japan enjoying growing and continuous trade surplus with the United States.

Thirdly, the low exchange rate of the Japanese yen to the dollar set by the United States in the early postwar years had played an important role in Japan's successful implementation of export-oriented economic strategy. The rate of 360 yen to 1 dollar lasted from 1949 to 1971. As the Japanese economy grew increasingly powerful over time, particularly after the mid-1950s, the yen became increasingly undervalued. Consequently, the undervalued yen amounted to a substantial indirect subsidy to Japanese export industries, which enabled Japanese companies to flood the world's markets with low-priced goods. The undervalued yen also functioned as one of a number of non-tariff barriers that protected Japan's market from competitive foreign products.

Fourthly, the United States allowed a "technological infusion" into Japan in the postwar years. Imports of foreign technology via technical cooperation with foreign (primarily US) firms grew rapidly, from 27 agreements in 1950 to 101 in 1951, 133 in 1952, 103 in 1953, and 82 in 1954.[5] A whole range of industries benefited from this technological infusion, which not only helped improve the technological levels of Japanese industries that adopted the imported technologies but also brought ramification effects on other related industries, thus constituting an important factor for Japan's postwar rapid economic growth and upgrading of its economic structure.[6]

Last but not least, the United States also helped Japan enter the capitalist world economy by sponsoring its membership in most important international economic institutions, including the IMF (1952), the International Bank for Reconstruction and Development (World Bank) (1952), and the GATT (1955). These international institutions, which were established in the early postwar years, constituted the basis of the liberal international economic order. It was this US-led and -maintained international economic order together with US military commitment to its allies that created a favorable and secure environment for rapid economic growth of the capitalist world economy in general and provided very favorable external conditions for Japan to pursue export-oriented economic policy in particular. In the meantime, the stable supply of cheap raw materials and energy needed for heavy and chemical industries provided further essential favorable conditions for Japan's export-led industrialization in the postwar years.

Such a favorable external environment remained quite stable from the 1950s throughout the 1960s. It was within this favorable international environment that Japan had managed to ascend to an economic superpower by the end of the 1960s. Starting in the early 1970s, however, global economic conditions were undergoing dramatic transformation in the context of the eroding US economic hegemony, the growing influence of third world oil-exporting countries, and the rise of East Asian NIEs.

The postwar Japanese economy experienced a first major blow in 1971, when Washington announced its New Economic Policy, dubbed the "Nixon shock," which abruptly brought an end to the postwar fixed exchange rate system and replaced it with a floating exchange rate system. Consequently, Japan was forced to appreciate the yen, ending the

22-year golden period of the fixed exchange rate of 360 yen to the dollar. Thereafter, the value of the Japanese yen continued to rise, from 308 yen to the dollar in 1971 to 210 yen in 1978, 128 yen in 1988, and 94 yen in 1995, before it slightly bounced back to a range of 108–125 yen through 2003.[7] As the low exchange rate of the yen had been one of the crucial conditions contributing to Japan's postwar export-stimulated rapid economic growth, the impact of the appreciation of the yen on Japan's economic growth was substantial. Table 4.1 shows Japan's remarkable improvement in export price competitiveness for the two decades of the 1950s–60s taken as a whole as compared to West Europe and the United States. This steady improvement in Japanese export competitiveness was largely attributed to the fixed exchange rate of 360 yen to the dollar during these two decades. As a result of the appreciation of the Japanese yen in 1971, however, Japanese export unit prices began to increase, reflecting the disappearance of the advantages incurred from the long-time over-devalued yen. The appreciation of the yen therefore not only directly slowed down Japan's export-led economic growth but also greatly affected the Japanese national psychology, as most Japanese became pessimistic about the continuing international competitiveness of the Japanese economy without the 360 yen exchange rate.[8]

The Nixon shock was soon followed by two oil crises in the 1970s, which triggered a world-wide stagflation and hit the Japanese economy even harder. As Japan was dependent on imported oil for three quarters of its primary energy supply, the massive hike of oil price dramatically

Table 4.1 International Comparison of Unit Value of Exports, 1951–77 (1963: 100)

Year	Japan	USA	Western Europe	Developing countries
1951	134	93	101	128
1955	103	95	95	111
1960	107	99	97	103
1965	98	104	104	103
1967	100	110	105	103
1970	111	114	112	109
1971	110	121	130	126
1975	165	201	223	233
1977	162	218	243	404

Source: T. Nakamura, *The Postwar Japanese Economy: Its Development and Structure, 1937–1994*, 2nd edn (Tokyo: University of Tokyo Press, 1995), p. 206.

altered the very foundation of Japanese economic growth. Particularly, the two oil crises of the 1970s hit Japan's energy-consuming industries like petrochemical and heavy industries hardest, as the expansion of Japanese industry during the 1950s–60s had centered mainly on the steel and petrochemical industries, which heavily relied on imported oil. It is the cheap oil during these two decades that had brought the rapid growth of these high-volume energy-consumption materials industries. Under the impact of the dramatic rise of the prices of both oil and other primary commodities, concurrent with the growing competition from NIEs, some of Japanese industries like textiles, steel, nonferrous metals, and shipbuilding fell into a long-term depression.

Under such circumstances, the Japanese government decisively made significant strategic adjustment of the nation's economic structure. In May 1978, the Ministries of Trade and Industry, Transport, and Labor adopted countermeasures for "structurally depressed industries," directed at the hardest-hit industries and regions, by which Japan timely began to move from the resource-intensive industries into the high-tech industries, especially semiconductors, computers, consumer electronics, and robotics. In the meantime, the tertiary industries were encouraged to expand as well. The result was the successful adjustment of the Japanese industry into high-tech areas. Starting in the 1980s, Japan further directed research and development toward supercomputers, optoelectronics, and next-generation fighter planes.[9] By the early 1990s, Japan had established itself as a new international power in high-tech industries. A 1990 report by the US Defense Department acknowledges a Japanese lead in five high-tech industries crucial to US national security, including semiconductors, superconductivity, robotics, supercomputers, and photonics.[10]

As a result of its successful adjustment of the economic structure in the face of the global economic turbulence, Japan further consolidated its position as an economic superpower in the capitalist world economy in the course of the 1970s–80s. The effects of the rising Japanese economic power were stretching well beyond the region and over multiple economic areas, increasingly challenging the US economic power, which had experienced relative decline since the 1960s. Consequently, the nature of US–Japanese relationship that had been established in the early years of the Cold War had been transformed.

US–Japanese relations started to erode and transform in the late 1960s. While the United States and Japan remained allies in the areas of geopolitics and security, the rise of Japanese economic power increasingly triggered acute economic conflicts between the two countries over trade and other economic issues. Similar economic conflicts also grew between Japan and other Western industrialized countries.

The economic conflict between Washington and Tokyo started in the trade area as a result of Japan's consistent huge trade surplus with the United States. Japan moved into trade surplus with the United States in 1965 for the first time in the postwar years. Thereafter, Japan persistently maintained and expanded its trade surplus with the United States (with the exception of 1975), which reached its peak of $71.5 billion in 2000.[11] Japan's persistent huge trade surplus with the United States has therefore become a major constant source of US–Japanese economic conflict, as the Americans see the root cause of the trade imbalance between the two countries in Japan's unfair trade practices, which Washington could no longer tolerate as in the 1950s.

The first major trade friction between Japan and the United States emerged in the 1960s over the Japanese textiles exports. Thereafter, frictions over trade between the two countries gradually intensified, moving from textiles products to Japanese exports of steel, televisions, machine tools, automobiles, semiconductors, and other products. These trade frictions led to a series of bilateral negotiations on "voluntary" agreements, under which Washington forced Tokyo to accept "voluntary export restraint" (VER) and quotas on Japanese shipments of the products to the US market. In exerting pressure on Japan, Washington frequently threatened to take retaliatory measures such as the Omnibus Trade and Competitiveness Act of 1988 and the Super 301 provision of that Act. These measures would allow automatic investigation of unfair foreign trade practices and the threat as well as the retaliatory implementation of trade sanctions by the US President. In some instances, Washington did unilaterally imposed temporary higher tariffs on selected Japanese goods as an act of retaliation.

Whereas frictions over Japanese exports continued between Japan and the United States, and between Japan and other Western countries as well, there was also growing criticism in the United States of Japan's protection of its own markets against imports from abroad. As such, Washington increasingly exerted pressure on Japan to open its market to US products and to liberalize and deregulate its domestic economy, particularly pointing to the distribution system, domestic and overseas price differentials, cross-holding of company shares, land use, enforcement of the anti-monopoly law, the balance between domestic savings and investments, and the highly protected agricultural market. The United States also criticized Japan for failing to open its financial and securities markets, for lack of intellectual property rights protection, and for restrictions on foreign bidding for contracts and procurement orders, especially in public works and telecommunications industry. The United States also attempted to increase US products' access to the Japanese market by pressuring Japan into setting numerical targets in certain key sectors of the Japanese economy. Underlying the trade frictions, however, was a much broader issue of Washington's call for Japan to play a more active and responsible role in aiding the recovery of the world economy by stimulating its domestic demand and increasing imports.

To counter US pressure on trade issues, the Japanese particularly argue that the Americans need to reform their own economic structure and strengthen their competitiveness by improving the balance between investments and savings, research and development, the quality of the labor force, corporate investment behavior, and corporate strategy. On the other hand, however, under mounting external pressures, Japan did announce in 1973 to liberalize trade, by which some measures were adopted to reduce the scope and degree of protectionism and to improve market access for foreign goods and investment, although in reality the Japanese government continued to maintain non-tariff barriers to protect a number of selected industries. In a similar fashion, Japan also began to move to increase domestic demand and reduce reliance on exports for economic growth.

In addition to the frictions over trade and what kind of role Japan should play in promoting global economic growth, there was also conflict over the exchange rate of the Japanese yen. Washington's New Economic Policy of 1971 was at least partly the result of this conflict. Particularly, while Japan had become a highly competitive industrial nation, the continuing maintenance of the yen's low exchange rate was resented by both the United States and the Western European countries. Whereas the 360-yen exchange rate was seen by Washington as exerting strong pressure on its balance of payments obligations, West European countries viewed the undervalued yen as the Japanese unfair stealing of their markets. Although Japan was forced to have the Japanese yen appreciated after the collapse of the fixed exchange rate system as a result of the Nixon shock of 1971, the friction on the currency exchange rate continued between Japan and other developed countries, the United States in particular.

In the course of mounting economic conflicts over an increasing range of economic areas, US–Japanese economic relations became politicized after the 1970s. Against this background, there was even emergence of criticism of Japan's free ride on US military protection. As such, while the two countries remained allies, Washington exerted growing pressure on Tokyo that Japan should take more responsibility for its own national defense. Under such circumstances, the external conditions that had contributed to Japan's rapid economic growth in the 1950s–60s began to undergo substantial transformation in the 1970s and beyond.

4.2   The Japanese state and economic development

Japan's national ambition since the Meiji Restoration (1868) was to catch up with the West through creating a "rich country, strong army" (*fukoku kyohei*). However, as the military dimension of Japan's ambition was completely dashed as a result of the defeat and surrender on 15 August 1945, the postwar Japanese leaders concentrated on the economic objective of turning Japan into a leading industrial power and overtaking the West. This economic ambition of the Japanese substantially defined Japan's subsequent national policy and received universal public support in Japan in the postwar years, allowing politicians, government officials, and industrialists to join forces for its achievement.[12] It was within this context that the Japanese government played a special and active role in managing the national economy, particularly through the Ministry of International Trade and Industry (MITI) and the Ministry of Finance, and deliberately designed an export-oriented development strategy based on the nation's unique conditions. Consequently, the postwar Japanese political economy was highly supportive of the nation's fast economic recovery and subsequent rapid economic growth.

At the end of World War II, Japan's economy had been substantially devastated with widespread destruction of housing, industrial plants, and infrastructures, a substantially reduced rice crop output that was only two-thirds of that in the prewar period, rapidly rising inflation, and some ten million people out of employment. The total material losses caused by the war were estimated at a quarter of total national wealth, which accounted for all the gains that had been obtained since 1935.[13] Under such circumstances, the top priority of the postwar Japanese government was to bring economic recovery as soon as possible. To achieve quick economic recovery, the Japanese government introduced a series of institutional initiatives. The Economic Stabilization Board was established in 1946 to coordinate production and, together with the Reconstruction Bank, to channel capital into such industries as food, fertilizer, coal, and iron and steel. In 1948, the Economic Stabilization Board drew up a five-year plan, which envisaged the recovery of production to the levels of 1934 by the end of 1953. But what was most significant for the Japanese political economy of the coming years was the creation of MITI in 1949, whose chief objective, according to its inaugural minister, Inagaki Heitaro, was to transform Japan into a leading world exporter.[14] Under the aegis of MITI, the Japan Export-Import Bank was set up in 1950 – which was renamed the Export Bank of Japan in 1952 – for promotion of exports by providing financial support for exporting firms. In 1951, the Japan Development Bank was established to replace the Reconstruction Bank, which was responsible for supplying Japanese companies with low-interest funds for investment and providing security for finance received from commercial banks, international financial institutions, and other sources. By the time of the Japanese economic recovery at the end of 1953, MITI had firmly established its authority and prestige in the administration of the Japanese economy. In this process of institution buildup, a basic policy framework had been established that involved such policy measures as the allocation of import quotas, foreign exchange control, price controls, and various tax, financing and foreign investment incentives. These policy measures were used to promote such government-designated priority sectors as infrastructure, fertilizer, electrical power, coal, iron and steel, and shipbuilding.

After the economic recovery was achieved by the end of 1953, the Japanese government continued to be actively involved in economic development through setting national economic plans, defining economic priorities, adopting a series of supportive policies (including monetary, fiscal, industrial, technology, and trade policies), protecting domestic industries, managing the foreign trade process, and providing guidance for investment.

The Japanese government formally set its first national economic plan for administrative guidance of the economy as early as 1955 through the Economic Planning Agency (EPA). While most of economic plans were five-year plans, the average lifespan of a plan was about two and a half years, as each of these plans was usually put forward by a newly elected Prime Minister, who liked to build up a new image for his cabinet after coming into office. These plans provided a measure of flexible guidelines in determining financial allocations in finance, foreign exchange, and imported technology and, equally important, highlighted the industries that the state sought to promote. In brief, these economic plans contained three major elements: (1) the desired direction of economic and social development; (2) the policy direction the government should take in order to achieve the set goals; and (3) behavior guidelines for people and for businesses. In general, these plans set policy standards and functioned as guidelines for various aspects of the economy, particularly for government policy management.[15] Over time, however, the practical effects of the plans decreased in importance, as the government's role in the economy declined. During the 1990s, economic plans tended to focus either on responding to economic stagnation or on economic restructuring. In 2001, the EPA was reorganized into the secretariat to the newly created Council on Economic and Fiscal Policy (CEFP).

While economic plans set general objectives of economic development, it is MITI that was primarily responsible for guiding the direction of national economic development through industrial policy. MITI began to engage in administrative guidance in the form of advisory curtailments as early as 1952. Thereafter, MITI's administrative guidance of the nation's economy became increasingly sophisticated and comprehensive, which later evolved into a set of policy measures under the rubric of "industrial policy." These policy measures were deliberately designed to expand the nation's industrial base, promote new priority industries, and protect and adjust declining industries. To achieve the objective of industrial policy, MITI particularly adopted a strategy of import substitution and export expansion, based on a series of policy incentives, including preferential finance, tariff protection and import quotas, taxation breaks, subsidies, import permits for foreign technology, waivers from the Anti-Monopoly Law, and provision of industrial infrastructure. As such, MITI became the key government body that engineered the Japanese economic miracle.[16]

In pursuing industrial policy, MITI not only was able to influence the pattern of industrial legislation, but more importantly possessed extensive discretionary powers and leverages. In the early postwar years, the Japanese state was the main source of industrial finance dispensed through public financial institutions, the Japan Development Bank in particular, and through commercial banks. The Japan Development Bank not only provided low interest loans but also functioned to insure the borrowings by Japanese companies. As such, access to the Japan Development Bank's financing was very crucial in the long-term capitalization of Japanese companies. As the loans of the Japan Development Bank were provided on the basis of MITI's recommendation and were channeled into those projects that MITI deemed to be of national importance, MITI's decision would therefore determine the fortune of many Japanese companies. In the meantime, MITI had similar control of the financial resources of the Fiscal Investment Loan Program, which were largely funded by the post office savings system. Moreover, MITI was responsible for the allocation of foreign exchange under the terms of the Foreign Exchange and Foreign Trade Control Law. Given that foreign capital equipment and inputs were urgently needed in the 1950s, MITI's leverage over individual companies and industries in this respect was similarly decisive.

In particular, from the very beginning the Japanese government took various policy measures to protect domestic industries from foreign competition. Among the important protection measures adopted were high tariffs, a comprehensive system of quantitative controls and outright import bans, and foreign exchange controls. By the end of the 1950s, "only about 20 percent of Japan's imports were free of bans or quotas."[17] In addition to formal import barriers, Japan also maintained various informal and invisible barriers to manufactured imports, including highly restrictive product standards, testing and certification procedures, customs practices, government procurement practices and other protective practices and measures as well as cultural and structural barriers.[18] While the foreign exchange control was primarily a system for restricting the total volume of imports, it actually offered another effective means of protecting domestic industries by imposing extreme restrictions on imports, thus assuring a secured domestic market from foreign competition. Especially under the import protection were those key industries as identified by MITI, including, for example, automobile industry, steel industry, and computer industry. While the domestic market was highly protected, the Japanese government adopted aggressive and predatory measures to promote exports. As Richard Barnet points out, "Even as she was being initiated into the US-designed free trade system of the capitalist world, Japan was developing the mercantilist approach that would bring her extraordinary returns. The state guided internal trade, limiting imports to the barest essentials and subsidizing exports, just as in the prewar period."[19] Thus, in terms of industrial production, Japan substantially benefited from a large and protected domestic market and relative open access to large foreign markets. This permitted Japanese industries to reap the cost advantages of high-volume production. Moreover, MITI also used its powers to support the formation of large and economically powerful conglomerates – *keiretsu* – as an additional means to improve the competitiveness of Japanese companies. In a similar fashion, MITI encouraged producers in several fields (cotton-spinning, followed by steel) to form cartels to improve competitiveness.

In pursuing industrial policy, MITI by and large managed to maintain a high degree of autonomy and was impervious to the influence and domination of any single industry or interest group. Particularly, MITI applied its authority with considerable professionalism and care.

What is especially unique is that MITI managed to elicit entrepreneurial cooperation and maintained extremely close relationship with the business community for effective administrative guidance. In this regard, the Japanese Federation of Economic Organizations (*keidanren*) played an important role. It mobilized political donations and acted as an alliance in front of the government, imploring it to pursue measures that were supportive of industry in general. By acting as an umbrella organization, *keidanren* helped to partially prevent the formulation of policies that would otherwise narrow sectional interests. In the meantime, industries were also represented in the Industrial Structure Advisory Committee (the Industrial Structural Council after 1964) whose subcommittees deliberated on matters relating to individual industries. By this, businesses were able to ensure that MITI's policy recommendations were usually not coercive and were in keeping with their interests.[20]

In addition to MITI's industrial policy, the Japanese government, through several other government agencies (the Ministry of Finance in particular), frequently adopted fiscal and monetary policies to provide economic infrastructure and promote capital accumulation for industrial development. The tax system was reformed in the postwar years to promote investment and technological innovation. A proportional tax system was introduced, which placed particular emphasis on special tax measures for the promotion of plant and equipment investment and exports. Other measures of tax reductions and exemptions were also adopted, including a special high-rate depreciation system for important machinery. All these measures were designed to promote capital accumulation and became the basis of the subsequent business tax system.

In the meantime, by discouraging consumerism the Japanese government was able to institutionalize a high rate of internal savings for investment. This policy was in conformity with the Japanese people's high propensity to save. As a result, Japan achieved a much higher savings rate than other developed countries. For instance, in 1976, Japan had a savings rate of 24.9%, as compared to 7.9% for the United States, 11.2% for Britain, 14.5% for West Germany, 12.3% for France, and 19.4 for Italy.[21] High savings rate ensured that much of the capital required for industrial investment was raised from domestic private sources, channeled through the banks and post office savings. Consequently, Japan's economic growth was facilitated by exceptionally high rates of investment.

The government's heavy involvement in the nation's economic development helped turn the country into the so-called "Japan, Inc." Indeed, from the very beginning there was a national consensus in postwar Japan that "economism" should define their foreign policy and that the country should undertake economic expansion at home and abroad without involving itself in complex international politics. The Japanese were determined to catch up and move into the ranks of the major industrial nations. With such a determination, the Japanese government, through economic planning and industrial policy, decided the direction of the nation's industrial development and promoted and protected Japanese business in the process of moving toward that direction.[22] Such governmental guidance and protection first took shape in the early 20th century when the Japanese government adopted measures to protect and develop the steel and shipbuilding industries. Consequently, it was within the context of a favorable international environment combined with a developmental state in guiding and promoting the growth of national economy that Japan ascended to an economic superpower in about two decades in the postwar era.

As Japanese industry became increasingly mature and as it was also required as a member of both the IMF and the GATT, the Japanese government started economic liberalization in the 1960s. In the course of the 1960s through the 1980s, the trade and financial controls were gradually loosened – trade barriers began to be reduced in the 1960s, liberalization of FDI in the country started in 1964, foreign capital began to be introduced in 1967, and by 1980 foreign exchange control was abolished. In the 1980s, Japan's money and capital markets were both liberalized and opened to foreign financial institutions. Foreign banks were allowed to move into the trust business and foreign securities companies were permitted to obtain membership on the Tokyo Stock Exchange. In the meantime, the revision of the Foreign Exchange Law (1979) and the removal of restrictions on currency conversion (1984) facilitated the outflow of Japanese capital. As economic liberalization was deepening and the economy became fully mature, MITI was also transformed, which no longer pursued industrial policy to the extent that it had done before. Starting in 1984, MITI used administrative guidance as a policy instrument less frequently. Instead, the government began to rely primarily on the issuing of "visions" – that is, the formulation of blueprints for a future industrial structure, while the range of subsidies, low-interest financing, and tax incentives was substantially limited. In accordance with the changed role of the government, contemporary industrial policy is redirected at redressing obvious market failures. Issues that are now within the government's purview include problems associated with declining sectors, the reduction of capital risks in research and development within high technology fields, the inadequacy of social overheads, the improvement of public services, the promotion of high-tech industries, and the enhancement of life quality. Reflecting its modified role in the context of the changed external and domestic economic conditions, MITI was eventually reorganized into the Ministry of Economy, Trade and Industry (METI) in 2001.

4.3 The rise of Japan as an economic superpower

Thanks to a developmental state that persistently pursued an export-oriented strategy through deliberately designed industrial policy within a unique favorable international environment, Japan achieved remarkable economic success in the postwar years.

Japan's rapid economic growth started very early in the postwar years. During the 1950s, Japan witnessed an average annual growth rate of 8.7%, which was followed by an even more impressive average annual growth rate of 10.4% in the 1960s, both doubling the average annual growth rates of industrialized countries as a whole (4.3% for the 1950s and 5.1% for the 1960s) and exceeding those of the United States (3.3% and 4.3%) by a wide margin.[23] With such rapid economic growth, Japan first regained its prewar economic levels by 1954 and then ascended to an economic superpower by 1969. The oil crises of the 1970s and the consequent global stagflation ended Japan's over two decades of rapid economic growth and brought a long-term impact on Japan's economy. However, the upward move of economic structure triggered by the oil crises soon helped resume Japan's economic growth, although the growth rate declined from the average 10.4% of the 1960s to an average annual growth rate of 5.0% during the 1970s, which was consistently higher than the average rate of 3.2% of industrialized countries and those of other major industrialized countries (1.9% of Britain, 2.6% of West Germany, 3.0% of Italy and the United States, 3.5% of France, and 3.9% of Canada).[24] Especially, during the 1980s Japan's advantage came from its more stable economic growth, while economic growth of other industrialized countries was subject to greater fluctuation, with much sharper swings in the business cycle than in Japan. As a result, Japan maintained an average annual growth rate of 4.0% in the 1980s, well above all other major industrialized countries (2.2% for West Germany, 2.4% for France and Italy, 3.0% for the United States, 3.2% for Britain, and 3.4% for Canada).[25]

As a result of rapid economic growth, Japan became the second largest economy in the world. While less than one-elevenths of the size of the US economy and about two-thirds of the size of the British economy in 1960, the Japanese economy became 73.5% of that of the United States and as large as that of the combined economy of Britain, France, and Germany in 1995. In the meantime, with only 2.2% of world's total population, Japan had an economy that accounted for 17.4% ($5149.2 billion) of world GNP in 1996, compared with 3.9% ($1152.1 billion) for Britain, 5.2% ($1533.6 billion) for France, 8.0% ($2364.6 billion) for Germany, and 25.2% ($7433.5 billion) for the United States. In 1988, Japan for the first time boasted a higher annual GNP per capita ($21,050) than that of the United States ($19,870); and by 1996 the respective figures were $40,940 for Japan and $28,020 for the United States. Due to the economic downturn that started in the early 1990s, however, the Japanese economy experienced shrink over the second half of the 1990s and early 2000s. Consequently, by 2003 Japan's GNP had reduced to $4360.8 billion and its share in world GNP dropped to 12.6%. At the same time, Japan's GNP per capita also reduced to $34,180 by 2003, as compared to $37,870 for the United States.[26] Despite the recent economic shrink, Japan remains the second largest economy in the world after the United States.

Japan's rapid economic growth was accompanied by a steady transformation of the economic structure (Table 4.2). Particularly, the industrial structure moved along a clear ladder of upward development. In the 1950s, Japan's textile industry was reestablished. From the mid-1950s through the end of the 1960s, Japanese companies moved beyond production of low-wage, technologically limited goods into much more advanced areas of steel production, shipbuilding, machine tools, plastics, petrochemicals, cameras, television sets, motorcycles, and automobiles, the industries that required large natural resources, and a big market to absorb their products. All these industries were protected by MITI

Table 4.2   Transformation of Japan's Economic Structure, 1950–2002 (% of GDP)

	Primary industry	Secondary industry	Tertiary industry
1950	26.0	31.8	42.3
1960	12.8	40.8	46.4
1970	5.9	43.1	50.9
1980	3.6	37.8	58.7
1990	2.4	35.7	61.8
2000	1.3	28.4	70.2
2002	1.3	26.4	72.3

Source: Calculated from Statistics Bureau (Japan), *Japan Statistical Yearbook*, various years (Tokyo: Japan Statistical Association and Mainichi Newspapers).

from foreign competition while they were establishing a market position within Japan. The *keiretsu* played a particularly dominant role in this process. Consequently, in the 1960s Japan became the world's third largest producer of crude steel and aluminum, the sixth largest exporter, and the largest shipbuilder, exceeding the combined production of its four closest competitors. By 1980, Japan surpassed the United States as the largest producer of automobiles. By 2002, Japan remained the largest shipbuilding nation and the largest producer of automobiles, and the second largest producer of iron and steel in the world.[27]

As Japan's rapid economic growth was especially propelled by the country's robust growth of manufacturing exports, the transformation of the Japanese industrial structure is accordingly reflected in changes of composition of Japanese exports. While about half of Japanese exports consisted of textile products in 1950, this figure was steadily dropping to 37.3% in 1955, 9.0% in 1970, 5.3% in 1975, and 2.5% in 1990. By 2003, textile products almost disappeared as an export item (0.2%). Over the 1950s, steel products became an important item of Japanese exports, rising to 34.0% by 1960. But subsequently steel exports also declined, falling to 14.7% in 1970, 11.9% in 1980, 4.4% in 1990, and by 2003 dropping to only 3.8%. Starting in the 1960s, machinery and transport equipment (particularly ships and automobiles) replaced steel as the leading exports, steadily rising from 12.3% of overall Japanese exports in 1955 to 23.2% in 1960, 31.2% in 1965, 40.5% in 1970, 62.7% in 1980, and 74.9% in 1990, and thereafter remaining stable at over 70% (74.3% in 2000 and 72% in 2003). Particularly important, between 1965 and 2003, nonelectric machinery exports jumped from 7.4% of Japan's total exports to 20.2%, exports of electric machinery, apparatus, and appliances from 9.2% to 23.6%, and exports of transport equipment from 14.7% to 24.3%.[28] Overall, Japanese exports are dominated by manufactured goods, incorporating 93% of Japan's total exports in 2003.[29] Consequently, Japanese products have successively dominated global markets in shipbuilding, steel, chemicals, consumer electronics, and automobiles since the early 1960s.

In contrast to the export of manufacturing products, Japanese imports concentrated on mineral fuels and raw materials for a quite long period of time. Although the pattern of Japanese imports has evolved over time with the relative importance of primary goods declining while imports of manufactured goods increasing, reflecting Japan's changing economic structure, the weighted average ratio of manufactures to total Japanese imports is still only 76% as compared to over 80% of most other developed countries.[30]

The transformation of the Japanese economic structure is also illustrated in the changing pattern of Japan's technology exports and imports. While as late as 1975, Japan's technology exports were still less than half of technology imports in terms of value, this pattern of technology exports and imports was reversed by 1980, which made Japan a net technology exporting nation. Thereafter, technology exports rose substantially and by 2003 became 2.7 times the technology imports in value. This trend can also be explained by the increasing number of business enterprises involved in technology exports and the decreasing number of business enterprises engaged in technology imports around the same period. It is also important to note that Japanese technology exports concentrate in manufacturing sectors, particularly in chemicals, electric machinery, and transportation.[31]

With such a structure of exports and imports, Japan has developed a triangular trade pattern over time, under which Japan runs trade deficits with some of its major raw material suppliers (including the Middle East, Australia, Canada, the Philippines, Brunei, Indonesia, Malaysia, and Brazil), while enjoying sizeable trade surpluses with the United States, Europe, rest of Asia, and other countries through venting its manufactured exports. In 1965, Japan achieved trade surplus for the first time in 20 years. Thereafter, Japan continuously enjoyed surpluses with most of its trading partners. Most spectacularly, Japan's trade surplus with the United States jumped from $113 million in 1965 to $40.6 billion in 1985 and reached a peak of $71.5 billion in 2000. By 2004, Japan enjoyed an overall trade surplus of $110.7 billion, including a surplus of $65.0 billion with the United States.[32]

With continuous trade surplus, Japan has enjoyed a stable balance of payments surplus since 1968 with the exception of 1973, 1974, and 1980 when the country was severely hit by the oil crises of the 1970s. By 2003, Japan achieved a balance of payments surplus under the current account that amounted to $136.2 billion, which was 2.5 times the second largest balance of payments surplus held by Germany ($54.9 billion). The sustained balance of payments surplus in turn enabled Japan to build up its gold and foreign exchange reserves and transform itself from a debtor to a creditor nation. By 2003, Japan had accumulated the largest ever foreign exchange and gold reserves in the world, amounting to $673.6 billion.[33] By the end of October 2005, Japan's foreign exchange and gold reserves reached $836.5 billion, of which foreign exchange reserves amounting to $824.3 billion.[34] By contrast, the United States experienced huge budget deficits, trade deficits, and the falling US dollar over the same period of time. The result was a massive transfer of financial power from the United

States to Japan. Consequently, Japan became a full-fledged competitor in search of outlets not only for its ever-growing industrial production but also for its immense surplus capital.

With a huge financial surplus, Japan rapidly moved into overseas direct and portfolio investment that mirrors the pattern of financial outreach of Great Britain in the 19th century and the United States between 1948 and 1980. Postwar Japanese outward FDI remained insignificant until the mid-1960s. By 1965, the accumulated amount of Japanese outward FDI had been only $949 million. After 1965, however, Japanese FDI outflows began to get momentum, rising from $159 million in 1965 to $904 million in 1970. It grew even more rigorously through the early 1970s and by 1975 Japanese annual FDI outflows reached $3.3 billion. The great boom in Japanese FDI came after 1980 as a result of continuous huge trade surplus and the high domestic savings rate. Particularly, spurred by the rise in the value of the yen following the 1985 Plaza Accord, Japanese outward FDI rose from $4.7 billion in 1980 to $22.3 billion in 1986 and reached a peak of $67.5 billion in 1989, which turned Japan into the largest current FDI source country, surpassing the United States ($40 billion) and Britain ($35 billion).[35] By the late 1980s, Japanese outward FDI accounted for around 17% of the world's FDI stock.[36] Starting in the early 1990s, however, Japan's outward FDI has been on decline, dropping from $57.7 billion in 1990 to $35.4 billion in 2004.[37] Consequently, by 2004 Japan ranked the sixth in terms of annual FDI outflows and the seventh in terms of outward FDI stock.[38]

The pattern of Japanese outward FDI with respect to industrial and geographical distribution evolved over time. Initially, Japanese FDI was concentrated on raw materials and on low-tech manufacturing facilities located in developing countries. By 1970, 40% of the Japanese FDI had been in resources, primarily the mining industry; 22% in labor-intensive industries or in local market-oriented sectors; and 38% in commerce and finance. In terms of geographical distribution, 25% of Japanese FDI was in North America, 22% in Southeast Asia, 18% in Europe, 16% in Central and South America, and 9% in the Middle East.[39] However, the surge of Japanese FDI outflows after 1980 was primarily concentrated in developed countries and in industries where Japan was exporting. Protecting export markets, which was only a modest motive in the 1960s, became a much more important factor after 1980. As a result, by 1989, the share of Japanese FDI in terms of value in mining dropped to 1.9% and the share in textiles, electrical equipment, and metals dropped to 9.7%, while 50.5% of Japanese FDI was in trade, finance, insurance, service, and transportation, a pattern that remained roughly the same throughout the early 21st century.[40]

In terms of geographical distribution, by 1989, 50.3% of Japanese outward FDI in terms of value was in North America, 21.8% in Europe, 12.2% in Asia, 7.7% in Latin America, and 6.8% in Oceania.[41] Especially, the rise of Japanese outward FDI was in conjunction with huge Japanese international surpluses and corresponding US deficits. The United States was the major destination of Japanese FDI, which absorbed 48.4% of Japanese total FDI at its peak in 1989.[42] The flooding of Japanese FDI into the United States was partly due to the rise in the value of the yen, which made investment in the United States much cheaper than in Japan, and partly due to the need to circumvent US protectionist measures such as VER imposed on Japanese imports. In this regard, Japanese automotive companies and electronic manufacturers were especially active in setting up plants to produce goods directly for the US market within the United States. In a further analysis, the boom of Japanese FDI in the United States, especially after the 1985 Plaza Accord, was also part of the broader process of globalization of Japanese business. But since the early 1990s, however, Japanese FDI going to North America was steadily declining and by 2004 it dropped to 13.6% in value. In contrast, Japanese FDI to Europe was steadily rising through the early 21st century from 21.8% in 1989 to a peak of 49.9% in 2000 before dropping to 36.5% in 2004. On the other hand, Japanese FDI to Asia rose from 12.2% in 1989 to 26.4% in 2004. The changing number of cases is also illustrative of this trend with the exception that the number of cases of Japanese FDI in Asia remained almost unchanged between 1989 and 2004 despite the doubling of Japanese FDI in value in the region. This indicates the increased average size of Japanese investment projects in Asia.[43]

Even more impressive is the rising Japanese influence in international financial and capital markets through the investment of Japanese surplus capital in a range of financial instruments. With huge international surpluses, Japan's portfolio investments rose from $4.1 billion in 1975 to $21.4 billion in 1980, and $145.7 billion in 1985. After the mid-1980s, as a result of the dramatic rise in the value of the yen after the Plaza Accord and the continuing high interest rates in the United States, there was even more rapid increase in Japan's foreign portfolio investments, which jumped to $563.8 billion in 1990, $938.3 billion in 1995, $1392.9 billion in 2000, and $1590.2 billion in 2003.[44] The majority of Japan's portfolio investments were in the United States. On the other hand, the United States, sinking to the status of the world's largest debtor, became increasingly dependent on Japan for financial resources as a major source in the US treasury bonds and other financial markets. By the end of June 2004, Japan's holdings of US securities (including equities, long-term and short-term debt securities) had amounted to $1019 billion, accounting for 20.5% of the total foreign holdings of US securities, which more than doubled the second largest holdings of $488 billion claimed by Britain.[45] Japan's huge portfolio investments in the United States indirectly helped to finance US huge trade and budget deficits. Moreover, Japanese financial power is both large and concentrated enough to affect global markets in substantial ways. For example, financial decisions by the Japanese were blamed for the collapse of world bond and stock prices in 1987 and also credited for their subsequent recovery.[46] Consequently, the growing financial power of Japan generated a strong sense and fear among many Americans of the US economy being overwhelmed by the Japanese.

As a result of the rapid growth of overseas direct and portfolio investments, Japan's net external assets dramatically expanded in about three decades, jumping from $7.0 billion in 1975 to $11.5 billion in 1980, $129.8 billion in 1985, $328.1 billion in 1990, $893.8 billion in 1995, $1234.5 billion in 2000, and $1490.7 billion in 2003, making Japan the largest creditor nation in the world.[47]

Equally significant, as the largest creditor nation, Japan also became an indispensable source of capital for developing countries and international financial institutions. With its huge economic capabilities and international surpluses, Japan played a growingly important role in foreign aid to developing countries. From 1973 onward, Japanese official development assistance (ODA) expanded rapidly under a series of mid-term plans, from $0.5 billion in 1970 to $1.1 billion in 1973, $3.7 billion in 1980, $10.5 billion in 1990, and a historic high of $17.5 billion in 1995. In 1989, Japan exceeded the United States in ODA for the first time, and remained the largest donor of ODA for ten consecutive years from 1992 to 2001. Thereafter, Japan maintained the position of the second largest donor after the United States.[48] By 2004, Japan disbursed $16.2 billion of ODA, which accounted for 17.5% of the total ODA provided by the countries of Development Assistance Committee (DAC).[49] Japan's ODA includes bilateral ODA in the form of grants and development lending as well as contributions to multilateral institutions. In terms of regional distribution, Japan's bilateral ODA has concentrated in East Asia, followed by South and Central Asia (Table 4.3). It is important to note that Japan's aids as well as investments in developing countries are closely tied to their import of Japanese products.

The rising economic power has substantially enhanced Japan's status and influence in global economic institutions. Japan was initially

Table 4.3 Japan's Bilateral ODA by Region, 1970–2005 (% of Total)

Year	Asia			Africa	America	Europe	Oceania
	Far East Asia	South & Central Asia	Middle East				
1970	74.5	23.8	3.3	2.3	–	–	–
1975	56.8	18.3	3.9	13.0	5.6	0.6	0.6
1980	39.1	29.3	2.5	18.5	5.9	0.2	0.6
1985	46.9	20.7	1.7	15.0	8.8	1.1	0.9
1990	46.8	14.1	1.5	15.8	8.3	4.8	1.7
1995	39.2	15.5	3.9	15.5	11.0	0.5	1.5
2000	42.5	13.3	3.4	11.0	8.5	2.3	1.6
2005	44.8	13.9	4.7	8.3	5.6	0.1	1.6

Source: OECD. Stat Development/Aggregate Aid Statistics/2b. ODA by Recipient by Region, http://www.sourceoecd.org/database/oecdstat, accessed on 25 January 2008.

sponsored by the United States to enter into three key institutions of the capitalist world economy – the IMF and the World Bank in 1952 and the GATT in 1955. Ever since, Japanese economic and political power within these multilateral institutions has increased through the expansion of its financial contribution and attendant voting shares. By October–November 2005, Japan had possessed 6.24% of total quotas in the IMF and 8.08% of total subscriptions in the World Bank, and accordingly had secured the second largest share of votes in both institutions – 6.13% in the former and 7.86% in the latter.[50]

Japan maintained a low international posture in the first three decades after World War II. With its rising economic power as well as the changed external conditions in the wake of the end of the Cold War, Japan has developed a much greater consciousness of its own power and willingness to apply that power to Japanese-defined goals. Consequently, since the 1980s Japan has been pursuing a more independent, and even assertive, foreign policy with greater international thinking in such areas as foreign aid, peace-keeping, and growing defense capabilities. Particularly, Japan plays an increasingly active role in the United Nations as the second largest financial contributor to the UN budget. In G-8 Summit, Japan also plays three overlapping roles of being a member of the Western camp, assuming the responsibilities of an international state and representing the interests of East Asia as the only non-Western member of the summit.[51]

4.4   Japan's reestablished economic dominance of East and Southeast Asia

As a hegemonic power in the postwar years, the United States maintained its economic dominance in East and Southeast Asia in the 1950s through the early 1970s. Over time, however, Japan was slowly reestablishing its economic hegemony in the region, while US economic dominance of East and Southeast Asia was weakening. The result is that since the early 1970s, East and Southeast Asia's dependence has gradually shifted from the United States to Japan in terms of aid, loans, import–export ratios, foreign investment, and capital flows.

Japan's postwar economic domination of the region was initially established through its ODA to East and Southeast Asian countries. From the very beginning, Japan's provision of ODA to the region had a clear strategic and political purpose, serving as a substitute for military power and helping to draw the states of the region into a relationship of both political and economic interdependence. Japan's ODA first came as reparations aids, which primarily took the form of the export of outdated technology and industrial plants. These aids allowed Japanese companies to reenter regional markets and to create the technological and production linkages between East and Southeast Asian countries and Japan in the 1950s–60s. Thereafter, Japan's ODA was directly linked to the purchase of Japanese goods and services, especially for those Japanese-aided large infrastructure projects. While the direction of Japanese ODA diversified in the 1970s and mid-1980s in attempts to guarantee oil supplies from the Middle East and to assist US allies in the Persian Gulf, Horn of Africa, Caribbean and bordering Afghanistan, East and Southeast Asia still received the largest share of Japanese bilateral ODA. Top recipients of Japanese bilateral ODA are mostly East and Southeast Asian countries (Table 4.4). For most East and Southeast Asian countries that receive ODA from developed countries, Japan ranks as the main aid donor.

Furthermore, Japan also plays a crucial role within the Asian Development Bank (ADB) as one of the two largest contributors with its subscribed capital amounting to 15.781% of the ADB's capital pool, having 12.942% of voting power as of 31 December 2004 – the United States is another country that holds the same percentage of subscribed capital and voting power.[52]

The MITI often conceived of ODA as a means to enhance the vertical integration of the regional economy into the Japanese economy in order to establish a regional division of labor. Consequently, Japanese ODA is frequently used to support the penetration of East and Southeast Asian

Table 4.4 Top Five Recipient Countries of Japanese Bilateral ODA, 1970–2004 (% of Total)

Ranking	1		2		3		4		5	
Year	Country	%	Country	%	Country	%	Country	%	Country	%
1970	Indonesia	33.9	South Korea	23.4	Pakistan	10.7	India	8.8	Philippines	5.2
1971	South Korea	28.8	Indonesia	25.9	Pakistan	8.1	India	7.8	Philippines	6.9
1972	South Korea	25.2	Philippines	23.1	Indonesia	23.0	India	6.0	Bangladesh	3.9
1973	South Korea	20.5	Indonesia	18.7	Philippines	18.5	India	9.0	Bangladesh	3.8
1974	Indonesia	25.1	South Korea	19.1	Philippines	8.3	India	7.4	Vietnam	6.2
1975	Indonesia	23.3	South Korea	10.3	Philippines	8.3	Malaysia	7.4	Egypt	5.9
1976	Indonesia	26.6	India	10.5	Philippines	10.0	Thailand	5.7	Malaysia	4.5
1977	Indonesia	16.5	South Korea	9.4	Egypt	7.5	Bangladesh	7.3	Thailand	5.8
1978	Indonesia	14.9	Bangladesh	7.8	Egypt	7.8	Thailand	6.8	Philippines	4.3
1979	Indonesia	11.5	Bangladesh	10.5	Thailand	9.1	Pakistan	8.5	Egypt	6.7
1980	Indonesia	17.4	Bangladesh	10.7	Thailand	9.4	Egypt	6.1	Pakistan	5.6
1981	Indonesia	13.3	South Korea	13.1	Thailand	9.5	Philippines	9.3	Bangladesh	6.4
1982	China	15.6	Indonesia	12.4	Bangladesh	9.1	Thailand	7.2	Philippines	5.8
1983	China	14.4	Thailand	10.2	Indonesia	9.7	Philippines	6.1	India	5.3
1984	China	16.0	Malaysia	10.1	Thailand	9.6	Indonesia	6.9	Philippines	6.6
1985	China	15.2	Thailand	10.3	Philippines	9.4	Indonesia	6.3	Malaysia	4.9

Year									
1986	China	12.9	Philippines	11.4	Thailand	6.8	Bangladesh	6.5	India	5.9
1987	Indonesia	13.8	China	10.8	Philippines	7.4	Bangladesh	6.5	India	5.9
1988	Indonesia	15.3	China	10.5	Philippines	8.3	Thailand	5.6	Bangladesh	5.3
1989	Indonesia	16.9	China	12.3	Thailand	7.2	Philippines	6.0	Bangladesh	5.5
1990	Indonesia	12.8	China	10.7	Philippines	9.5	Thailand	6.2	Bangladesh	5.5
1991	Indonesia	12.0	India	10.1	Egypt	7.0	China	6.6	Philippines	5.2
1992	Indonesia	16.2	China	12.5	Philippines	12.3	India	5.1	Thailand	4.9
1993	China	16.5	Indonesia	14.1	Philippines	9.3	Thailand	4.3	India	3.6
1994	China	15.3	India	9.2	Indonesia	9.2	Philippines	6.1	Thailand	4.0
1995	China	13.1	Indonesia	8.4	Thailand	6.3	India	4.8	Philippines	3.9
1996	Indonesia	11.6	China	10.3	Thailand	7.9	India	6.9	Philippines	5.0
1997	China	8.7	Indonesia	7.5	India	7.4	Thailand	7.1	Philippines	4.8
1998	China	13.5	Indonesia	9.6	Thailand	6.5	India	5.9	Pakistan	5.7
1999	Indonesia	15.3	China	11.7	Thailand	8.4	Vietnam	6.5	India	6.0
2000	Indonesia	10.1	Vietnam	9.6	China	8.0	Thailand	6.6	India	3.8
2001	Indonesia	11.5	China	9.2	India	7.1	Vietnam	6.2	Philippines	4.0
2002	China	12.3	Indonesia	8.0	India	7.3	Vietnam	5.6	Philippines	4.7
2003	Indonesia	18.0	China	12.0	Philippines	8.3	Vietnam	7.6	India	5.1
2004	China	16.3	Vietnam	10.4	Malaysia	4.3	Philippines	3.6	Pakistan	2.3

Source: OECD. Stat Development/Aggregate Aid Statistics/2a. ODA by Recipient by Country, http://www.sourceoecd.org/database/oecdstat, accessed on 14 December 2005.

markets and the creation of extended production networks by Japanese multinational companies. Accordingly, Japanese ODA is usually complemented by the development of Japan's FDI and trade links through activities of Japanese multinational companies in the region.[53]

Like ODA, Japanese FDI is also an important vehicle that helped to rebuild links between Japan and the region. Japanese FDI was initiated in East and Southeast Asia in the 1950s–60s as part of the effort to secure supplies of natural resources, with major investments in resource extraction in Southeast Asia. However, Japanese FDI during this period was limited due to restrictions on the convertibility of the yen. The first major upsurge of Japanese FDI in the region came in the late 1960s and early 1970s as a result of changed conditions and government policies, including the nation's achievement of balance of payments surplus in 1965, a total lifting of foreign investment restrictions in 1971, a 14% of yen appreciation in 1973 following the Nixon shock, easy access to finances at low interest rates, increasingly strict pollution controls and pressure from the Japanese public to move heavy and polluting industries overseas, significant rises in labor costs in Japan, adoption of foreign investment promotion policies in East and Southeast Asia, and the ASEAN states' imposition of import restrictions on Japanese goods as part of their import-substitution development policies. These developments encouraged and even forced Japanese companies to restructure and invest abroad to reduce production costs and remain competitive. As a consequence, Japanese FDI in East and Southeast Asia jumped from $165 million in 1970 to $1.1 billion in 1975. A large proportion of this FDI was concentrated in industries such as textiles (30–40%) and electronics (15–30%), with most production intended for re-export to third countries, the US market in particular.[54] But the Japanese FDI boom of the late 1960s and early 1970s was ended by the first oil crisis of 1973, which suddenly worsened both internal and external economic conditions. After the nation had overcome the negative effects of the oil crisis through economic restructuring and seeking to lower costs, Japanese FDI outflows took off again after 1980. In this process, Japan's FDI in the region increased rapidly from around $1.2 billion in 1980 to $1.4 billion in 1985, $7.0 billion in 1990, and peaked at $12.4 billion in 1995. In the wake of the Asian financial crisis of 1997–98, Japan's FDI in East and Southeast Asia dropped to $6.2 billion in 1998, $7.0 billion in 1999, and $6.0 billion in 2000, but resumed to $9.2 billion in 2004.[55] More importantly, Japanese FDI outflows in the region since the 1980s have been concentrated in electronics, automobiles, and manufacturing assembly. Japanese companies have moved beyond a traditional interest in low-tech/low-wage manufacturing toward production of sophisticated equipment for local markets and for export beyond the region. The result is a growing trend toward the organization of Asian markets and production by the Japanese companies.[56]

In accordance with the pattern of Japanese ODA and FDI in East and Southeast Asia, Japan has also been deepening its trade linkage with the region. Whereas the United States remains Japan's largest individual trading partner over time, Japan's combined trade with the region has experienced a general upward trend, rising from 19.1% of the total in 1970 to 24.0% in 1980, 28.2% in 1990, 39.7% in 2000, and 45.2% in 2004. Particularly, Japan's total trade with East and Southeast Asia has constantly surpassed Japan–US trade since 1990, and by 2004 the total volume of Japan's trade with the region was 2.4 times that with the United States.[57] In 2004, Japan was the largest individual trading partner for Taiwan, Indonesia, the Philippines, and Thailand; the second largest for China and Malaysia;[58] and the third largest for South Korea, Hong Kong, and Singapore. In the meantime, Japan was the largest source of imports for China, South Korea, Taiwan, Malaysia, and Thailand; and the second largest for Hong Kong, Indonesia, the Philippines, and Singapore.[59] Particularly, an increasing proportion of these trade flows resulted from Japan's growing absorption of manufactured goods from the region, which rose from 25% of total Japanese imports from the region in 1984 to 73% in 1998. By 2004, 78.8% of Japanese imports from East and Southeast Asia were manufactured products.[60]

It is particularly important to note that a distinctive triangular pattern of trade relations has been formed over time between Japan, East and Southeast Asia, and the United States, under which while East and Southeast Asian economies enjoy trade surplus with the United States, they persistently run a combined trade deficit with Japan, which continuously rose from $227 million in 1960 to $1.9 billion in 1970, $2.0 billion in 1980, $22.7 billion in 1990, and peaked at $71.1 billion in 1995. By 2003, the region still maintained a trade deficit of $49.4 billion with Japan.[61] The only few East and Southeast Asian countries that enjoy trade surplus with Japan are those on which Japan relies for their resources, which include Indonesia, Brunei, and China. Japan's trade surplus with the region derives entirely from its huge surplus in the export of manufactured goods. Japan's exports to East and Southeast Asia consist of 100% of manufactured goods and technology. This implies that Japan primarily plays a role as an exporter of technology goods to East and Southeast Asia, while the United States remains the largest absorber of manufactured products of the region. As such, the United States remains an important source of the economic growth of East and Southeast Asia.

4.5   The Japanese political economy in the 1990s and beyond

Japan emerged from the Cold War as an economic superpower with substantial economic wealth and growing political influence. Starting in 1992, however, the Japanese economy experienced protracted stagnation. While the Japanese economy has been still growing, the pace of growth is much below the previous average. This "growth recession" is well reflected in Japan's 1.3% of average annual growth rate for the 1990s, as compared to 4.0% for the 1980s. The recession continued into the early 21st century, with GDP for 2000–01 shrinking by 0.6% and that for 2001–02 growing at only 0.3%. On the whole, in a period between 1990 and 2002, Japan had an average annual growth rate of only 1.3%, well below the world average of 2.7%. Japan's growth rate during this period was also the lowest among G-7 countries, a phenomenon that had never happened in the postwar years.[62] In a similar fashion, incomes continued to rise and jobs continued to be created, but at a rate much less than the expected. In the meantime, the size of Japan's government debt has been growing, surging from $1495.5 billion in 1990 to $4969.7 billion in 2000, and $6065.3 billion in 2003. Accordingly, the government debt continuously rose from 48.2% of GDP in 1990 to 104% in 2000 and 140.3% in 2003.[63] This makes the Japanese government the biggest borrower among the major industrialized powers.

This protracted recession is the direct result of the burst of economic bubbles that had been accumulated since the mid-1980s, characterized by the steep rise in stock and land prices. These bubbles, which dominated the Japanese economy from the mid-1980s to the early 1990s, were created by people's expectation of higher prices based on the perceptions of a bullish market. As Japan maintained high, sustained economic growth rates in the postwar era, there was an established expectation that high levels of growth would continue indefinitely. Slowly and subtly, investors began to act upon this expectation instead of a realistic assessment of current and future economic fortunes.

The bubbles first occurred in the property market for land and real estate, known as "property bubbles." Since Japan has a very high population density, land has long been expensive and land-intensive products are extremely costly in the country. The sustained economic growth brought growing funds to be spent on luxuries, which continuously pushed land prices up. Under such circumstances, investors bought land with the conviction that it could be sold out at higher prices later. Consequently, real estate prices soared and property bubbles formed and inflated, creating a mountain of financial wealth.

Very soon, contagion occurred when investors used the inflated value of their property as collateral for loans, which were then used to invest in Japan's stock market. The property bubbles therefore fueled stock market bubbles. In a similar fashion, investors were buying stocks based only upon the expectation of future price rises, not based upon the profitability of the underlying businesses. The Tokyo stock price index doubled between 1983 (647.41) and 1986 (1324.26), and then nearly doubled again in 1989 (2569.27) – a growth of stock prices that exceeded the growth of the Japanese economy by an astronomical amount.[64]

Economic bubbles can only sustain themselves as long as the expectation continues to rise. A sudden shift in the expectation would inevitably lead to sell-off and price collapse. This happened first in the property market. As there were growing concerns that real estate prices would not continue to rise, Japanese investors began to sell off their property holdings before the fall of price. Consequently, a panic ensued and the Japanese land market collapsed. As the stock market bubbles were supported in part by loans based upon high property values, the fall of real estate prices in turn forced investors to sell off their stock holdings too. Consequently, the burst of property bubbles led to the crash of the stock market. Japanese stocks lost over 50% of their value during 1990–92 with the Tokyo stock price index falling from 2569.27 in 1989 to 1359.55 in 1992. By 2003, the Tokyo stock price index dropped to 918.86, a drop of over 60% from its peak in 1989. By 2004, the figure stood at 1120.07.[65]

In the process, Japanese banks were caught in the middle of the property and stock bubbles. They had accepted property as collateral and lent money to those who bought stocks. As both real estate and stock bubbles burst, many banks were left with huge liabilities and few assets of real value. As a result, a banking crisis emerged and developed, bringing even more serious consequences for the Japanese economy.

Banks are in many ways the key economic institutions of the Japanese postwar miracle. One of the unique characteristics of Japan's economic system is its dependence upon banks rather than markets as a form of financial organization. Most personal savings take the form of low-interest bank deposits, which are then funneled through banks to the government and business at a lower cost than in other countries, where financial markets rather than banks serve this function. On the other hand, the Japanese government maintained very close ties with banks and provided them with many benefits when the Japanese economy was growing rapidly and when property and stock bubbles were building. Such a close relationship between the government and the financial community exacerbated problems during the collapse and its aftermath. Insolvent banks were propped up and kept functioning by the government rather than being shut down or forced to merge with sound banks. As a result, the debts grew bigger and bigger and the banks went further and further into the red. When the government finally acted, the cost had already been very high.

While the government was slow to respond to the emerging crisis, the *keiretsu* made the problem even more complicated and difficult. During the boom years, the *keiretsu* were seen as the key to Japan's rapid growth. At the heart of each of the *keiretsu* was a banking system that was obliged to channel funds to those member companies that needed them regardless of their performance. As long as the economy was growing rapidly, the *keiretsu* had plenty of financial resources to cover and subsidize short-term losses in order to support their long-term investment strategies. As the Japanese economy slowed down and eventually contracted, these banks within the *keiretsu* realized that their role was in direct violation of the fundamental principles of sound finance. But *keiretsu* banks are supposed to continue to provide money-losing member companies with loans even during a recession so as to keep these problematic companies afloat. As the economic slowdown persisted and intensified, the financial condition of *keiretsu* banks got dramatically worse until the late 1990s, when the banks themselves finally began to fail. Consequently, the economic crash incurred thereby became all the more severe and widespread.

In a further analysis, the burst of the Japanese economic bubbles reveals fundamental structural problems of Japan's developmental state. According to critics, the malfunctioning of the Japanese economy actually derives from Japan's economic structure and mode of operation, which is characterized by "crony capitalism" rather than real liberalism. As a matter of fact, the ongoing Japanese economic stagnation is accompanied by a series of political corruption scandals and partisan realignments. Moreover, scandals also involve senior bureaucrats from the respected ministries of finance, health, and trade. This calls into question not only the wisdom of bureaucratic policies, but also the legitimacy of Japan's system of bureaucratic governance that is believed to be the foundation of Japan's postwar economic success. As such, rather than a team of devoted politicians, competent and autonomous bureaucrats, and efficient businesses that pursue the shared national goal of making

Japan an international power, the Japanese political economy actually represents a tight network of personal and professional relationships that systematically exploits and manipulates the public interest for the gain of a small group of elite at the expense of the majority.

Japan's problems were striking in the sense that these problems were persistent over a decade since the early 1990s. An analysis of the four basic sources of economic stimulus – consumption, investment, exports, and the structure of the Japanese political economy – shows that it was far from an easy job for the Japanese government to move out of the protracted stagnation and resume economic growth. In the first place, to increase consumer expenditures as a source of economic recovery seemed to be out of the question in Japan. Unlike the United States, domestic consumer spending was never a driving force for economic growth in Japan. This is because Japan has a tradition of high savings rates. During the boom years, high savings rates were seen as a distinct advantage, which substantially contributed to high investment rates in Japan's economy. On the other hand, high savings rates also served to inflate property and stock bubbles in the second half of the 1980s and the early 1990s. At the time of economic uncertainty of the 1990s and the early 2000s, Japanese consumers were even more reluctant to spend. Rather, worried people would put their money in the safest place in case they might need it at hard times in the future.

Likewise, it was not easy for investment spending to provide a boost for the Japanese economic recovery either. This is because Japanese investors had lost enormous sums in the burst of property and stock bubbles. As the key players in the Japanese economy, *Keiretsu* were neither willing nor able to make huge investment due to both the stagnant economy and their internal financial problems. Even when the Bank of Japan made bold attempts to stimulate domestic investment by driving interest rates down to 1%, then to 0.5%, and finally to 0% in 1998–99, for example, there was still no strong demand for investment loans!

As the Japanese economic growth was quite dependent on exports for long, it is logical that Japan would look to higher exports to solve its problems. However, the promotion of exports as a source of economic growth no longer works today as effectively as before. This is because Japanese exports are not so large compared to the entire Japanese economy as thought. Like the United States, Japan has most of its products consumed domestically rather than being exported. Many of the Japanese goods that are purchased by foreigners are not exported from Japan but are made in Japanese-owned factories overseas. As such, it would be difficult for Japan to rely solely on more exports to dramatically turn its economic fortune. On the other hand, as Japan's financial crisis intensified and the Japanese financial system weakened, many Japanese investors brought their overseas investments back home to shore up their domestic accounts. Doing so, they actually helped to push the value of the yen upwards, which made Japan's products more expensive and more difficult to export. Moreover, the promotion of more exports as a source of economic recovery also became increasingly difficult when Japan faced stern international pressure to address its huge trade surplus, particularly Washington's strong pressure to reduce its persistent huge trade surplus with the United States.

In a final analysis, the nature of the Japanese political economy constituted a fundamental structural obstacle to a quick recovery of the Japanese economy. As the fundamental problem of the Japanese economy derived from an interest-group structure of the so-called "iron triangle," which involved strong connections of political and bureaucratic institutions with the business community, it was difficult, if not totally impossible, for the Japanese government to take decisive actions to destruct the country's tightly woven and corrupt economic system and to restructure the economy in substantial and fundamental ways. Without such a dramatic and painful restructuring of the Japanese political economy, which would inevitably face the fierce resistance of some most powerful groups in Japanese society, fundamental reforms, which were the very key to revitalizing the Japanese economy, could hardly be possible. In a similar fashion, the same domestic constraints also prevented Japan from playing a greater leadership role in the world economy, as such a leadership role would require that the Japanese government have its economic strategy adjusted from export-led growth to domestic stimulation and importation of foreign goods, an adjustment that would inevitably meet strong resistance of domestic powerful interests.

It was within this context that Junichiro Koizumi came to office as Japanese Prime Minister on 26 April 2001, promising to revitalize the Japanese economy through structural reform under the slogan of "without reform there will be no growth." Under Koizumi, Japan entered "the intensive adjustment period" (FY2002–FY2004), during which Koizumi pushed not only for restructuring of the corporate sector and economic reforms, aiming to act against nonperforming loans (NPLs) and privatize the postal savings system, but also for reorganizing the factional structure of the ruling Liberal Democratic Party (LDP). In the meantime, Koizumi moved LDP away from its traditional rural agrarian base toward a more urban, neoliberal core. In addition to the privatization of Japan Post, the Koizumi government also slowed down its heavy subsidies for infrastructure and industrial development in rural areas.

As a result of the structural reform in "the intensive adjustment period," the Japanese economy was slowly reviving from a decade of economic stagnation following the burst of the economic bubbles in the early 1990s. From 2002 to the end of 2005, output had increased at an average annual growth rate of more than 2% (3.3% excluding the negative contribution from the public sector).[66] In the meantime, the target of reducing major banks' stock of NPLs, which amounted to 8.4% of their total lending in March 2002, by half by March 2005 was achieved.[67] The corporate sector also made progress in overcoming the problem of excess-employment, excess-capital stock, and excess-liabilities. As a result, the corporate structure was strengthened and corporate profits were improving. The economic growth and corporate recovery, in turn, helped to boost employment and improve income situations of household sectors.[68]

Despite these positive developments, however, Japan still faces a number of challenges in pursuing sustained economic growth and ensuring rising living standards. The first challenge is entrenched deflation, reflected in continuing decline of land prices since the early 1990s and continuing fall of bank lending. The second challenge is high gross public debt, which amounts to 160% of GDP, the highest among OECD countries. As the Japanese population is rapidly aging, the high public debt, which has been caused by large government budget deficits, brings the issue of Japan's fiscal sustainability. The third challenge is a lack of fiscal discipline at the local government level, which is contributing to the run-up in debt. The fourth challenge is the continuing existence of a number of structural problems, including weak competition in some sectors. The fifth challenge is aging population, which is not only posing growing financial pressure on the government but also reducing the size of the workforce. The last major challenge is increasing dualism in the labor market, which creates both efficiency and equity concerns.[69]

It is under such circumstances that the Japanese economy has now entered "the concentrated consolidation period" (FY2005–FY2006), during which the Japanese government is attempting (1) to establish a small and efficient government, (2) to establish a foundation that will allow Japan to overcome the two most important environmental changes for the Japanese economy in the 21st century, that is, the trend of declining birth rate and an aging society, and the trend of globalization, with an eye to the new dynamic era, and (3) to overcome deflation and to secure sustained economic growth driven by private demand.[70]

In the meantime, the Japanese government is committed to further structural reform, which, among other things, involves privatization of Japan Post, reform of policy-based finance, strengthening management of government assets and debts, decentralization of financial power from the central government to local government, introduction of "market testing" to improve the efficiency of public services, reform of the budget system, administrative reform of central and local government, reform of the social security system, adoption of measures to reverse the declining birth rate, education reform, strengthening global strategy, reform of the financial system, and revitalization of regional economies.[71]

In September 2004, a special board of enquiry was established by the CEFP to draft "Japan's 21st Century Vision," which was formally published in April 2005. The report clarifies the shape of the 21st-century Japan that is supposed to be realized by structural reform. The document covers a wide range of possibilities up to 2030. It first points out four scenarios that must be avoided: (1) economic activity stagnates and contracts; (2) government becomes a weight and a burden on economic activity; (3) Japan is left behind in globalization; and (4) an increasing number of people lose hope and society becomes unstable. The report then presents a vision of how things should be like in 2030, which include the following: (1) an open, culturally creative nation; (2) healthy life expectancy of 80 years enjoyed by people with the luxury of free time; and (3) contended public, small government. The strategy and specific actions recommended by the report for achieving the specified future vision include the following: (1) to create a virtuous cycle of rising productivity and growing income; (2) to take maximum advantage of globalization; and (3) to create systems to provide public values as selected by the citizenry. In the meantime, the document envisions an economy in which rising labor productivity will sustain growth, and the real GDP growth rate will be somewhere in the order of 1.5%.[72]

Indeed, the Japanese political economy is at the turning point in the early 21st century.

5
The South Korean Political Economy Since 1945

5.1 The Cold War, US hegemony and the South Korean political economy

After Japan was defeated by the Allied powers in 1945, the Korean peninsula came under the joint occupation of the Soviet forces in the north and the US forces in the south with the 38th parallel as the demarcation line, as agreed between the United States and the Soviet Union before the end of the war. The Allied occupation was seen at the time as a temporary measure for the Koreans to prepare for election of their own government and regain independence. However, with the spread of the Cold War from Europe to the Far East, it gradually became clear that a peninsular-wide election was no longer possible. Eventually, the Korean peninsula was formally divided into two separate states along the 38th parallel in 1948 with the establishment of the Republic of Korea (hereafter referred to as South Korea) and the Democratic People's Republic of Korea (hereafter referred to as North Korea). With the breakout of the Korean War (1950–53), the United States and South Korea formally formed an alliance. In 1954, the two allies signed the Mutual Security Treaty, by which Seoul was officially incorporated into Washington-led anti-communist security framework in the Far East. The US–South Korean Mutual Security Treaty thereafter became the cornerstone of America's military commitment to South Korea, while South Korea took a development path that was vastly different from that of North Korea.

Like that of the Japanese political economy, the transformation of the South Korean political economy in the postwar years was substantially influenced by Washington's geopolitical strategy in the region. Following the communist victory in mainland China in 1949 and the outbreak of the Korean War in 1950, the strategic importance of South Korea became all the more evident for Washington. Therefore, soon after the end of the Korean War in 1953, South Korea was formally incorporated into America's strategy of containing communism and isolating China and the other socialist countries in the Far East. This policy was clearly reflected in Washington's National Security Council (NSC) policy document, NSC 154, approved by the President on 3 July 1953, which laid out various interim courses of action designed to maintain economic and political pressures on China and North Korea and to support South Korea's defense and security.[1] As an integral part of this policy, Washington decided to substantially boost its aid to help South Korea with its economic reconstruction and development, a policy that was specified in the NSC policy document on postwar economic and military aid for South Korea (NSC 156).[2] The US aid was crucial for the very survival of South Korea at the time, a country that had been totally devastated by the war.

As such, the United States provided huge amounts of military and economic aid for South Korea in the postwar years.[3] In August 1953, 1 month after the end of the Korean War, Washington established the US Office of Economic Coordinator for Korea to coordinate US economic and military aid so that the aid funds were used efficiently. From 1946 through 1976, South Korea received $12.6 billion in US military and economic aid.[4] Including $1.9 billion from the international financial institutions and about $0.8 billion from Japan, South Korea received a total of over $15 billion in aid during this period, equivalent to $600 per capita, a per capita aid figure that was only surpassed by South Vietnam and Israel.[5] Particularly in the period 1953–61, the US aid, which accounted for 95% of total foreign aid the nation received, helped South Korea finance the government budget and capital formation, ease balance of payments deficits, and reduce the inflationary pressure. The US economic aid amounted to 100% of the South Korean government budget in the 1950s,[6] 80% of the fixed capital formation, 8% of GNP, and 70% of total imports from 1953 through 1962. Moreover, the US military aid programs not only helped the construction of roads, bridges, and other infrastructure but also contributed to the formation of valuable human capital through the training of South Korean military personnel in organization, management and technical skills, who, after leaving military service, went to work in industrial and service sectors, especially in government-owned enterprises.[7] Consequently, for the two decades from the mid-1940s to the mid-1960s the US economic and military aid constituted a critical factor not only for South Korea's survival as an independent state but also for its economic recovery and early industrialization, which in turn laid the foundation for the nation's rapid economic growth in the subsequent years.

After the mid-1960s, while its direct aid reduced in significance, the United States played a crucial role in absorbing South Korean goods.[8] While tolerating South Korea's highly protective policies and practices, Washington adopted liberal and benevolent trade policies toward South Korea and brought it into the liberal international trade regime. America's huge open market and relatively liberal markets in other industrial countries made it possible for South Korea to successfully switch to implement an export-oriented development strategy from the early 1960s onward.

The US investment and technology transfer also played an important role in South Korea's economic development. Particularly, after the United States shifted its economic aid from grant aid to loan aid in the mid-1960s, the South Korean government switched to rely on huge foreign borrowings (governmental loans as well as commercial loans) to finance its series of economic development plans and maintain a vigorous pace of investment activities. Moreover, supported by the United States, South Korea joined the IMF and the World Bank on 26 August 1955, which further facilitated the flow of foreign capital into the country. From 1962, when the first FDI project was approved by the South Korean government to the end of 1976, South Korea received a total of $950 million in FDI. The FDI inflows in South Korea were dominated by US companies until 1968, and thereafter they became predominantly Japanese.[9] The foreign investment, together with foreign aid and loans, contributed to the expansion of the export manufacturing industries. By the 1970s, exports and foreign private capital had replaced US aid to become the major sources of foreign exchange earnings to finance the country's industrialization. Equally significant, the US aid made a considerable contribution to the transfer of technology through project financing, development loans, and the provision of large numbers of technical experts. In the meantime, South Korea also acquired modern industrial technology through US investment and technological licensing agreements with US companies. To help South Korean industry with the adoption and adaptation of modern technology, the United States aided the creation of the Korean Institute of Science and Technology (KIST) in 1966.

The United States also provided South Korea with technical assistance through being heavily involved in government economic decision-making regarding the allocation of aid sources. After the mid-1960s, the United States showed more concerns for research, economic planning and policy, and export programs. It financially supported a series of economic and social studies of problem areas in the South Korean economy, such as the financial system, grain marketing, and land tenure conditions.[10] In 1971, Washington used its aid to support the creation of the Korea Development Institute (KDI), which was to assist the South Korean government with research and analysis of critical economic policy and planning problems.

Given the high degree of hostility between the north and the south, the US military protection not only provided South Korea with a secure external environment for its economic development, but also helped the country reduce the burden of its military expenditures so that South Korea could use more resources on economic development. On the other hand, South Korea also earned huge amounts of foreign exchange from South Korean troops' participation in the Vietnam War and from local procurement by US forces stationed on its soil, which were then used to pay for imports needed for the country's industrialization. According to Edward Mason *et al.*, the foreign exchange earnings from these sources were even larger than regular export earnings in the period before 1962.[11]

Using its influence, Washington pressured South Korea for a series of reforms and policy adjustment, which later proved conducive to the country's economic recovery and subsequent rapid growth. The land reform in South Korea was initiated by the US occupation authorities after 1945 and was later completed by the South Korean government under America's strong pressure after the country's independence. More significantly, to push the South Koreans to increase their ability of earning foreign exchange to finance the nation's development, Washington pressured Seoul to switch its import-substitution development strategy of the 1950s to the export-oriented development strategy after the 1960s. The US influence was also reflected in a high proportion of the senior personnel in the government, business, and academics who were exposed to US training under either the economic or military aid programs.

While the United States most substantially influenced the trajectory and pace of South Korea's postwar political economy in the context of the Cold War, Japan, encouraged by Washington, also played an important role in providing capital and technology for South Korea in its economic development after the normalization of diplomatic relations between the two countries in 1965. In the meantime, Japan also became the second largest market for South Korean exports after the United States for decades, contributing to the success of South Korea's export-oriented development strategy. It is important to note that from the very beginning South Korea's economic ties with Japan were built into a pattern of triangle economic relationship that involved the United States, Japan, and South Korea, within which the United States functioned as a major market to absorb South Korean products, Japan provided South Korea with capital and technology, and South Korea produced goods aimed at the US market. This pattern of trilateral economic relationship continued thereafter.

Obviously, America's military and economic support for South Korea in the context of the Cold War provided crucial external conditions for South Korea to achieve economic recovery and fast economic growth. By the end of the 1980s, however, the external conditions had substantially transformed. Particularly, with the end of the Cold War and the relative decline of the US economic power, Washington modified its previous Cold War foreign policy that subordinated its economic interests to its geopolitical objective to a new approach that pursues both economic and geopolitical interests. On its side, South Korea, with the achievement of industrialization and economic boom, had substantially improved its position and confidence as a nation by the end of the 1980s. Under such circumstances, the US–South Korean relationship gradually transformed in the period 1980s–90s. While the two countries continued to maintain their political and strategic alliance, there was the emergence of conflict over a range of economic issues. Especially, the economic success that had its roots in the early 1960s continued throughout the 1980s and culminated in the rapid expansion of South Korean exports to the US market in the late 1980s and resultant South Korea's swelling trade surpluses with the United States. As a result, economic frictions and tensions emerged between the two allies. In defense of its own economic interests, Washington growingly treated South Korea as an economic competitor and exerted increasing pressure upon the nation.

Despite the rising economic power, however, South Korea continued to have a high stake in its relationship with the United States. This is not only because South Korea continued to need its alliance with the United States for protection of its security and for maintenance of regional stability, but also because the United States remained the largest export market for South Korean products until very recently and the nation's largest source of FDI. As such, South Korea's relationship with the United States remained the top priority in Seoul's policy agenda.

5.2 The South Korean state and economic development

When the Korean peninsula was formally divided into two states in 1948 with the establishment of the Republic of Korea in the south and the Democratic People's Republic of Korea in the north, nearly all the power-generating capacity and almost two-thirds of heavy industry was left in the north. The subsequent Korean War of 1950–53 further destroyed the tiny industrial base that had been newly created in the south. Consequently, South Korea faced mounting social, economic, and political problems in the immediate postwar years, including a flood of penniless refugees from the north, a high unemployment rate, a severe housing shortage, a completely destroyed administrative and economic infrastructure, and political instability.

Despite the immediate huge task of the nation's reconstruction and rehabilitation in the aftermath of the war, however, President Syngman Rhee was preoccupied with the consolidation of his political power and the reunification of the peninsula on his own terms. Although efforts were made for the reconstruction of the nation's industrial base and infrastructure and for the promotion of domestic import-substitution production, little attention was given to the country's long-term economic development. Moreover, with almost no domestic savings, South Korea relied heavily on foreign aid, US aid in particular, for all its reconstruction needs. As a result, the economic growth remained stagnant until the military coup in 1961.

The real transformation of the South Korean economy started only after the 1961 military coup led by Park Chung-hee, which brought in a military-controlled authoritarian government in 1962. While the new government resorted to authoritarian rule by declaring martial law, dissolving the National Assembly, imposing press censorship, and suspending party political activities, it initiated a major shift in policy focus toward economic growth. This major policy shift was based on President Park Chung-hee's belief that building of a strong economy and improvement of people's living standard would best enable the country to withstand the threat from the north and protect it from domestic communist insurgence. But to build such a strong nation, according to Park, a strong authoritarian government was essential. Consequently, the Park government concentrated on the promotion of rapid economic growth at the expense of development of a democratic political system.

The new political leaders were therefore highly committed to economic development and initiated a series of organizational reforms that aimed at the construction of a capable institutional structure for economic planning and management. Particularly important under these initiatives was the establishment of the Economic Planning Board (EPB) in 1961, a key body that was to be responsible for economic planning, central budgeting, foreign capital management and statistics and that was to have the authority to coordinate policies and programs among all the functional ministries involved in economic affairs. The role of the EPB was particularly strengthened through an institution-alized arrangement under which the minister of the EPB concurrently served as the deputy prime minister, who oversaw relevant ministries involved in economic matters.[12] In the meantime, the Office of Planning and Coordination was also established under the prime minister in 1961, which was to assist the prime minister in monitoring the performance of major projects and policies. This framework of planning and policy-making was highly centralized and streamlined. It is important to note that in South Korea the actual policymaking process usually involved only a small number of government officials, although policies were dis-cussed at the Economic Ministers Consultation Meeting. As such, policy decisions could be made quite rapidly in South Korea.

With a sound institutional structure in place, the South Korean gov-ernment played a very significant role in the course of the nation's economic development through formulating economic development plans, designing and implementing appropriate development strategies, allocating budgetary and financial resources in support of economic development, and providing leadership and guidance for the private sec-tor with respect to the direction of industrialization. In the meantime, the government also formed a cooperative alliance with the business in pursuing industrialization.

It was under such circumstances that in 1962 South Korea started to implement the first (1962–66) of its series of five-year economic development plans that were to transform the nation's economy in the subsequent years. These five-year plans set out the government's policies and objectives and played a significant role in guiding and coordinating the direction of industrialization. As South Korean leaders were very prag-matic, these economic plans were designed in a way that responded to changing domestic and external conditions at the time. It is important to point out that while economic planning exerted a substantial influence on the private sector by providing a framework of guidance and direction of industrialization, the South Korean government still primarily relied on the market mechanism for its economic policymaking and was com-mitted to maintaining an economy in which the private sector played a central role. What the government mainly did was to offer incentives to those companies that complied with economic plans, while final cooper-ate decisions were still left in the hand of private companies. Since 1962, the series of government five-year plans has substantially contributed to the country's rapid industrialization and economic growth.

As South Korea had scant natural resources, a small domestic market and weak capability of earning foreign exchange, the Park government, soon after coming to power, switched from the import-substitution development strategy of the 1950s to an export-oriented development strategy that was designed to achieve industrialization by focusing on the production and export of labor-intensive manufactured goods, of which South Korea had comparative advantage at the time. This development strategy would not only help increase employment and income but also help provide much needed foreign exchange earnings and a sound base for further economic development. In pursuing this development strategy, the South Korean government followed Japan's footsteps by vigorously adopting industrial policy to identify the priority industries that the government saw most important for the private sector to develop. Although the government did not always dictate policies to the private sector, it exerted substantial influence on private firms through various policy measures. As such, throughout the process of industrialization, the South Korean government played a significant role in shaping the nation's industrial structure.

In response to changes in both domestic and external conditions, South Korea's industrial policy was timely adjusted and redesigned. During the take-off period 1962–72, the focus of South Korea's industrial policy was to promote exports and to construct basic industries and social infrastructure. To achieve these objectives, the government adopted a series of policy measures, including an exchange rate system under which the Korean won was pegged to the US dollar, drastically raised interest rate to increase domestic savings, anti-inflation fiscal and monetary stabilization policies, various incentives to promote exports, and high tariff and a negative list system that imposed restrictions on imports. These policy measures brought rapid export increase, economic growth, and the establishment of basic industries such as steel, fertilizer, cement, oil refining, and electricity and the social and economic infrastructure such as highways, harbors, and irrigations facilities, which had basically transformed South Korea from an agricultural economy into a manufacturing-centered economy by the early 1970s.

The South Korean government timely moved to a new industrial policy in 1973, issuing the Heavy and Chemical Industry Declaration. The new industrial policy was intended to promote such strategic heavy and chemical industries as iron and steel, nonferrous metals, shipbuilding, industrial machinery, electronics, and petrochemical processing industries. To support the development of these heavy and chemical industries, the government provided not only direct and indirect administrative assistance but also preferential financial resources in support of the construction of plants and facilities. A National Investment Fund was created to provide low-interest loans for investment in the heavy and chemical industries. The proportion of financial resources allocated to the heavy and chemical industries much exceeded those to light industries. In the meantime, preferential tax policies, such as exemptions and reductions of corporate taxes, were also employed to support the heavy and chemical industries. Furthermore, the heavy and chemical industries were protected by the government as "infant industries" from international competition through prohibitive tariffs and import restrictions. Particularly, the South Korean government encouraged monopolistic production in certain of these industries on the ground that this would strengthen their competitiveness through economies of scale. Consequently, *chaebol* grew rapidly at the expense of small- and medium-sized companies. With the aid of these policy measures, the heavy and petrochemical industries had been solidly established by the end of the 1970s with their share in the manufacturing sector increasing from 38% in terms of value added in 1973 to 54.5% in 1980, and exports exceeding 50% of total exports by 1983. The heavy industrialization in turn helped promote the nation's economic growth.[13]

During the 1970s, the South Korean government also attempted to modernize the rural sector, which had fallen behind the urban sector during the process of rapid industrialization. In order to promote the development of the rural sector, the government launched the *Saemaul* (New Community) Movement in 1971, which aimed to boost agricultural production and productivity and to raise the income of farmers and fishing workers. While the government's efforts to boost rural productivity and income were quite successful, the policy of price support for agricultural produce greatly contributed to the government's chronic budget deficits and the nation's inflation in the 1970s.

By the end of the 1970s, there had been changed domestic and external conditions. Domestically, there was rising domestic inflation due to the government's inflationary policy to finance the nation's industrialization over the 1970s. In the meantime, there was lack of economic rationale of the heavy industrialization, as it was pursued for national-security as well as economic reasons rather than based on comparative advantage, over-concentration of economic power among several major corporations and subsequent economic inequality. There was also political instability following President Park's assassination in 1979. Externally, the worldwide recession following the oil crises of the 1970s dealt a heavy blow to the South Korean economy. The development of the heavy and chemical industries was based on the consumption of huge amounts of energy, which was 100% imported from abroad. As a result, with ever-growing heavy and chemical industries South Korea became increasingly vulnerable to fluctuations in global energy prices. Consequently, the impact of the oil crises of the 1970s on the South Korean economy was devastating. The nation's crude oil import bill increased to the equivalent of 9.2% of GNP in 1980 from 2.2% in 1972.[14] In the meantime, South Korea was facing mounting pressure of the developed countries from above and developing countries from below. Whereas industrialized countries became increasingly protectionist against foreign products, including South Korean products, as a result of their loss of comparative advantage in many traditional manufacturing industries, developing countries, such as China and Southeast Asian countries, began their rapid industrialization by specializing in the production of low-skilled, labor-intensive goods, which challenged South Korean products in these sectors.

Facing the new challenges under such concurrent changes in domestic and external conditions, the government adjusted its economic policy in the early 1980s to focus on price stability, balanced economic growth, and market liberalization. In the meantime, the government conducted structural readjustment of the heavy and chemical industries through mergers, cancellation of some investment projects, and promotion of product specialization in power-generating equipment, automobile assembly, heavy electrical motors, electronic switchboard systems, diesel engines for marine use, and copper smelting. To improve the competitiveness of South Korea's companies, the government started to retreat from its previous practice of providing heavy and chemical industries with preferential loans as a direct policy measure of support. While continuing to provide directions of growth, the government allowed market forces to play a growingly important role. Investment was still encouraged in the heavy and chemical industries, but these industries were no longer protected by the government's import restrictions and tariffs. As part of the government's commitment to liberalization and internationalization, domestic markets were opened up to foreign goods and services, and in 1986 the regulations that prohibited foreign investment in South Korea were removed. The tax exemption enjoyed by these industries was ceased. In order to improve efficiency, the government promoted market competition and established a competitive environment by enacting the Anti-Monopoly and Fair Trade Act in 1981, which was aimed at eliminating market monopoly and preventing the concentration of economic power in a handful of large conglomerates. An important measure to promote competition was to start the process of liberalization during this period and reduction of tariffs. In the meantime, the government began to encourage growth of small- and medium-sized companies by offering them incentives to increase their investment and marketing activities. In a similar fashion, the government also made efforts to move industrial facilities into rural areas to promote more equitable distribution of wealth between the urban and the rural areas. The result of these policy measures was an overall improvement in economic performance over the 1980s.

Entering the 1990s, the government's policies aimed to transform the nation's economy and lay the groundwork for the reunification of the Korean peninsula by stimulating technological and managerial innovation, boosting R&D spending, increasing expenditure on social infrastructure, and easing labor shortages. In the meantime, the government also promoted social development, which involved developing rural areas, improving social welfare, enhancing socio-economic equity, expanding the nation's housing stock, and curbing real estate speculation.

In the process of industrialization, the South Korean government was actively engaged in fiscal management to pursue its industrial policy. The most important reform in fiscal management seemed to be the establishment of the Office of National Tax Administration in 1966, which thereafter became a powerful government body that supervised business performance and steered businesses toward objectives of the government's industrial policy. In general, South Korea adopted a fiscal policy that was characterized by restrained government expenditure, a small public sector, a balanced budget, comparatively low taxes, liberal use of tax incentives for investments, heavy reliance on indirect taxes, increased public savings, small expenditures on social services (but rising sharply in recent years), high expenditures on education, and the use of significant resources for industrial development. The government adopted various short-term policies to address such areas as aggregate demand management, taxes, exchange rates, interest rates, preferential credit, farm prices, and industrial promotion. These policies were usually initiated or designed by various relevant ministries, such as the Ministry of Finance, the Central Bank, the Ministry of Agriculture and Fisheries, and so on.

The South Korean government's tax policy was designed not only to mobilize resources for capital formation in the public sector but also to encourage investments in the private sector. The South Korean government applied various tax incentives to promote industrial development and export growth. These tax incentives were particularly provided for those heavy and chemical industries and export industries. In general, investment-incentive policies were employed to affect the sectoral allocation of investment resources. Through numerous tax reforms in the process of industrialization, the government provided businesses with increasingly favorable tax treatment, including tax exemptions, investment tax credit, accelerated depreciation, and continuously lowered tax rates.

Since the adoption of its first economic plan in 1962, the South Korean government has pursued a systematic economic policy of export-led growth. This was a highly logical policy for a country that lacked natural resources and sizable domestic market. To promote exports, the government set export targets for each sector and provided those companies engaged in exports with various policy incentives including tax exemptions, reduced public utility charges, low interest loans, tariff rebates on imports for re-export, and simplified customs procedures for import of raw materials to be processed for re-export. Companies that met or exceeded the government-set targets would receive even more favorable treatment, whereas companies that failed to meet their quotas would face sanctions and tax investigations. Consequently, exports functioned as the engine of South Korea's economic growth and industrialization. At the same time, the export structure of South Korea also substantially transformed alongside its industrialization. During the 1960s, as the only available resource South Korea possessed was huge, cheap, and skilled labor force, the government adopted a strategy of promoting export of labor-intensive light manufactured goods, which provided a sound economic base from which South Korea could start to develop heavy and chemical industries in the 1970s. Entering the 1980s and 1990s, South Korea's exports switched from labor-intensive products to capital- and technology-intensive products.

South Korea's trade policy was quite systematic. Its basic trade policy was characterized by balanced expansion of external trade, diversification of foreign markets, development of brand names and product image, and expansion of multilateral cooperation. As a nation that heavily relied on foreign trade, South Korea pursued active trade diplomacy, participating in multilateral trade negotiations under the framework of GATT/WTO and holding regular talks with major trading partners such as the United States, Japan, and more recently China.

A unique feature of the South Korean political economy was a long-time mutually profitable relationship between the government and big business. As in Japan, the South Korean government dominated its relationship with business, encouraged the development of a handful of conglomerates, *chaebol*, through various policy incentives, and provided a favorable environment for business. Especially, the government exerted extensive influence on business activities by owning financial intermediaries and controlling access to foreign capital. But before and after the government made decisions regarding policies and targets, business leaders were usually consulted. On the other hand, the *chaebol* gave their support to the government in return and seized the opportunities provided by the government. So it was the combined efforts of the government and the private sector that produced South Korea's economic success. This government–business relationship was well supported by the cultural orientation of the Korean people, who have long been psychologically oriented toward powerful leadership by an elite and a centralized hierarchical bureaucracy. Under such an arrangement, the South Korean economy was dominated by a handful of powerful *chaebol*, which produced a wide range of goods for both export and domestic sale. The *chaebol* therefore played a vital role in South Korea's industrialization and economic growth.

In summary, the South Korean government played a crucial role in helping achieve the country's economic success through adoption of an outward-oriented development strategy, providing various incentives by resorting to the market mechanism, supporting the big business groups, and providing social and political stability through authoritarian rule. Although the process of democratization, which started in 1987 with the restoration of the multiparty political system following rising popular demonstrations and pressure for democracy since the early 1980s, eventually led to the nation's successful transition to democracy by 1992 with the election of Kim Young-sam as the nation's first civilian president following 32 years of military rule, the South Korean government, as a fully functioning modern democracy, still maintains an active role in promoting the national economy as was during the authoritarian period. In a final analysis, such persistent influence of the state in the nation's economic development might probably be explained by some unique social and cultural conditions of South Korea like a strong sense of national identity, loyalty, collectivism, paternalism, and acceptance of authority.

5.3   The rise of the South Korean economy

At the end of the Korean War in 1953, South Korea inherited an economy that had been devastated by the war, an impoverished population, and a country that lacked resources. Furthermore, the division of the peninsula along the 38th parallel had left most of the nation's industry and natural resources in the North, while the South possessed a backward agrarian economy with agriculture, forestry, and fishing accounting for 47% of GNP and manufacturing for less than 9%.[15] With such unfavorable economic and social conditions, together with a constant security threat from the north, it seemed to be an extremely difficult task at the time for South Korea to bring economic recovery and build a sound economy. After over five decades of development, however, South Korea has transformed dramatically from a small, stagnant agricultural subsistence economy into a modern industrialized economy, achieving what is called the "Miracle on the Han River."

In retrospect, there has been a clear trajectory of the rise of the South Korean economy over the past five decades. During the first postwar decade, South Korea remained locked in the so-called "vicious cycle" of poverty. Although the reconstruction of the infrastructure and factories that had been destroyed in the war was completed by mid-1957, the South Korean leaders failed to take effective measures timely to promote economic growth. In the meantime, the government adopted an import-substitution industrial policy and made limited attempts to promote exports. As a result, the economic growth during 1953–61 was quite modest with the average annual growth rate being 3.7% and the average annual per capita GNP growth rate being 0.7%.[16] Exports were stagnant during this period, rising only from $39.6 million in 1953 to $40.9 million in 1961, which was equivalent to no more than 1% of GNP.[17] Consequently, by 1962 the South Korean economy remained largely agrarian, with about two-thirds of the population working in the primary sector, per capita GNP being only $87, virtually no exports and domestic savings, and a population growing at a faster rate than the economy.[18] As a result, South Korea lagged behind North Korea in terms of per capita income and industrial production capacity.

The nation was put on the right track of fast economic growth only after the establishment of a development-oriented military-influenced authoritarian government under Park Chung-hee in 1962. Seeing the failure of the import-substitution development strategy adopted in the previous decade, the Park government switched to an export-oriented development strategy that would promote such labor-intensive industries as textiles, toys, footwear, and plywood for exports in which the nation enjoyed comparative advantage. As a result, South Korea achieved rapid economic growth after 1962 with the real growth rate rising from 2.1% in 1962 to 13.8% in 1969, an average annual growth rate of 8.7%.

The performance was even more impressive in terms of per capita GNP growth, which rose from $87 in 1962 to $210 in 1969, an average annual growth rate of 12.5%.[19] The result of this rapid growth was the doubling of the nation's GNP. More significantly, the rapid economic growth was accompanied by steady structural changes of the economy with the share of the manufacturing sector rising from 16% of GNP in 1962 to 21% in 1970 while that of the primary sector declining from 37% to 26%.[20] By the early 1970s, the construction of the basic industries such as steel, fertilizer, cement, oil refining, and electricity and the infrastructure such as highways, harbors, and irrigations facilities had been either completed or underway. As a result, South Korea had been well on the way from a traditional agriculture-based economy to a modern manufacturing-centered economy.

It is particularly important to point out that much of the high economic growth rate was attributed to the rapid growth of exports, which increased from $54.8 million in 1962 to $658.3 million in 1969, an average annual rate of 41.5%. In the meantime, imports also grew at an average annual rate of 24.7%, rising from $390.1 million in 1962 to $1650.0 million in 1969.[21] Notably, there was a changing structure of exports, which represented the resonance of the transformation of the nation's economic structure. Initially, South Korea's exports consisted only of low-skilled, labor-intensive products such as wigs, plywood, footwear, toys, and low-quality textiles. By the end of the 1960s, however, they diversified into higher-skilled, labor-intensive goods such as electric products. The remarkable performance in export growth brought huge amount of foreign exchange earnings, contributed to the high economic growth and helped accelerate industrialization.

Moreover, the rapid economic growth during this period also benefited from huge investment, most of which was financed by foreign capital, as the domestic savings rate remained well below the investment rate. As such, the government encouraged private companies to borrow foreign loans from international commercial banks and provided guarantees on foreign borrowings under the Foreign Capital Inducement Act of 1966.

In the early 1970s, South Korea experienced changed domestic and international economic conditions. Domestically, the rapid economic expansion of the 1960s led to a growing shortage of skilled workers, which, together with soaring inflation, caused a rapid rise of real wages. While its competitive advantage was eroding in many labor-intensive export industries as a result of the rising labor costs, South Korea faced growing competition from a number of other East and Southeast Asian developing economies, particularly Taiwan and Singapore. Moreover,

South Korean exports also encountered a worsening market condition resulted from rising protectionism in the world economy and the world-wide stagflation triggered by the first oil crisis. Facing the loss of its competitive advantage in export-oriented light industries, the South Korean government timely pushed for strategic restructuring of its economy and establishing a new niche in the world economy by promoting heavy and chemical industries, including shipbuilding, iron and steel, automobiles, machinery, petrochemicals, and electronics.[22] As a result, the share of heavy and chemical products expanded from 12.8% of total exports in 1970 to 38.5% in 1979, while the share of primary products dropping from 17.5% to 10.1%, and light industry products from 69.7% to 51.4%. With the successful transformation of heavy and chemical industries into new export sectors, South Korea continued to maintain rapid export growth at an annual rate of about 40% throughout the 1970s with the total amount of exports rising from less than $1 billion in 1970 to $15 billion in 1979. In the meantime, South Korea also promoted construction and manufacturing exports to the oil producing countries in the Middle East. Particularly, the construction orders from the Middle East amounted to $3.4 billion in 1977, $8 billion in 1978, and $6 billion in 1979 respectively, as compared to $0.8 billion in 1975, which not only helped improve the domestic employment but also brought a new source of foreign exchange earnings. The rapid export growth in turn contributed to a continuing high economic growth rate, which was averaged at 8.6% per year throughout the 1970s. Equally impressive, per capital GNP jumped from $243 in 1970 to $1636 in 1979.[23] As a result, South Korea emerged by the end of the 1970s as one of the four NIEs in the region, along with Taiwan, Singapore, and Hong Kong.

However, the process of South Korea's industrialization during the 1960s–70s was accompanied by chronic inflation, piling-up of foreign debt, and persistent huge trade and current account deficits. These problems, together with the effects of the assassination of President Park Chung-hee (October 1979), the second oil crisis and a disastrous harvest, finally brought a heavy blow on the South Korean economy, turning its growth rate into the first ever-negative figure of 2.1% in 1980. Under such circumstances, the post-Park Chun-hee government undertook a series of structural adjustment measures to streamline the economy. The policy adjustment measures, added by low oil prices, low international interest rates and low exchange rates of the won, paved the way for resumed rapid economic growth in the 1980s, averaging at 7.5% per year. Especially, economic growth was accelerated at a spectacular rate after 1986 with the growth rate of 1987 reaching 13.0%, one of the highest growth rates in the world. Accordingly, per capita GNP increased from $1598 in 1980 to $5185 in 1989, an average annual increase rate of 12.2%. Particularly significant, in 1986 South Korea achieved its first substantial trade and current account surpluses in its 38-year history of the Republic.[24] In the meantime, the domestic savings rate also increased from 24.4% in 1980 to 37.6% in 1989, exceeding the domestic investment rate. As a result, investment was increasingly financed by domestic funds.[25]

Starting in the early 1990s, South Korea entered a new stage of development through improving product quality, upgrading technology, and producing high-tech, high value-added goods. Propelled by export of high-tech, high value-added products, such as semiconductors, electronics, and automobiles, South Korea's economic growth continued in the 1990s. During the period 1990–96, the nation maintained an average annual growth rate of 7.6%, which helped increase per capita GNP from $5886 in 1990 to $12,197 in 1996. After experiencing the worst consequences of the financial crisis in 1997–98, during which the economy grew at a reduced rate of 4.7% in 1997 but shrank by 6.9% in 1998, the nation soon recovered and regained economic growth by 9.5% in 1999 and 8.5% in 2000 respectively.[26] As a result, South Korea still achieved an average annual growth rate of 5.7% between 1990 and 2000.[27]

As in the previous two decades, the remarkable performance of the South Korean economy during the 1980s–90s was well reflected in the nation's export performance. South Korean exports rose tenfold from $17.4 billion in 1980 to $171.8 billion in 2000.[28] According to United Nations Conference on Trade and Development (UNCTAD), the nation's overall world market share increased from 1.5% to 2.5% between 1985 and 2000. Most importantly, South Korea's export success during this period was largely based on high- and medium-technology exports with the exports of high-tech products jumping from 14% to 38% and the exports of medium-tech products rising from 22% to 29%. Its five high-tech exports (semiconductors, computers and parts and accessories, telecom equipment, and electrical machinery and apparatus) accounted for over one-third of all exports. Moreover, passenger cars represented another significant export item. In the meantime, South Korea also improved its market share in products based on natural resources. Consequently, South Korea increased its market share in all ten of the principal export products, seven of which are dynamic in world trade (Table 5.1).[29]

The rapid economic growth of the 1980s–90s also benefited from accelerating FDI inflows during these two decades, which helped bring foreign capital, technology, know-how and access to the global market. FDI inflows remained insignificant until the mid-1980s due to the restrictive foreign investment policy imposed by the government. After the liberalization of foreign investment was initiated in the mid-1980s, there was rapid rise of FDI inflows into the country. The average annual FDI inflows

Table 5.1 The Republic of Korea's Competitiveness in the World Market, 1985–2000

Product	Category		1985	1990	1995	2000
Market shares			*1.5*	*1.9*	*2.2*	*2.5*
Primary products[a]			0.3	0.5	0.5	0.4
Manufactures based on natural resources[b]			0.7	0.8	1.2	2.0
Manufactures not based on natural resources[c]			2.3	2.6	2.9	3.2
Low technology[d]			5.0	4.7	3.0	2.8
Medium technology[e]			1.1	1.6	2.2	2.5
High technology[f]			1.8	2.5	3.8	4.2
Others[g]			0.5	0.7	1.4	1.2
Export structure			*100.0*	*100.0*	*100.0*	*100.0*
Primary products[a]			4.8	3.2	1.9	1.7
Manufactures based on natural resources[b]			9.3	7.4	9.1	12.0
Manufactures not based on natural resources[c]			84.7	88.0	86.7	84.4
Low technology[d]			48.7	41.7	22.5	16.9
Medium technology[e]			21.7	25.9	31.3	29.2
High technology[f]			14.4	20.5	32.9	38.4
Others[g]			1.1	1.3	2.2	1.8
10 Principal exports (SITC Rev.2)	*A (h)*	*B (i)*	*21.6*	*28.0*	*47.0*	*54.3*
776 Thermionic valves and tubes and other semiconductors, n.e.s.	*	+	4.8	7.3	16.7	16.4
752 Automatic data processing machines, units thereof	*	+	0.9	3.4	3.4	6.8
781 Passenger motor cars (excl. public service type)	*	+	1.4	3.1	5.1	6.8
764 Telecommunications equipment, n.e.s.	*	+	3.2	3.4	3.8	6.6
334 Petroleum products, refined		+	2.1	0.5	1.8	4.3
759 Parts, n.e.s., of and accessories for 751 and 752[j]	*	+	0.7	1.1	3.4	3.7

583 Polymerization and copolymerization products	*	+	0.7	1.2	2.9	3.1
653 Fabrics, woven, of man-made fibers		+	4.0	4.4	5.0	2.5
674 Universals, plates and sheets, of iron or steel		+	2.7	2.3	2.3	2.5
778 Electrical machinery and apparatus, n.e.s.	*	+	1.2	1.3	2.4	1.7

Source: UNCTAD, *World Investment Report 2002: Transnational Corporations and Export Competitiveness* (New York: United Nations, 2002), Table VI.16, p. 177.
Notes: [a] Contains 45 basic products that are simple to process, includes concentrates.
[b] Contains 65 items: 35 agricultural/forestry groups and 30 others (mainly metals, excluding steel, plus petroleum products, cement, glass, etc.)
[c] Contains 120 groups representing the sum of low, medium, and high technology.
[d] Contains 44 items: 20 groups from the textile and garment category, plus 24 others (paper products, glass and steel, jewellery).
[e] Contains 58 items: 5 groups from the automotive industry, 22 from the processing industry, and 31 from the engineering industry.
[f] Contains 18 items: 11 groups from the electronics category, plus another 7 (pharmaceutical products, turbines, aircraft, optical and measuring instruments).
[g] Contains 9 unclassified groups.
[h] Groups (*) belonging to the 50 most dynamic in world imports, 1985–2000.
[i] Groups in which South Korea gained (+) world market share, 1985–2000.
[j] 751 refers to office machines; 752 refers to automatic data processing machines and units thereof.

increased from $105 million in the 1970s and $133 million in 1981–85 to $676 million in 1986–90. Entering the 1990s, FDI inflows increased even more rapidly, particularly after the mid-1990s. By 1999, the nation received $9.4 billion FDI, which was followed by $8.6 billion in 2000. While the annual FDI inflows dropped to around $3.0–$3.8 billion in 2001–03, it jumped again to $7.7 billion in 2004 (Table 5.2). Accordingly, the stock of FDI inflows increased from $1.3 billion in 1980 to $5.2 billion in 1990, $37.2 billion in 2000, and $55.3 billion in 2004.[30] These FDI inflows helped to contribute to the country's export growth,

Table 5.2   South Korea: FDI Inflows, 1971–2004 ($ millions)

1971–75	1976–80	1981–85	1986–90	1991	1992	1993	1994	1995
550	495	665	3382	1130	563	539	788	1250

1996	1997	1998	1999	2000	2001	2002	2003	2004
2012	2640	5040	9448	8591	3692	2975	3785	7687

Source: UNCTAD, Key Data from WIR (*World Investment Report*) Annex Tables, http://www.unctad.org, accessed on 18 February 2006.

particularly in the 1990s, although South Korean *chaebol* are responsible for the bulk of the country's exports.

The economic success of South Korea is indeed very remarkable. While the nation's GDP expanded from about $2 billion to $688 billion between 1962 and 2004, per capita GNI rose from $87 to $14,162 during the same period.[31] Especially noticeable, today South Korea has far surpassed North Korea in every aspect of the economy with its GDP almost 40 times and per capita GNP almost 20 times those of North Korea.[32] More significantly, South Korea has followed a clear path of upward movement along the ladder of economic development with the nation's economic structure undergoing a dramatic transformation. For the past four decades, the manufacturing sector has been the focus of development and the primary source of growth. During the 1960s, the government promoted the development of export-oriented light industries such as textiles, toys, and footwear. Entering the 1970s, due to increasing labor costs and competition from other developing countries, the South Korean government shifted its attention to the growth of heavy and chemical industries such as shipbuilding, iron and steel, automobiles, machinery, petrochemicals, and electronics. During the 1980s–90s, the government focused on the development of technology- and capital-intensive industries, including electronics, semiconductors, automobiles, and machines. As a result, between 1960 and 2003 the share of the manufacturing sector in the economy rose from 14% to 23%, while the agricultural sector falling from 37% to 3%.[33] In this process, South Korea has transformed from a mere assembler of a range of manufacturing products under contract with Western and Japanese transnational corporations (TNCs) to a major player in its own right that designs and develops its indigenous brands and models.

By the early 21st century, South Korea has emerged as an economic power in the world economy. In 2003, for example, with 0.8% of the world population, South Korea produced 1.7% of world GDP and ranked 11th in the world in terms of the economic size, ahead of Australia, Netherlands, and Russia. In the meantime, South Korea was the 12th largest export nation as well as the 12th largest trading nation.[34] Furthermore, the nation established a strong presence in a range of key industrial sectors, including automobiles, shipbuilding, iron and steel, electronics, petrochemicals, machinery, and construction. By the early 21st century, South Korea was the fifth largest producer of passenger cars after the United States, Japan, Germany, and France (2001); the second largest shipbuilding nation next only to Japan (2001), including both tankers and other sea-going merchant vessels; the ninth largest iron and steel producing country (2001); the third largest TV set producer after China and Malaysia (2001); the fifth largest cement producer (2000); the fourth largest producer of household-use refrigerators (2000); and the fifth largest producer of household-use washing machines (2000).[35] Moreover, South Korea was also the second largest memory chip and the third largest semiconductor producer in the world.[36]

In projecting the nation's growing economic might, South Korean *chaebol* have played a crucial role. These large business conglomerates, supported by the government, are involved in a variety of business activities, ranging from heavy and chemical industries to high-tech and services industries. Leading *chaebol* include Samsung, LG, Hyundai, Daiwoo, and SK. They are actively engaged in the production and export of a wide range of products through their affiliated companies. According to UNCTAD, three South Korean companies were among the top 50 nonfinancial TNCs from developing countries in 2003, of which Samsung Electronics Co., Ltd. ranked the 4th, LG Electronics Inc. the 9th, and Hyundai Motor Company the 35th. Samsung Electronics Co., Ltd. was also among the world's top 100 TNCs.[37] Actually, *chaebol* are the driving force behind the rapid export-led growth of the South Korean economy.

In parallel with the growing economic power of South Korea and the rise of *chaebol* is the acceleration of South Korea's outward FDI. South Korean FDI did not become important until the mid-1980s. After South Korea achieved its first significant current account surplus in 1986, its outward FDI began to accelerate, jumping from $124 million in the period 1971–80, $972 million in 1981–85 to $4.0 billion in 1986–90. Entering the 1990s, there was a surge of South Korean FDI outflows, reaching its annual peak of $5.0 billion in 2000 (Table 5.3). Accordingly, the nation's accumulated FDI outflows rose from $127 million in 1980 to $2.3 billion in 1990, $26.8 billion in 2000, $39.3 billion in 2004.[38] Today,

Table 5.3 South Korea: FDI Outflows, 1971–2004 ($ millions)

1971–80	1981–85	1986	1987	1988	1989	1990	1991	1992	1993	1994
124	972	1227	515	643	598	1052	1489	1162	1340	2461

1995	1996	1997	1998	1999	2000	2001	2002	2003	2004
3552	4670	4449	4740	4198	4999	2420	2617	3426	4792

Source: UNCTAD, Key Data from WIR (*World Investment Report*) Annex Tables, http://www.unctad.org, accessed on 18 February 2006.

South Korea is the fourth largest outward FDI nation among developing economies, after Hong Kong, Singapore, and Taiwan.

In terms of sectoral distribution, the share of South Korean FDI that went to exploit natural resources in developing countries decreased from the mid-1980s onwards, while manufacturing FDI increased in importance. By the end of 1998, 52.0% of South Korea's total accumulated FDI outflows had been in the secondary sector, 6.9% in the primary sector, and 41.1% in the tertiary sector. In terms of geographical destination, 45.9% of the South Korean outward FDI had been in Asia, 28.3% in North America, 10.0% in Western Europe, and 15.8% in the rest of the world. By 1998, South Korean TNCs had established a total of 8450 overseas affiliates, of which 66.6% (5631) was in the secondary sector, 3.2% (266) in the primary sector, and 30.2% (2553) in the tertiary sector. In terms of geographical distribution, 1243 South Korean overseas affiliates (14.7%) were in North America, 278 (3.3%) in Western Europe, 6027 (71.3%) in Asia, and the remaining 902 (10.7%) were in the rest of the world.[39] By investing abroad, South Korean companies are primarily motivated by obtaining cost advantages through relocating industries, overcoming trade barriers in other countries, gaining access to new markets and high technology, and obtain competitiveness over domestic rivals.[40]

Probably, the rise of the South Korean economy is most illustratively reflected in Seoul's accession to OECD in 1996, by which the economic might of South Korea was formally recognized by Western powers. Hence, South Korea, following the steps of Japan ahead of it, became the second Asian country that was admitted to this rich countries' club. In 2004, South Korea joined the trillion-dollar club of world economies.

As economic development continued, there were increasing calls for political reform and democratic developments to match the economic gains. The 1987 presidential election, a direct popular election, was a big step toward a more democratic system of government, which led to the first peaceful transfer of power in the history of the Republic in 1988. The presidential election of 1992 saw the election of the first civilian leader in three decades in South Korea, which led to the nation's successful transition to democracy. Since then, democracy has been gradually consolidated in South Korea.

5.4   South Korea's transformed regional economic relations

In the process of the rise of the South Korean economy, the nation's economic relations with major neighboring countries evolved in the postwar years, reflecting changing international, regional, and domestic conditions. For over a decade after the Korean War, South Korea's economic exchanges with the neighboring economies in East Asia were quite limited. Particularly, the Cold War prevented South Korea from establishing economic as well as political contact with China and other communist states in the region. On the other hand, Seoul's historical animosity and political distrust of the Japanese blocked development of economic ties with Japan. It was the normalization of South Korean–Japanese diplomatic relations in 1965 that finally paved the way for the reestablishment of economic ties between these two countries. Thereafter, South Korea's regional economic relations primarily focused on Japan. Although the bilateral political relations between Seoul and Tokyo continued to be shadowed by the Koreans' persisting bitterness and bad feeling against the Japanese harsh colonial rule in 1910–45, the bilateral economic relations experienced very rapid development. Mimicking the structure of bilateral economic relationship during the Japanese colonial era, the post-1965 economic ties between South Korea and Japan assumed a similar one-sided pattern, under which Japan provided South Korea with ODA, investment and technology while South Korea exported their products to the Japanese market. As a consequence, the Japanese ODA, investment, technology and market played an important role in the economic success of South Korea.

The close economic ties between South Korea and Japan in the post-war years were initially reestablished on the basis of Japanese aid to South Korea. As part of the deal for normalization of bilateral relations in 1965, Japan paid South Korea $300 million as an indemnity for the harm incurred on the Koreans under Japan's 35 years of colonial rule before World War II. In the meantime, Japan further provided $200 million in long-term low interest government loans and $300 million in commercial loans in assistance of South Korea's economic development over a period of 10 years. The result of this arrangement was sizable financial flows from Japan to South Korea after 1965. The Japanese grants were used by South Korea to purchase Japanese equipment for developing marine and agricultural sectors, textile, steel, and machinery industries, while the Japanese government loans were used for the construction of railways, motorways, and dams. In 1971, Japan extended new aid to South Korea, which amounted to 107 billion yen in grants and 317 billion yen in loans over a period up to 1980. In a 1983 agreement on aid, Japan further promised to provide $4 billion for the period 1982–89, which was divided into $1.85 billion yen-denominated ODA loans, $350 million yen bank loans, and $1.8 billion Export-Import Bank dollar-denominated loans. Japanese ODA loans were used by South Korea for the construction of modern urban infrastructure and for programs of agricultural and marine research. By the early 1990s, as a well-established mature economy, South Korea had ceased to receive Japanese aid. Thereafter, the focus of bilateral interest shifted to investment and technology transfer.[41]

Alongside Japanese aid was the rising Japanese investment in South Korea after the mid-1960s, which led Japan to become a major investor in the country. During the period 1965–70, the Japanese FDI accounted for 33.3% of total amount of FDI inflows in South Korea. The Japanese share rose to 61.6% in the period 1971–80 but dropped slightly to 49.5% in 1981–85. After the mid-1980s when the South Korean government relaxed its FDI policy and the appreciation of the yen as a result of the Plaza Accord, the Japanese share remained high until 1989, when it began to decline. According to South Korean statistics, Japanese investment in South Korea mainly focused on the production of components and intermediate goods and on export production for third markets. With rising labor costs and deteriorating labor relations in South Korea, however, Japanese companies began to look elsewhere for production sites in the late 1980s, particularly in China and Southeast Asia. Consequently, entering the 1990s, Japanese FDI to South Korea began to decline (Table 5.4).

As South Korea's major investor and source of imports, Japan also quickly became a principal supplier of foreign technology and capital goods to South Korea. From 1962 to June 1991, for example, South Korea imported 3683 Japanese technologies (51% of the total imported technologies), which were valued at $1.5 billion (31% of the total).[42]

Trade played a most important role in South Korean–Japanese economic relations after 1965. Before the normalization of diplomatic relations, bilateral trade was extremely limited between the two countries with the total trade volume standing at only $211 million in 1965. By 1970, however, the volume of South Korean–Japanese trade had grown to $1.4 billion. By 1980, the figure had jumped to $8.9 billion.[43] Despite some stagnation in the early 1980s, trade between the two countries rose rapidly again after the mid-1980s, which reached $31.2 billion in 1990, $49.7 billion in 1995, $52.3 billion in 2000, and $67.8 billion in 2004.[44] Especially, it is important to note that South Korean–Japanese trade relations after 1965 were part of a trade triangle among the United States, Japan, and South Korea. Over time, Japan replaced the United States as South Korea's main source of imports and the United States replaced Japan as its main export market. Consequently, with the exception of

Table 5.4   South Korea's FDI Inflows by Geographical Origin, 1965–2003 (% of Total)

	Japan	USA	Western Europe-5*	Others
1965–70	33.3	46.1	8.7	11.9
1971–80	61.6	21.7	7.4	9.3
1981–85	49.5	32.9	8.8	8.8
1986	39.1	35.3	16.1	9.5
1987	46.7	23.4	19.6	10.3
1988	54.3	22.2	17.1	6.4
1989	42.7	29.3	18.4	9.6
1990	29.3	39.6	23.0	8.1
1991	16.2	21.2	56.5	6.1
1992	17.3	42.4	28.4	11.9
1993	27.4	32.6	27.3	12.7
1994	32.5	23.6	16.7	27.2
1995	21.8	33.0	17.8	27.4
1996	8.0	27.3	19.7	45.0
1997	3.8	45.8	28.7	21.7
1998	5.7	33.6	29.5	31.2
1999	11.3	24.1	36.4	28.2
2000	16.1	19.2	26.8	37.9
2001	6.9	34.4	23.0	35.7
2002	15.4	49.4	10.9	24.3
2003	8.4	19.2	24.3	48.1

Source: Calculated from National Statistical Office (Republic of Korea), statistical database (KOSIS), http://www.nso.go.kr, accessed on 19 February 2006.
* Western Europe-5 refers to UK, Germany, France, Netherlands, and Switzerland.

1983, the United States was South Korea's largest export market until 2003, when it was replaced by China, while Japan often well behind the United States. On the other hand, with the exception of 1982–83, Japan maintained its position as South Korea's leading source of imports while the United States in the second place until 2004, when China overtook it as the second largest source of South Korea's imports.

A significant feature of South Korean–Japanese trade is a bilateral trade structure that produced substantial bilateral trade imbalance that was constantly in favor of Japan. Under this trade structure, South Korea predominantly exported low value-added and labor-intensive industrial products such as textiles, and agricultural and fishery products to Japan, but imported high value-added Japanese capital goods and technology. Although the specific goods that flowed between the two countries changed over time, this structure remained basically unchanged. For example, during the 1960s–70s, South Korea imported textile machinery and synthetic fibers from Japan and exported textiles mostly to the United States and secondly to Japan. After South Korea moved into ship-building in the 1970s–80s, the nation began to import steel, engines, and heavy electrical machinery from Japan. During the 1980s–90s, South Korea's electrical and electronic consumer goods and chemical goods relied heavily on Japanese components and assembly-line equipment. Consequently, the process of upward movement of South Korea's indus-tries along the technological ladder was accompanied by the import of relevant equipment and components from Japan. This trade pattern reflected South Korea's heavy dependence on Japanese components and intermediate parts as well as Japanese technology and know-how for the nation's industrial development. In many sectors, the introduction of technology from Japan brought in complete Japanese factory lines and production systems that relied on imported Japanese components and intermediate materials. Although the South Korean government attempt-ed to reduce their trade deficit with and their import dependence on Japan, their concerted efforts to obtain Japanese technology (by implica-tion, creating their technological dependence on Japan) actually helped to aggravate rather than improve trade balance and increase rather than reduce dependence on Japanese technology.

South Korea's trade dependence on Japan was reflected not only in the trade structure but also in the share of its trade with Japan. For example, trade with Japan accounted for 19.7% of South Korea's total trade in 1985. By comparison, trade with South Korea represented only 3.7% of Japan's total trade for the same year. South Korea's trade with Japan remained around 20–25% of its total trade until the mid-1990s before it began to decrease to around 15%. On the other hand, Japan's trade with South Korea maintained about 4–6% of its total trade during the 1990s through the early 21st century.[45] South Korea's trade dependence on Japan was even more pronounced with respect to imports, which accounted to 34.3% of South Korea's imports in 1986. Although this dependence decreased in the following years due to South Korea's efforts to reduce its trade deficits with Japan, it still stood at 20.6% of its total imports for 2004.[46]

The trade deficit with Japan has regularly accounted for the lion's share of South Korea's total trade deficits. In 1991, for example, South Korea's trade deficit with Japan reached 8.8 billion, equivalent to 91.7% of South Korea's total trade deficit of $9.6 billion for that year. In 1995 and 1996, South Korea's trade deficit with Japan reached $15.5 billion and $15.7 bil-lion respectively, which were even larger than the nation's overall trade deficits for these 2 years ($9.8 billion for 1995 and $12.7 billion for 1996).

By 2004, South Korea's trade deficit with Japan reached a peak of $24.4 billion.[47] The persistent trade imbalance with Japan and Tokyo's reluctance to further open its markets to South Korean goods or to provide the advanced technology needed by South Korean manufacturers turned to be a constant source of frictions between the two countries.

On the other hand, however, with successful industrialization, which was greatly based on Japanese technology and components, South Korea also became increasingly in competition with Japan in global markets for significant market shares for its ever-growing industrial capacities. Over time, the South Koreans followed the Japanese into the US market and other markets by offering a similar mix of products and trying to undercut Japanese products. This competition started in cutlery and textile goods in the 1960s and thereafter involved an ever-increasing list of products such as ocean vessels, steel, electronics, and cars.

In the course of rising economic power, South Korea achieved remarkable success in exporting to overseas markets and significant trade surpluses. This led to increasing economic frictions with major developed countries, the United States in particular. As a result, South Korean exports increasingly faced trade barriers and protectionist measures in the United States and other Western developed countries. Particularly, Washington criticized South Korea for not making enough progress in economic liberalization, lack of enforcement of copyright and patent protection, the existence of a number of non-tariff barriers (such as overstrict testing and quarantine procedures for imported goods), and restrictions on foreign access to South Korea's financial, telecommunications, distribution, and service industries. On the other hand, there was also mounting economic conflict with Japan. Under such circumstances, South Korea began to seek diversification of its foreign economic relations so as to rectify its dependence on the United States and Japan. It was within this context that Seoul modified its foreign policy by adopting the "northern policy" in the late 1980s and early 1990s. While political considerations of reaching rapprochement with communist giants and stabilizing its relations with North Korea were well behind this policy change, Seoul's intention to diversify its economic relations was apparently an important factor for the adoption of the new foreign policy. As a result, the early 1990s saw a dramatic change in Seoul's foreign policy from a strong anti-communist posture in the 1960s to the normalization of diplomatic relations with the Soviet Union in 1990 and with China in 1992. The improved relations with the two communist giants not only helped greatly increase Seoul's status in the international arena, but also broadened its external economic space. In this process, China was especially an important target of Seoul's efforts to diversify its foreign economic relations.

For political reasons, South Korea and China were completely closed of each other both politically and economically for over four decades during the Cold War era. However, the establishment of diplomatic relations in 1992 paved the way for rapid expansion of economic ties between the two countries. The highly complementary economic structures of the two countries provided a strong impetus for accelerating bilateral economic relations. Moreover, the geographic proximity, shared cultural background, similar security and trade interests and common experience with the Japanese provided additional favorable conditions for the rapid development of bilateral economic relations. Especially, the huge Chinese market as a result of China's rapid economic growth became increasingly important for South Korea's economic growth and future.

The rapid expansion of South Korean–Chinese economic ties since 1992 was most phenomenally illustrated by the rapid growth of bilateral trade, which jumped by 18 times from \$4.4 billion in 1991 to \$79.3 billion in 2004. By 2004, China had surpassed the United States as South Korea's largest trading partner. In this process, the share of South Korean exports to China out of the nation's total exports increased from 1.4% in 1991 to 19.7% in 2004, while the share of South Korea's imports from China rose from 4.2% of the country's total imports to 13.2% during the same period. Particularly significant, China surpassed Japan to become South Korea's second largest export market in 2001, and subsequently overtook the United States in 2003 to become the largest market for South Korean exports and remained so in 2004. Most importantly for the South Korean economy, the nation has enjoyed persistently expanding trade surplus with China since 1993. In 2004, South Korea's trade surplus with China reached a record of \$20.2 billion, which accounted for 70.4% of the nation's total trade surplus (\$28.7 billion) for the year.[48]

The pattern of South Korean–Chinese trade reflected the complementarity of economic structures of the two countries. On the one hand, South Korea mainly exported to China such industrial intermediate goods as electrical machinery, nuclear reactors and boilers, plastics, petrochemical products, and iron and steel. On the other hand, South Korea's imports from China underwent structural change over time, reflecting the rapid industrialization of the Chinese economy. As a result, the share of South Korea's import of raw materials from China decreased from

67.8% to 37.4% in the period 1995–2003, while the share of capital goods increased significantly from 8.1% to 33.4%, and the share of consumption goods increased slightly from 24.2% to 29.2%.[49]

The rapid expansion of South Korean–Chinese economic ties was also reflected in the rising flows of FDI from South Korea to China. South Korean companies began to invest in China in the late 1980s. However, the initial South Korean investment in China was small and exploratory in nature. It was only after the establishment of diplomatic relations between the two countries in 1992 that there was rapid rise of South Korean investment in China. Notably, the investment protection treaty that was signed between Seoul and Beijing soon after the establishment of diplomatic relations in 1992 paved the way for the subsequent mounting of South Korean investment in China. According to South Korean statistics, South Korean FDI to China experienced the first wave of rapid increase in the period 1992–96, from $6.4 million in 1989 to $141.1 million in 1992 and $901.2 million in 1996. As a result, after 1994 China became the second favorite investment destination of South Korean companies after the United States. South Korean FDI to China subsided significantly after 1997 due to the devastating financial crisis. As the South Korean economy began to recover from the financial crisis, South Korean FDI to China started to show resurgence in 2000, increasing by 75.8% from the previous year. In 2003, China overtook the United States as the largest destination of South Korean FDI, receiving an annual amount of $1.3 billion, which accounted for 37.1% of total South Korean FDI for the year. In the meantime, the number of South Korean projects in China reached 1757 in 2003, which accounted for 59.7% of the total number of South Korean foreign investment projects for the year. As a result, the cumulative South Korean FDI in China reached $8.0 billion by the end of 2003, which represented 18.0% of total South Korean FDI outflows, while the cumulative number of South Korean FDI projects in China rose to 9075, which was equivalent to 46.0% of the total number of South Korea's overseas investment projects.[50] In the process, South Korea's giant companies such as LG, SK, Hyundai, and Samsung, together with small- and medium-sized enterprises (SMEs), increased their investment, taking advantage of low labor costs in China. According to Lee Chang-kyu, South Korean FDI to China contributed to increasing South Korean exports to China because South Korean affiliates in China imported large amounts of intermediate goods and components from the home country. According to a survey study conducted by the Korea International Trade Association (KITA), South Korean FDI in China was estimated to create a trade surplus of $3.46 billion, which accounted for

54.5% of South Korea's actual trade surplus with China in 2002. Cheap goods manufactured by South Korean (or joint venture) companies in China were mostly exported to third countries such as the United States and Japan, while some of these goods were also exported to and take a sizeable market share back in South Korea. As such, South Korean FDI in China served as a main channel for bilateral trade between the two countries.[51]

As a result of expanding economic ties with China for over a decade, South Korea's previous excessive partner concentration in the United States and Japan substantially transformed by the early 21st century. While the relative share of US and Japanese markets was on the decline, China became a significant market for South Korean exports. During the period 1986–2004, while the US share of South Korea's total exports drastically decreased from 40.0% to 17.0% and the Japanese share dropped from 15.6% to 8.6%, the Chinese share rose from almost none to 19.7%, which made China the largest market for South Korea.[52] In the meantime, South Korean FDI flows to China helped restructuring of the South Korean economy into a more technology-intensive and high value-added industries. The growing importance of China for the South Korean economy was also reflected in a "China boom" that South Korea is currently experiencing. A growing number of South Koreans are studying the Chinese language and traveling to China, and public opinion polls show that a growing number of South Koreans have favorable views of China, which is in contrast of a sharp decline in favorable views of the United States and Japan. These developments will inevitably bring substantial impact on the political economy of East Asia.

5.5   The South Korean economy rebounding from the Asian financial crisis

Entering the 1990s, while continuing to achieve rapid, although reduced, economic growth, the South Korean economy suffered major setbacks again as a result of rising production costs, increasing protectionism in key export markets, and fierce competition from developing countries. Domestically, the democratic reform in 1987 led to the free formation of autonomous trade unions for the first time in the nation's history. As a result, the increased collective bargaining power of South Korean workers led to rapid wage increases that far exceeded the increase in productivity. In the meantime, the prolonged and sometimes violent labor disputes affected both South Korea's production and exports. On the other hand, the rapid appreciation of the won against major currencies further weakened the competitiveness of South Korean exports. Consequently, under the combined effect of wage increases and currency appreciation, South Korean exports lost their competitiveness in the global market. While South Korean products became unable to compete with the products of other East and Southeast Asian economies on price in the lower end of the market, they were not yet in a position to challenge Japanese products on quality at the top end of the market. In the meantime, the liberalization of domestic markets in the 1980s brought a surge in imports of both capital and consumer goods.

As a consequence, the nation's current account balance turned into deficit from 1990 onward. Especially, the 1996 current account deficit reached $23.1 billion, equivalent to 4.1% of GDP. Total foreign debt also widened from $29.4 billion at the end of 1989 to $104.7 billion at the end of 1996.[53] On the eve of the Asian financial crisis in June 1997, the total foreign debt amounted to $116.7 billion, of which $67.8 billion (58.1% of the total debt) was short-term debt.[54] Notably, from the beginning of 1997, NPLs of South Korean banks had rapidly accumulated as a result of a string of large corporate insolvencies.

Behind the mounting problems were the fundamental structural weaknesses characterized by an excessively indebted corporate sector and a poorly supervised, fragile financial system. These weaknesses derived from the close ties between the government, banks, and corporations, which had formed a web of implicit guarantees and a mentality of "too big to fail." This so-called "crony capitalism" resulted in excessive financial borrowings and high risky over-investment without sufficient attention to credit and exchange rate risks. Finally, the shaky financial system was unable to sustain the shocks of the Asian financial crisis that started in Thailand on 2 July 1997.

Characterized by large-scale capital flight, the plummeting exchange rate of the won (dropping from about 1150 won to the dollar at the beginning of December 1997 to almost 2000 won at the end of the year) and sharply falling stock and property markets, the financial crisis of 1997–98 soon evolved into an overall economic and social crisis, bringing a most severe blow to the South Korean economy in the Republic's history. As a result of the crisis, economic growth dropped from 7.0% in 1996 to 4.7% in 1997 and finally shrank by 6.9% in 1998. Per capital GNP dropped substantially from $12,197 in 1996 to $7355 in 1998.[55] In the meantime, with the loss of 1.2 million jobs the unemployment rate climbed from 2.2% to 7.0% between the summer of 1997 and June 1998.[56]

On the verge of defaulting on its debts as a result of the financial crisis, South Korea turned to the IMF for emergency aid in November 1997. In the following month, Seoul signed an agreement with the IMF, which promised to provide a record standby of $57 billion loan under the condition that the South Korean government would adopt a series of tight macroeconomic policies – including monetary and fiscal policies – to restore economic stability and confidence. In the meantime, as part of the agreement with the IMF, South Korea also undertook a wide range of painful structural reforms to further liberalize the economy and to create a more effective governance structure to supervise and regulate financial institutions and the corporate sector. The programs of restructuring the financial sector and corporate sector aimed at enhancing the soundness and profitability of the two sectors by adopting measures to rejuvenate troubled financial institutions and companies, improve the financial structure of viable financial institutions and companies, and strengthen management transparency.

The restructuring of the financial sector was conducted through two stages, during which the financial sector was reorganized through market competition and financial companies shrank by about 30% in terms of both the number of companies and the number of employees with a number of insolvent financial institutions cleaned up. The result was the substantial improvement in the soundness, profitability, and efficiency of financial companies, which was reflected in various productivity indices, including assets per capita, net profit per year, and return on assets. Moreover, the government poured huge amounts of public funds into banks to help eliminate bad loans, facilitate capital expansion, and secure profitability, which helped South Korean banks substantially improve their Bank for International Settlements (BIS) ratios and bad-debt rations from 12.9 in 1999 to 2.4 by June 2002, approaching the level of advanced countries. In the meantime, all 15 commercial banks and 5 noncommercial banks turned from the red to the black and achieved a net profit of 4.1 trillion won during the period, which indicated that South Korean banks acquired the ability to absorb by themselves NPLs that could arise in the future.[57] The recuperated financial system in turn set the stage for economic recovery.

The restructuring of the corporate sector involved the early disposal of insolvent companies, improvement of companies' financial structure, and adoption of an ongoing evaluation system for corporate credit risk. These measures helped improve the financial soundness, efficiency, management transparency, and corporate governance of companies. As a result, the ratio of ordinary profits to sales increased from 2.2% to 7.6% between the first 9 months of 2001 and those of 2002, which marked the highest recorded profit. At the same time, the financial structure of companies greatly improved with debt and cross shareholdings reduced. The debt ratio of the manufacturing sector dropped from 396% in 1997 to 130% by the end of September 2002. By 2003, the restructuring of the corporate sector was successfully completed.[58]

As a result of the sound macroeconomic policies and restructuring of financial and corporate sectors, the South Korean economy soon achieved an impressive recovery from the financial crisis and the severe recession of 1997–98 with most of its macroeconomic indices recovering to pre-crisis levels. By the end of 1998, the economy had stabilized, setting the stage for a resumption of growth in the following years. In 1999, the nation achieved economic growth by 9.5%, which was followed by a growth rate of 8.5% in 2000. Although the growth rate reduced to 3.8% in 2001 in the midst of a global recession, the South Korean economy posted a rebounded growth rate of 7.0% in 2002. Thereafter, South Korea's growth rates remained around 4% (3.1% for 2003, 4.6% for 2004 and 4.0% for 2005).[59] In the process of economic recovery, the corporate sector slashed employment and wages, reduced its debt burden, and recorded profit gains, leading to a rise in fixed investment. Export growth also picked up, reflecting the increased competitiveness of South Korea following the depreciation of the won. Particularly noteworthy was the information technology industry, which was the fastest growing industry sector in recent years, accounting for some 10% of GDP and 30% of total exports in 2002.[60] As the economy continued its rapid recovery, the unemployment rate declined each year after 1998, hanging around 3.3–4.0% in 2001–05.[61] In the meantime, South Korea reversed its chronic current account deficit in 1998 and maintained a surplus thereafter. Most significantly, the nation turned itself around from a net debtor country to a net creditor country in 1999 and has remained this net creditor position ever since. With all this success, South Korea had its IMF debts completely cleared in 2002.

While the post-crisis economic recovery of South Korea was impressive, however, there were still some apparent problems. Most notably, some of the troubled financial institutions and large companies were not sufficiently restructured, and state financial institutions still did not enjoy managerial autonomy. Moreover, judged by international standards, South Korea's financial sector remained fragile in terms of soundness, profitability, software level, market transparency, fairness, and corporate financial soundness.[62] On the other hand, despite successful cooperate reorganization, a small number of *chaebol* continued to dominate the corporate environment, with the top 30 of them accounting for about 40% of manufacturing output and 50% of exports.[63] Moreover, the nation's external dependence increased as a result of market liberalization and securing of foreign capital in the process of economic reforms. Besides, the tight macroeconomic policies and restructuring programs brought about adverse social effects like the deepening gap between the rich and the poor.

Despite the problems that continued to exist, however, the remarkable recovery of the South Korean economy from the financial crisis of 1997–98 was indeed primarily due to the supportive fiscal and monetary policies and economic restructuring programs. More fundamentally, South Korea's quick recovery reflected the underlying dynamism of the South Korean economy. The sound macroeconomic policies and reform efforts simply helped capitalize this very dynamism of the South Korean economy by strengthening the mechanisms for resource allocation through market forces and altering the legal and institutional settings to improve governance.

6
The Taiwanese Political Economy Since 1945

6.1   The Cold War, US hegemony, and the Taiwanese political economy

Like that of Japan and South Korea, the trajectory of Taiwan's political economy in the postwar years was substantially influenced by the United States in the context of the unique postwar international conditions in the region. The United States not only secured the physical survival of the Nationalist state in the postwar years through its military commitment but also substantially affected postwar Taiwan's political and economic development through its massive economic and military aid, advice, market, capital, technology, training and education, and political support.

When the Nationalist government was defeated by the Communist forces and forced to retreat to Taiwan in 1949, Washington was initially prepared to see the fall of Taiwan to the newly established Communist regime in Beijing.[1] With the breakout of the Korean War in June 1950, however, Washington quickly revised its strategy in the Far East and saw Taiwan as a key strategic bastion in its new strategy of containing communist expansion in East Asia. As such, Washington immediately decided to defend Taiwan and dispatched the Seventh Fleet to the Taiwan Straits to protect the island from a possible attack from the mainland, a military commitment that was later institutionalized in the US–ROC Mutual Defense Treaty signed in 1954. It was precisely America's protection that provided an essential precondition for Taiwan's political stability, economic recovery, and subsequent rapid economic growth in the postwar years.

Once the strategic relationship with Taiwan was established, Washington provided the Nationalist government with massive

economic and military aid to help build Taiwan into a strong strategic ally in the region. In the period 1951–65, Washington provided
Taiwan with over $1.5 billion in economic aid, which was equivalent to
$10 per capita per year, and about $2.5 billion in military aid.[2] US aid
brought much needed capital and resources at a critical time of Taiwan's
economic development and security.

The US economic aid to Taiwan was carefully targeted to help stabilize
the Taiwanese economy and construct a sound economic foundation
during the 1950s–60s. US assistance started with large shipments of
daily necessities of life and materials that Taiwan desperately needed
for economic revival, including chemical fertilizer, wheat, cotton, and
raw materials. In the meantime, US programs helped stabilize inflation in the early years. In the following years, almost half of US aid
was used for construction and improvement of vital infrastructure such
as roads, harbors, railways, thermal and hydroelectric power stations,
communications, and other public works, which in turn provided a
foundation for Taiwan's subsequent economic development and political stability.[3] Moreover, US aid was also used to pay for the import of
essential capital goods, machinery, and technical services at a time when
Taiwan was in severe shortage of foreign exchanges.[4] Equally important, massive US aid helped Taiwan to turn its own domestic savings
into productive investment. Overall, during the period 1951–65, US economic aid averaged about 6.4% of Taiwan's GNP and about 34% of
total gross investment in Taiwan. Taiwan achieved an average annual
rate of growth in real GNP of around 7.5% while per capital GNP
increased at the astonishing annual rate of 4.2% despite high defense
expenditure and a high rate of population growth. According to Neil
Jacoby, because of US aid, Taiwan reached living standards in 1964 that
would otherwise have been achieved by 1995.[5] Obviously, massive US
aid substantially contributed to Taiwan's quick economic recovery and
subsequent rapid economic development. Very few developing states
had their economic growth generated by foreign aid at such a scale.
Moreover, US military aid provided Taiwan with most of its heavy military equipment, including ammunition, artillery, aircraft, tanks, ships
and vehicles as well as budgetary support, technical training and advice,
airfields, roads, and telecommunications facilities.[6] According to Samuel
Ho, US aid enabled Taiwan to pursue three conflicting objectives of
rapid economic growth, stable prices, and a strong military force at the
same time.[7] By the time US aid ended in 1965, a sound foundation
had been well established for Taiwan's subsequent rapid self-sustained
growth.

While US aid phased out by the mid-1960s, the US market played an increasingly important role in supporting Taiwan's export-driven industrialization. By the 1960s, as the growth based on agricultural exports to Japan and elsewhere reached its limit, Taiwan switched to industrialization based on exporting manufactured goods to the United States. Taiwan not only enjoyed free access to the huge US market but was also the largest beneficiary of US Generalized System of Preferences (GSP) from 1976 to 1988, which permitted 3000 Taiwan-made products to enter the United States duty free.[8] As a result, the exports to the United States substantially increased from only 3.5% of Taiwan's total exports in 1952 to 38.1% in 1970, making the United States surpass Japan to become the largest market for Taiwan's exports. By 1984, the proportion of Taiwan's exports to the US market reached a peak of 48.8%. It is no exaggeration to say that it was the US market that made the success of Taiwan's export-oriented industrialization possible. Whereas the United States allowed Taiwan's exports to have free access to its market, it tolerated the island's highly protected market to US exports. Consequently, the imports from the United States continuously declined from 45.7% of Taiwan's total imports in 1952 to 38.1% in 1960, 23.9% in 1970 and 23.7% in 1980, and remained at an annual average of 23.3 % throughout the 1980s. The result of this trade pattern was that Taiwan developed continuously growing trade surplus with the United States throughout the 1970s–80s – peaking at $16.0 billion in 1987,[9] which brought an effect that was equivalent to massive US aid in the 1950s through the mid-1960s.

The US aid as well as military protection also provided a very favorable condition for foreign investment inflows in Taiwan. In the 1950s–60s, the United States was the dominant source of foreign investment in Taiwan. US investment amounted to $4.3 billion or 28.4% of total $15 billion of foreign investment in Taiwan between 1952 and 1991, and accounted for over 90% of the total FDI in Taiwan in the 1950s, over 60% for the period 1952–70, and 27.5% in the period 1952–90.[10] US investment brought Taiwan not only much needed capital but also technology and access to the global markets for Taiwanese products.

It is important to note that in conjunction with massive economic and military aid, Washington sent a powerful group of US advisors to Taiwan, who substantially influenced Taiwan's policymaking and implementation over a range of policy issues, including agriculture, financial and social stability, infrastructure, development strategy, human resources, industry, and defense. Using its economic and military aid as leverage, Washington forced through a number of important reforms in Taiwan.

For example, the land reform was engineered by the US–Taiwan Joint Commission for Rural Reconstruction (JCRR), which frequently over-ruled the Taiwanese government's objections to reform by a combination of incentives and threat to withhold aid.[11] Another example is Taiwan's switch to the export-oriented industrialization in the late 1950s and early 1960s, which was partly the result of Washington's pressure on Taiwan for improving its own ability to earn foreign exchanges in place of US aid.

Taiwan's economic development in the postwar years also benefited from access to the US education system and US-sponsored advanced technical training programs. A large number of Taiwanese, from govern-ment officials to professionals in various areas, obtained their degrees in the United States and later came back to Taiwan to play an important role in Taiwan's economic success. Equally important, some important US values, standards, and practices – like free market, private property, individual incentives, freedom of enterprise, free trade, human rights, democracy, and so on – substantially influenced Taiwan's society from the top right down to the grass roots, which led to the development of a well-functioning capitalist economy and the eventual end of the author-itarian governance. Internationally, the United States provided valuable support to help Taiwan establish its creditworthiness with international financial institutions and gain technical assistance from the UN and its agencies. Notably, Taiwan's economy was also boosted by US military operations in East and Southeast Asia, the Korean War, and Vietnam War in particular, through supplying the US forces with equipment, food, and ammunition.

In the early 1970s, however, Washington began to improve its rela-tions with Beijing for strategic considerations at the expense of Taiwan. By 1 January 1979, Washington switched its diplomatic recognition from Taipei to Beijing and abrogated the US–ROC Mutual Defense Treaty as of 31 December 1979. Despite Washington's adjustment of its Taiwan policy, however, the US Congress passed a special Taiwan Relations Act (TRA) in April 1979. The TRA committed the United States to provide Taiwan with modern defensive weapons and equipment and to continue existing economic, educational, and cultural relationships with Taiwan. Most significantly, the TRA, through US implicit commitment to pro-tect Taiwan, was intended to deter China from any attempt to use force against Taiwan. Though assuming no form, the TRA contained the true substance of a continuing strategic alliance between the United States and Taiwan. According to Gary Klintworth, the TRA proved to be very close to the spirit and intent of the US–ROC Mutual Defense Treaty.[12]

By the mid-1980s, however, there had been substantially transformed global and regional political and economic conditions. While the United States continued to maintain its implicit commitment to Taiwan's secur- ity under the TRA, there had been the rise of economic conflicts between Washington and Taipei over Taiwan's huge trade surplus with the United States and Taiwan's failure to protect intellectual property rights. In 1987, Taiwan's trade surplus with the United States reached $16.0 billion, mak- ing Taiwan the second largest perpetrator of the US trade deficit after Japan but with four times Japan's surplus with the United States in per capita terms. As a result, there was mounting criticism of Taiwan from the US Congress and labor unions for causing unemployment in the United States and hurting certain US industries. Under the circum- stances, Washington not only terminated special tariffs for Taiwan under the GSP in 1988 on the ground that the island had graduated from devel- oping countries, but also turned Taiwan into a target of possible trade retaliation for its illiberal trade and other policies and unfair trade prac- tices. Under Washington's strong pressure, Taipei was forced to address US concerns by liberalizing its market and financial services, appreciating its currency against the US dollar, reducing tariffs and trade restrictions, sending purchasing missions to the United States, banning the purchase of certain goods from other countries, and giving US exporters various kinds of preferential treatment. These measures, together with relocating labor-intensive export industries into mainland China, helped reduce trade surplus with the United States substantially from $16.0 billion in 1987 to $5.6 billion in 1995, and thereafter stabilized at a range of $6.3–$11.5 billion throughout 2006.[13]

The most significant consequence of the US–Taiwanese trade conflict, however, was to set Taiwan on a course of diversification of its trade and economic relations. As a result, the proportion of Taiwan's exports going to the US market steadily declined from the mid-1980s onward, from the peak of 48.8% in 1984 to14.4 % in 2006. In the meantime, the share of US imports also slipped to 11.2% by 2006. Most symbolically, the US position as Taiwan's largest market was replaced by Hong Kong in 2002 and in 2004 the US market slipped further to the third place for Taiwanese exports after China overtook Hong Kong as Taiwan's largest market. In the meantime, the US position as Taiwan's largest trading partner since the 1950s was overtaken by Japan in 2003. In 2004, the United States further declined to the island's third largest trading partner after China became the second largest trading partner of Taiwan. By 2006, the United States remained as the third largest trading partner of Taiwan after China and Japan.[14]

Entering the 21st century, the United States and Taiwan continued to share some basic strategic and economic interests and the American ties continued to occupy a central position in Taiwan's external political and economic relations. On the other hand, however, Taiwan's political economy was being substantially transformed to become subject to novel external forces of globalization and economic regionalism. Moreover, cross-Taiwan Straits relations were also exerting growingly powerful influence on Taiwan's political economy.

6.2   The Taiwanese state and economic development

When the Nationalist government retreated to Taiwan from the mainland in 1949 as a result of the loss in the civil war with the Communist forces, the island was very poor with almost no natural resources, a severe shortage of capital, a very unfavorable land-to-population ratio, an inflation rate of around 3,000%, and the loss of its export markets in both Japan and China. Moreover, the influx of about 2 million people who came to the island along with the Nationalist government made the economic situation of the island even more severe. On the other hand, because of its harsh treatment of the Taiwanese after the island was returned to China in 1945, the Nationalist government was discredited and unpopular among the Taiwanese people, which made economic reconstruction on the island even more difficult. Finally, the possible invasion from the Communist forces on the mainland posed a constant threat on Taiwan. As such, Taiwan was seen at the time as barely having any economic prospects.

After arriving in Taiwan in 1949, however, Chiang Kai-shek was determined to establish Taiwan as a base for the eventual recovery of the mainland from the Communist control. To this end, Chiang Kai-shek reorganized the ruling party, the army, and the civil service and strengthened the authoritarian structure of the state through emergency legislation, which was justified by the state of conflict across the Taiwan Straits. While the state excised authoritarian power over society and suppressed opposition activities, the Nationalist government also made major efforts to prevent the development of widespread corruption, a costly lesson that had been learned from its loss of power on the mainland. Particularly, the Nationalist government realized the very importance of economic development, which was seen crucial not only for the survival of the regime in the face of the constant threat from the Communist mainland but also for justification and consolidation of its rule on the island. As such, economic development was top on the government agenda.

It was under such circumstances that the Nationalist government took it as its emergent task to control the ongoing rampant inflation and to stabilize the economy. The first body that was established in 1949 to coordinate economic policy for stabilizing the Taiwanese economy was the Taiwan Production Board. Through a number of policy measures including currency reform, increase of interest rates, control of money supply, and conservative fiscal policies of balanced budgets, skyrocketing inflation was curtailed. The control of inflation helped stabilize the island's economy, which paved the way for subsequent economic recovery and development.

While the emergent measures to control inflation and stabilize the economy were still under way, the government began to launch land reform on the island. Learning from its past experience on the mainland where its loss of peasant support had largely contributed to its loss of power, the Nationalist government now saw farmers as crucial for consolidation of its power in Taiwan. Moreover, the need to feed Taiwan's rapidly growing population also warranted the development of agriculture. As such, the government, under US advice, embarked upon an ambitious program of land reform. From the very beginning, the land reform was well conceived. As the Nationalist government was not politically beholden to the landlord class in Taiwan in the way that it had been on the mainland, it was able to pursue the land reform seriously and thoroughly. The JCRR played a key role in planning and carrying out the land reform and other reforms affecting agriculture. The land reform was conducted through three stages. In 1949, rent was reduced from around 50% to 37.5% of the main crop. Then in 1951 the government sold out 96,000 hectares of public land to 156,000 tenant farm families at 2.5 times the value of 1 year's crop. Finally, in 1953 the Land to the Tiller Act was promulgated, under which landlords were allowed to keep only 2.1 hectares of paddy field and twice as much of dry land but forced to sell the rest of the land they did not farm themselves.[15] While small farmers were provided with credit for purchase of land, the landlords who sold their land were compensated with land bonds or shares in public enterprises. The result of the land reform was the rise of owner-cultivated land from 51% to 79% between 1949 and 1953.[16]

The land reform greatly helped stimulate farmers' incentives to work hard and make efforts to improve land quality and increase output. After the successful completion of the land reform, the government continued to support agricultural development by creating farmers' associations, initiating a government-sponsored fertilizer-for-rice exchange program, and sponsoring other activities that helped farmers. In the meantime, the government also encouraged farmers to grow new crops and helped farmers to use new farming techniques.

The land reform and the agriculture-supportive policy helped substantially increase agricultural productivity, greatly promoted agricultural production, and increased rice yields. During the 1950s, Taiwan achieved an impressive average annual growth rate of 14% in agricultural production.[17] As a result, Taiwan's agriculture made significant contribution to the island's economic development in the early years. Notably, the rapid agricultural growth helped provide cheaper food and improve the diet of the Taiwanese people. By the mid-1960s, Taiwan's farmers provided the population with a level of food consumption superior to that of any country in Asia except Japan. In caloric content, Taiwan surpassed Japan a few years later. More important, the rapid agricultural growth helped produce an agricultural surplus that could be used to finance industrialization. Taiwan's industrialization was greatly facilitated by taxes collected from the rural areas, farmers' savings (40% of capital formation in the 1950s), and their purchases of manufactured products, including consumer goods, farm tools, machineries, fertilizers, and others. In the meantime, during the 1950s and early 1960s, half of Taiwan's foreign exchange earnings came from agricultural exports. Equally important, improved agricultural productivity allowed more rural labor force to move out of the agricultural sector to the industrial sector, which was in much need of labor. As a result, during the 1950s–70s, nearly half of the new labor used in nonagricultural production came from the rural areas.[18] All these paved the way for a quick economic recovery and subsequent rapid industrialization. Politically, the successful land reform and rapid agricultural growth helped the Nationalist government gain support in the countryside.

With the economy stabilized and agriculture put on the right track, the Nationalist government moved to focus on the promotion of industrialization. Like other developmental states in East Asia, the Taiwanese state played a crucial role in the process of industrialization through an institutional framework of economic planning and management. The government not only designed and implemented economic development plans but also pursued its objective of national development by adopting a well-designed and timely adjusted suitable development strategy and a wide range of supportive policy measures.

First of all, the government developed an institutional framework of economic planning and management that provided an organizational foundation for state involvement in promoting rapid economic growth. The most important bodies included the Council for Economic Planning and Development (CEPD), the Ministry of Economic Affairs (MOEA), the Central Bank of China, the Ministry of Finance (MOF), and the China External Trade Development Council (CETRA).

The CEPD originated from the Council for US Aid (CUSA), which was founded on the mainland in 1948 to coordinate and allocate US aid. CUSA was reorganized into the Council for International Economic Cooperation and Development (CIECD) in 1963. In 1973, CIECD was transformed into the Economic Planning Council (EPC) to strengthen the Executive Yuan's economic planning and research functions. In 1977, EPC was merged with the Executive Yuan's Finance and Economic Committee to form CEPD. CEPD, similar to South Korea's EPB, was aimed at strengthening the effectiveness of national economic planning and promoting comprehensive national economic development. Thereafter, CEPD played a crucial role in the formation of Taiwan's economic policy, responsible for the overall planning for national economic development, evaluating projects and programs for the Executive Yuan and monitoring the implementation of development projects, measures and programs, and coordinating the economic policy-making activities of related ministries and agencies.

The MOEA was another important government body, which was first established on the mainland in 1937. After the Nationalist government retreated to Taiwan in 1949, MOEA was reorganized several times. Through its 14 powerful agencies, MOEA covered sectoral division of the economy, responsible for industrial regulations, cross-sectoral coordination, export promotion, and industrial estates including the Export Processing Zones (EPZs) and public corporations.

During 1949–61, it was the Bank of Taiwan (a commercial bank controlled by the Taiwan provincial government) that functioned as a central bank in Taiwan. In 1961, the Central Bank of China, which had been the central bank on the mainland before 1949, was reestablished. Largely autonomous, the Central Bank of China was responsible for monetary and foreign exchange policy. On the other hand, the MOF was responsible for fiscal policies, tax collection, the customs, and supervision over the regulation of Taiwan's financial markets.

In 1970, the government helped create the CETRA, an organization that helped Taiwan's small- and medium-sized companies in export through providing a range of training facilities in foreign languages and economics, providing overseas market information, organizing both trade exhibitions and trade delegations, and more recently promoting quality initiatives and quality image of Taiwan's products abroad.

Through these well-constructed institutions staffed with highly competent and devoted professionals, many of whom had received Western education, the Taiwanese state was actively involved in promoting economic growth. The role of the state in Taiwan's economic development was first and foremost reflected in the government's economic development plans. The government began to adopt medium-term economic development plans in 1953, and by 2008 14 such economic plans have been adopted. These plans addressed the most important economic issues at the time, set economic goals, and provided guidance for the direction for almost all sectors of the economy, including the business community, farmers, and others.[19]

Particularly important, through these economic development plans the Taiwanese government pursued a clear development strategy that was deliberately and well designed to reflect both the external and the internal conditions of the time. In the early 1950s, because of the loss of the traditional Japanese market, a shortage of foreign exchanges, overvalued currency, lack of capital and technology, and a serious unemployment problem, the government adopted an import-substitution strategy by promoting the development of local industries. To pursue this development strategy, the government adopted various policy measures – including an overvalued currency, high tariffs, foreign exchange controls, import quotas and other import controls, and favorable financial treatment for selected domestic producers – to protect domestic industries from foreign competition and discourage the purchase of foreign goods.

Taiwan's import-substitution development strategy successfully helped control the inflation, stabilize the economy, conserve precious foreign exchanges, and absorb excess labor. This strategy contributed to the rapid development of such industries as textiles, leather goods, food processing, fertilizer, and chemicals in the 1950s. During the period 1952–59, the rapid growth of these industries helped increase industry's share in the overall GNP by 6%. In the meantime, light manufacturing industries and some other industries such as sheet glass, nonmetal mineral products, machinery, equipment, and rayon also began to develop and grow during this period.[20]

By the end of the 1950s, however, the import-substitution strategy had reached its limit under changed conditions. In the first place, the domestic market had become saturated for domestic industries under the government's protectionist policy. On the other hand, in the process of import-substitution industrialization, Taiwan gradually obtained competitive advantage in some industries as well as in labor quality and costs. Under such circumstances, the government timely switched to an export-oriented development strategy by the end of the 1950s and early 1960s. Thereafter, Taiwan pursued a vigorous policy of promoting exports.

To promote export-led growth, the government modified its previous policies by abolishing the dual exchange-rate system, devaluing the currency, reducing tariffs, and establishing laws and regulations in favor of export companies. In the meantime, taxes, interest rates, regulations on import of raw materials, and foreign investment policy were also changed to accommodate the new strategy. In order to promote exports, the government also established EPZs, administered by MOEA, where tariffs and non-tariff barriers were removed and red tapes were reduced.

Initially in the early 1960s, the export-oriented development strategy was primarily based on the labor-intensive industries that produced consumer goods, including textiles, processed food products, leather goods, wood products, and paper products. This export-oriented policy was quite successful. As a result, exports rose from $164 million in 1960 to $1481 million in 1970.[21] In the meantime, the rapid development of export industries helped absorb considerable excess labor, bring needed foreign exchanges, and attract increasing foreign investment inflows. More important, export industries contributed to the rapid economic growth.

By the 1970s, economic conditions had changed again. With continued economic growth, there was the emergence of a labor shortage, which was driving labor costs to rise dramatically. On the other hand, investment capital became more easily available. Under the circumstances, the government dramatically moved away from labor-intensive industries to capital-intensive industries such as electronics, electrical products, chemicals, machinery, instruments, and metal products. The textile industry continued to exist, but it moved to the higher level of fashion and better grades while cheap textiles were gradually phased out. Consequently, there was a change in the quality, sophistication, and price of Taiwan's exports. Whereas the government helped and, in many cases, forced companies to move out of labor-intensive production into the areas of capital- and knowledge-intensive products, it also gave considerable attention to quality control. All this helped contribute to the continuing growth of exports. Moreover, facing the oil crises of the 1970s, the government timely adopted adjustment policies to diversify energy sources, encourage conservation, store more energy, and promote less energy-intensive industries.

Entering the 1980s, as domestic labor costs were rising further, the competitive advantage of Taiwan's traditional industries began to erode. As such, the government helped establish the Hsinchu Science-Based Industrial Park as a strategic base for new technologies and industries and provided support for the computer and other knowledge-intensive industries. This paved the way for the rapid development of high-tech industries in Taiwan in the 1990s and after.

In the 1990s, the government moved to strengthen the infrastructure of the economy by assigning top priority to the implementation of 12 major construction projects, covering transportation, culture and education, improvement of living standards, water resources development, and environmental protection. Furthermore, the government introduced the concept of transforming Taiwan into a modern industrialized society and adopted a plan to develop Taiwan into an Asia-Pacific Regional Operations Center (APROC).

Entering the 21st century, Taiwan further moved away from the earlier labor- and capital-intensive industries as a key driver of economic growth toward further transformation and upgrading of the island's industrial structure, investing heavily in human resources, logistics networks, and the environment, with the objective of developing Taiwan into a silicon-based economy.

To achieve the objectives of its development strategy, the government adopted a range of supportive policy measures. The government helped boost domestic savings by adopting a high interest rate policy. The high savings provided an important source for financing investment, particularly in the 1950s through the 1980s. On the other hand, however, Taiwan's high savings also implied the absence of a social welfare system and an undeveloped consumer credit system.

In the process of industrialization, the government promoted exports as the driving force for rapid economic growth, particularly after the early 1960s, by employing a series of supportive policies, including tariffs, rebates, subsidiary, easy credit, preferential taxes, and so on. A system of tariffs and rebates was also available for some items of imports that were subsequently re-exported. In 1966, the government established the first EPZ at Kaohsiung, which was designed to attract foreign companies with minimum regulations and low-wage labor force in return for exporting all of their production. Thereafter, the EPZs played an important role in promoting Taiwan's exports. Moreover, the government also paid particular attention to the quality of Taiwan-made products and prohibited the export of inferior goods.

Unlike Japan and South Korea, Taiwan adopted preferential policies to attract foreign investment to help improve the infrastructure and build new factories. In the mid-1950s, the government introduced new investment laws, which permitted foreign companies to bring equipment and build plants in Taiwan. In 1959, tax incentives were introduced to attract foreign investment. In the mid-1960s, EPZs – a Taiwan's invention – were established, within which foreign companies enjoyed free-port status for imports and exports, relief from many government regulations and controls, and access to good harbors. These government policies helped bring a marked increase in foreign investment in Taiwan. As a result, while the surplus in the agricultural sector and US economic aid were the primary sources of capital accumulation during the 1950s–60s, very soon Taiwan's economic growth was facilitated by a large amount of foreign investment inflows together with high domestic savings. Foreign investment not only helped create more jobs, provide worker training and upgrade workers' skills, but also helped facilitate the development of new industries and the transfer of technology. In 1995, Taiwan's stock market was also opened for foreign investment, which opened a new channel for bringing in considerable investment funds from abroad.

In promoting economic growth, the Taiwanese government paid great attention to science and technology. In order to acquire more advanced foreign technology and to diffuse it across the private sector, the government created the Industrial Technology Research Institute (ITRI) in 1973 with a view to developing research and development and attracting more Taiwanese scientists back from abroad. The Electronic Research and Service Organization (ERSO), which was affiliated with ITRI, played a key role in transferring foreign technology into Taiwan. By licensing foreign technology and then sub-licensing it, ERSO helped prevent competition between domestic companies for technological advantage. The government also encouraged the cooperation between the public and the private sector and used quasi-governmental organizations to act as agents of technology transfer to the private sector. These policies were important in helping the leading Taiwanese corporations achieve key positions in the global market. In the meantime, the policy of attracting foreign investment also helped facilitate technology imports. Foreign companies brought new production techniques to Taiwan while stimulating research and worker training. Moreover, Taiwan's education system was designed in a way that promoted technology absorption by training young people to learn new technology.

The Taiwanese government also invested heavily in constructing a sound economic infrastructure that provided electricity, energy, roads, railroads, airports, harbors, ports, and communications for rapid economic development. In the meantime, the government also created a favorable social infrastructure for economic growth. Special attention was paid to education. From the 1960s onward, the government took a series of policies on the provision of primary, secondary, and tertiary education, preparing students either for technical or vocational colleges or for higher education. The government also promoted higher education. Emphasis on education helped produce a quality workforce. Moreover, labor policy was pursued in a way that helped produce a cheap, highly disciplined, and skillful labor force. During the period of Taiwan's rapid industrialization, the government adopted a number of laws and regulations that generally favored management and sought to maintain a passive labor force by banning strikes and discouraging labor organization and collective bargaining. Nevertheless, in 1958, the Labor Insurance Act was passed, and, in 1994, the Labor Safety and Health Law. However, the Labor Standards Law – the most important piece of legislation – went into effect in 1984, which provided comprehensive guarantees and rights to workers and defined many unclear provisions in labor-management relations. This law covered 40% of the labor force, including agricultural workers.[22] The government made sure that productivity must exceed wage increases.

Compared to Japan and South Korea, Taiwan had a very strong public sector. The public sector played an important role in economic development. In 1945, the Nationalist government took over most of the large manufacturing enterprises left over by the Japanese. Later, the government also created a number of public enterprises. Although the Nationalist government was committed to the market economy, it believed at the time that the government's control of large industries was very important for the economy and national security. Moreover, the government also used public enterprises to pursue integrated research programs and enter into new fields with potentially high entry barriers and risks. As such, in the 1950s, public enterprises dominated such industries as fuel, chemicals, fertilizer, food processing, textiles, and utilities. In 1954, the private enterprises accounted for only 43.4% of industrial production. But gradually, the government introduced privatization and began to sell off many public enterprises. By 1962, there had been a noticeable increase in the private sector's percentage of industrial production. By 1972, this percentage reached 80% and by the mid-1980s, nearly 90%.[23] By 1988, there were 122 enterprises that remained controlled by the government, which accounted for just 16% of all enterprises on the island.[24] Today, while the percentage of private enterprises reached 95%, mostly in the form of small family-owned businesses,[25] there were still seven important public corporations that dominated such sectors as sugar, power, petroleum, shipbuilding, aerospace, water supply, and steel.

The macroeconomic policies of Taiwan were designed to promote economic growth while maintaining macroeconomic stability. The government pursued a conservative monetary policy, low taxes, sound fiscal policy, and foreign exchange policy. The government also wisely regulated banking and financial institutions, and maintained social and political stability. While the government began financial liberalization in the 1970s and moved to privatize a number of the state-owned banks, the process was still far from complete.

In general, the role of the Taiwanese state evolved over time in the process of industrialization, reflecting changing domestic and international conditions. In the early years of development, the state played a more direct role in intervening in economic development by using executive orders, controlling credit and finance, and running public corporations. The government played an important role in guiding and designing economic development through economic plans, forecasting, and advice for farmers, small- and medium-sized companies, and business leaders. The government adopted and modified the development strategy several times to keep the island's development on the right track. As such, under the state guidance, Taiwan followed a very clear path of development: development of agriculture in the first place, followed by a short period of import-substitution development, and then the timely switch to export-led economic growth based on the island's comparative advantages. As the economy became increasingly mature and democracy was gradually established and consolidated in Taiwan in the course of the 1980s–90s, the government began to introduce economic liberalization and internationalization, and the role of the state in economic development was steadily weakened. As a result, the government gradually moved to play a more indirect role in economic management, such as provision of infrastructure, promotion of effective functioning of market, provision of social welfare, protection of environment, and so on. Today, Taiwan basically has a free market economy in terms of trade policies, taxation, government consumption, monetary policy, wage and price controls, property rights and regulations, foreign investment, and banking.

6.3   The rise of the Taiwanese economy

As a result of its defeat in World War II, Japan was forced to return the sovereignty over Taiwan to the Nationalist China in August 1945. The consequent severing of the island's economy from the Japanese economy, however, hit Taiwan severely. The Nationalist government, which was preoccupied with the civil war against the Communists on the mainland at the time, hardly paid attention to the economy of the recovered island. As a consequence, Taiwan's economic productivity declined precipitously across nearly all sectors. By 1946, overall production had fallen to less than half of what it had been.[26] In the meantime, the island was suffering a shortage of consumer products, widespread poverty and disease, deteriorating education system and public services, rampant inflation, war-damaged infrastructure, and a shortage of foreign exchanges. In just over 1 year from November 1945 to the beginning of 1947, the price of food jumped 700%, fuel and construction materials 1400%, and fertilizer 25,000%.[27] On top of that, there was an influx of about 2 million refugees from the mainland, which further deteriorated the existing problems in housing, employment, and infrastructure. To make the situation worse, precious resources were further diverted to prepare for defense of the island against possible invasion from the mainland. It seemed at the time that Taiwan would hardly have economic future.

Despite the huge problems of the early years, however, Taiwan was soon back on the right track in the early 1950s and thereafter maintained sustained rapid economic growth, thanks to the favorable external environment provided by the US hegemon in the context of the Cold War, the government's commitment to economic development and adoption of a suitable development strategy, and macroeconomic stability.

Taiwan's rapid economic growth since the early 1950s was very remarkable. During the 1950s, the island's economy grew at an average annual rate of 8.2%, which was followed by an expanded average annual rate of 9.2% in the 1960s. In the 1970s, despite the oil crises and the worldwide recession, Taiwan, through timely policy adjustment, achieved an even higher two-digit average annual growth rate of 10.2%.[28] The rapid economic growth continued relatively unabated in the more protectionist atmosphere of the 1980s through the 1990s. The 1980s witnessed an average annual growth rate of 8.2%, much higher than the world average of 3.3% and the OECD average of 2.7%. In the 1990s, although Taiwan experienced a reduced annual growth rate of 6.4%, this economic performance still much exceeded that of the world average (2.7%) and the OECD average (2.6%).[29] Particularly important, Taiwan achieved this growth rate in the context of the Asian financial crisis in the late 1990s. During 2000–06, Taiwan's annual growth rate remained at 3.8%.[30] As a result of rapid economic growth, Taiwan's GDP jumped 217 times over five decades, from $1.7 billion in 1952 to $364.4 billion in 2006. In the meantime, per capita GNP rose from $197 to $16,471 during the same period.[31] Consequently, Taiwan was transformed from a very poor and small economy to a newly industrializing economy.

Particularly impressive is that Taiwan's rapid economic growth was achieved with low unemployment, low inflation, a relatively equitable distribution of national income, and a healthy balance of payments surplus. Unemployment rate was kept below 2.0% for most years after the mid-1960s through the 1980s and it averaged 2.0% in the 1990s and 4.3% in 2000–06. Inflation also remained low with consumer prices rising at an average rate of 4.3% per year in the 1970s despite the oil crises, 3.0% in the 1980s, 2.9% in the 1990s, and 0.8% in 2000–06. Taiwan's rapid economic growth was also accompanied by relatively equal income distribution, thanks to a range of governmental redistribution policies. Although the Gini coefficient – the ratio of the highest 20% of income to the lowest 20% – increased from 4.17 in 1980 to 6.04 in 2005 largely due to a decrease in the size of households in the lower income groups and rising unemployment in recent years, Taiwan remained one of the economies that had the lowest income disparity in the world.[32] Moreover, in the process of economic growth, Taiwan also avoided such problems that plagued many developing countries as a large external debt, dislocation of certain sectors, and political instability. For example, in 2004 Taiwan's external debt as the percentage of GNP was only 24%, compared to 35% of Thailand, 53% of Malaysia, 61% of Indonesia, and 73% of the Philippines.[33]

The rapid economic growth of Taiwan was largely driven by exports, particularly after the 1960s. In 1952, Taiwan's total volume of exports was only $116 million. After the launching of an export-oriented development strategy in the early 1960s, it began to rise rapidly from the 1960s onward and by 2006 the total volume of Taiwan's exports reached $224.0 billion. This implies that Taiwan achieved an astounding average annual export growth rate of 35.8% between 1952 and 2006. In a similar fashion, the growth of overall trade (imports and exports) was also momentous by any standard. In 1952, the total volume of Taiwan's trade was only $303 million. But by 2006, Taiwan achieved a total annual volume of trade of $426.7 billion, which implies an average annual growth rate of 26.1% between 1952 and 2006.[34] As the statistical data show, exports were the most important source of Taiwan's economic growth (Table 6.1).

Consequently, Taiwan became a highly trade-oriented economy with the ratio of its overall trade to GNP rising from 18% in 1952 to 114% in 2006.[35] Taiwan's per capita trade volume also jumped substantially, from $38 to $18,765 during the same period.[36] In a similar fashion, the ratio of exports to GNP rose rapidly from 6.9% in 1952 to 59.8% in 2006.[37]

Table 6.1 Sources of Economic Growth: Expenditure Side (Contribution to Economic Growth Rate), 1952–2006 (%)

Period	Economic growth rate (Increase in real GDP)	Domestic demand					Net exports		
		Subtotal	Private consumption	Government consumption	Gross fixed capital formation	Increase in inventory	Subtotal	Exports of goods and services	Less imports of goods and services
1952	100.00	127.18	85.95	23.80	13.84	4.09	−27.68	0.33	28.01
1955	100.00	66.06	45.78	39.32	−13.31	−3.73	31.94	12.69	−19.26
1960	100.00	104.40	52.59	11.63	29.11	11.07	−4.40	11.71	16.12
1965	100.00	105.48	62.07	16.33	17.88	9.91	−5.48	20.11	25.59
1970	100.00	101.29	51.73	22.26	17.67	9.64	−1.29	37.98	39.27
1975	100.00	69.24	56.60	55.22	80.20	−122.78	30.76	−0.25	−31.01
1980	100.00	89.41	40.56	21.83	39.27	−12.25	10.59	34.68	24.09
1985	100.00	62.96	64.52	24.29	−15.92	−9.93	37.04	15.32	−21.71
1990	100.00	137.26	79.78	40.46	25.29	−8.28	−37.26	4.70	41.96
1995	100.00	82.75	52.09	9.81	26.59	−5.74	17.25	81.51	64.26
2000	100.00	66.26	48.58	1.80	35.89	−20.00	33.74	155.33	121.59
2005	100.00	32.71	39.79	2.87	0.81	−10.76	67.29	114.44	47.15
2006	100.00	22.40	17.94	−0.61	4.30	0.77	77.60	139.88	62.28

Source: CEPD, *Taiwan Statistical Data Book, 2007* (Taipei: Council for Economic Planning and Development, Republic of China, 2007), Table 3-10a, p. 63.

High levels of savings and investment also contributed to Taiwan's rapid economic growth, especially after the 1960s. The gross national savings rose slightly from 15.3% of GNP in 1952 to 17.7% in 1960, but thereafter increased rapidly at a steady pace to 25.4% in 1970, 31.8% in 1980, and 38.0% and 38.1% respectively in 1986 and 1987. In recent years, however, gross national savings were falling as a result of rising consumption that accompanied the higher income, reduced corporate savings due to rising business costs, and rising government expenditures for social welfare. Consequently, gross national savings dropped to 24.2% in 2001 and remained at 27.8% in 2006.[38] High levels of savings helped bring high levels of gross domestic investment (capital formation), which rose from 15.3% of GNP in 1952 to 20.1% in 1960, 25.4% in 1970, and 33.8% in 1980. A high level of capital accumulation helped transform the Taiwanese economy to be more based on capital- and knowledge-intensive industries. As Taiwan had become a capital surplus economy by the 1990s, however, the gross domestic investment rate fell to 17.1% in 1986 but rose to 25.5% in 1993. By 2006, the figure remained at 20.7%.[39]

Taiwan's rapid economic growth was also driven by FDI. After US economic assistance reduced in importance as a main source of foreign capital in the 1960s, Taiwan began to adopt a number of measures to attract foreign investment. As a result, large amounts of needed capital came through FDI inflows. While in 1952 the total amount of FDI was only insignificant $1 million, it reached $16 million in 1960, $139 million in 1970, $466 million in 1980, $2302 million in 1990, and $7608 million in 2000, and $13,969 million in 2006. By 2006, the accumulated approved FDI reached $78.7 billion.[40] The most important investors were the United States, Japan, and Overseas Chinese. Much of the foreign investment was in export sectors, which directly stimulated the rapid export-led economic growth of Taiwan.

The expansion of the labor force was another important factor in Taiwan's rapid economic growth in the postwar years. Because of Taiwan's rapid population growth from 8.1 million in 1952 to 22.7 million in 2006, the labor force tripled, increasing from 3.1 to 10.5 million during the same period, while employment rose from 2.9 to 10.1 million between 1952 and 2006. Significantly, the percentage of the working age population (age of 15–64) ranged between 55.2% and 71.9% in the period 1952–2006, which was very high by international standards.[41] More importantly, the level of skills and education of the labor force improved rapidly, especially relative to labor costs. For instance, in the period 1981–2006, those with junior high education and below (including illiterate and primary education) dropped from 68.8% of the total labor force to 27.0%, while those with senior high and vocational education increased from 20.4% to 35.9% and those with junior college education and above jumped from 10.9% to 36.7%.[42] The high quality of Taiwan's labor force constituted a critical factor in the island's competitiveness and rapid economic growth.

In the process of rapid economic growth, labor productivity in industry improved substantially since the early 1950s. Initially, Taiwan's industrial productivity benefited from the low labor costs, a high level of skills and education of workers, and hard-work ethic. Later, however, rising labor productivity was growingly driven by efficient organization of labor, labor-saving measures, and rapid capitalization of production. Consequently, the index of the labor productivity in manufacturing industry was rising continuously, for example, from 76.36 in 1993 to 134.47 in 2006 with 2001 as 100.[43]

Taiwan's rapid economic growth was accompanied by fundamental transformation of the economic structure. As a result, agriculture's contribution to the economy declined markedly over time, while the industrial sector grew rapidly and became the engine of Taiwan's economic growth after the late 1950s. By the mid-1970s, Taiwan had become more industrialized than any other country in Asia except Japan.[44] In statistical terms, the share of agriculture in GDP continuously decreased from 32.1% in 1952 to 1.5% in 2006, whereas the share of industry in GDP steadily rose from 19.5% in 1952 to 44.8% in 1986 and then began to decline, dropping to 26.8% in 2006. On the other hand, the share of the service sector in GDP rose from 48.4% to 71.7% between 1952 and 2006, reflecting that with industrialization achieved in the 1980s Taiwan was moving toward a service-based economy.[45]

The transformation of the economic structure was also shown in the transformation of the employment structure with a massive shift of employment from agriculture to industry and services over time. The employment in the agricultural sector (primary industry) dropped from 56.1% to 5.5% between 1952 and 2006, while industrial employment rose from 16.9% in 1952 to 42.8% in 1987 before declining to 36.6% in 2006. Meanwhile, the employment in the service sector increased from 27.0% to 57.9% during the same period and will be the major source of new jobs for the coming years.[46]

Significantly, in the process of economic transformation Taiwan, like Japan and South Korea, was moving upward along the ladder of industrial production from labor-intensive industries of the 1950s–mid-1980s toward capital-intensive, high value-added heavy and high-tech industries and service industries from the mid-1980s onward in line with the island's changing comparative advantage. From the 1950s through the 1970s, the textiles played a particularly important role as Taiwan's largest industry in terms of value of production, volume of exports, and source of employment. As labor costs increased and foreign competition intensified, Taiwan gradually moved out of the textile industry. In the meantime, from the 1960s onward Taiwan's electrical equipment and electronics industries also began to grow, initially involving electric fans, integrated circuits, and other labor-intensive products. With the rising labor costs, these industries gradually became capital-intensive and moved upward to the production of household appliances, communication equipment, and consumer electronics. Over time, Taiwan became a major producer of radios, tape recorders, televisions, video-cassette recorders, stereo equipment, calculators, video games, electrical equipment, and semiconductors. Moreover, Taiwan also developed such industries as food processing, tobacco, alcoholic beverages, fertilizers, pharmaceuticals, rubber products, cement, glass products, wood products, and paper products, and bicycles.

Beginning in the 1970s, Taiwan promoted the development of a range of capital-intensive, high-tech and knowledge-intensive industries, including petrochemicals, metals (including steel, aluminum, copper, and other metals), shipbuilding, yacht, telecommunication equipment, precision tools, optical machines and supplies, sporting and fitness goods, automobiles, and motorcycles. The construction industry was also booming, driven by the government's ambitious public works projects as well as people's growing demand for better housing due to increasing standards of living. As a consequence, Taiwan established a quite comprehensive economic structure, capable of producing a range of sophisticated products.

The structural transformation of the Taiwanese economy was most illustratively reflected in the transformed structure of Taiwan's trade over time. While agricultural commodities such as sugar, rice, tea, and canned and tropical fruits accounted for the bulk of Taiwanese exports in the 1950s, after the 1960s manufactured products increasingly became a major source of exports. Consequently, the share of agricultural exports (including agricultural products and processed agricultural products) dropped from 91.9% of Taiwan's total exports in 1952 to insignificant 1.0% in 2006, while the share of manufactured exports jumped from 8.1% to 99.0% during the same period.[47] In recent years, Taiwan became a net importer of agricultural commodities. Significantly, the structure of manufactured exports was also transformed with the portion of capital-intensive, high-tech, and knowledge-intensive products increasing as Taiwan's major exports. By 2006, as the most important exports, electronic and IT & C products accounted for 32.1% of Taiwan's exports, while machinery, electrical machinery products and transportation equipment 15.3%, iron, steel, iron and steel products and other metal products 11.3%, optical, photographic, measuring and medical instrument 6.6%, and chemicals 5.0%. These products, combined, accounted for 70.3% of Taiwan's exports. On the other hand, such products as textiles, footwear, toys, and food became negligible as export items.[48] In terms of import composition, agricultural and industrial raw materials constantly accounted for the bulk of Taiwan's total imports (a range between over 60% and less than 80%) over the years, followed by capital goods and consumer goods.[49]

As a result of the rapid economic growth, Taiwan substantially improved its overall economic strength and significantly increased its influence in the global economy. Having a GNP of $364.0 billion, Taiwan, with only about 0.4% of the world population, ranked the 17th largest economy in the world in 2005. In terms of per capita GNP, Taiwan had $16,067 for the same year, making it one of the wealthiest states in Asia.[50] In 2003, Taiwan was the world's 13th largest trading nation, or the 15th largest exporter and the 12th largest importer.[51] Moreover, as one of the important trading economies in the world, Taiwan, with a population of 22.7 million, secured solid market shares in major OECD economies. In 2003, for example, Taiwan had 2.5% of market share in the United States, 3.7% in Japan, 1.0% in Germany, 1.0% in the United Kingdom, 0.4% in France, 0.6% in Italy, 1.1% in Canada, and 2.6% in Australia respectively.[52]

Particularly impressive, after recording its first trade surplus in 1971 Taiwan was enjoying continuous trade surplus since 1976 with the surplus reaching $22.6 billion in 2003 and $21.3 billion in 2006.[53] The result of persistent huge trade surplus made Taiwan possess the third largest foreign exchange reserves in the world after China and Japan by 2006, with an amount of $266.1 billion, ahead of all other East Asian NIEs.[54] As a consequence, Taiwan became a new important source of capital and the second-largest intraregional investor in East and Southeast Asia after Japan. In 1989, Taiwan's outward FDI reached a peak of $7.0 billion. While there were fluctuations of Taiwan's outward FDI thereafter due to a resurgence in domestic investment, it bounced back to $7.1 billion in 2004 and $7.3 billion in 2006.[55]

With its economy reaching high levels of sophistication in terms of technology and value-added products, Taiwan significantly improved its position in the international division of labor with a growing number of skill-intensive, high value-added industries becoming increasingly competitive at world market standards of cost and product specifications. Consequently, Taiwan established an international presence in a number of high-tech industries and became one of the leading producers in a wide range of high-tech related products.[56]

Moreover, in the process of industrialization a quite number of Taiwanese companies obtained global name recognition for growth, good management, and quality of products, including Taiwan Semiconductor, Acer, Evergreen Marine, Formosa Plastics, EVA Airways, President Enterprises, Nan Ya Plastics, Cathay Live Insurance, Far Eastern Textiles, and Chinatrust Commercial Bank.[57] A number of Taiwanese companies have moved into Original design manufacture (ODM). Taiwan's computer industries have established brand names such as Acer, Microtek, and Enta Technologies.

In the meantime, Taiwanese companies sought to go multinational, looking for cheaper labor in developing countries. In 2002, three Taiwanese companies were among the top 50 nonfinancial multinational corporations from developing economies, of which United Microelectronics Corporation ranked the 32nd, Nan Ya Plastics Corporation 35th, and Advanced Semiconductor Engineering Inc. 48th.[58] More important, Taiwan began to focus on the Pacific Rim for sustenance and markets. Particularly, Taiwan became rapidly integrated with the Chinese economy. By moving manufacturing offshore, Taiwan was now focusing on services, especially financial services on the island.

With increasing economic power, Taiwan was gaining growing confidence and was playing an increasingly important role in both the regional and the world economy. Taiwan sought to play a greater role in a range of economic forums and was a member of the Asia-Pacific Economic Cooperation (APEC), the Pacific Basin Economic Council (PBEC), and the Pacific Economic Cooperation Council (PECC). Especially significant, Taiwan obtained its WTO membership in January 2002. In line with its increased economic affluence, Taiwan also played an important part in promoting economic development through aid programs around the world. In 1989, Taiwan set up the International Economic Cooperation Development Fund (IECDF) to sponsor financial and technical development projects around the world. In 1996–97, IECDF, together with the Committee of International Technical Cooperation (CITC) – a body that was previously responsible for organizing and managing Taiwan's agricultural and fisheries missions in developing countries – was reorganized into the International Cooperation and Development Fund (ICDF), which thereafter became the principal body that oversaw Taiwan's overseas development aid programs. Taiwan provided aid primarily for its allies in Central and South America, the East Caribbean, Africa, the Asia-Pacific, and Europe. Its aid programs involved a range of activities, including loans for construction of economic and social infrastructure, agricultural development projects, private sector development and emergency recovery projects, direct and indirect investment projects in local businesses, credit guarantees, technical assistance projects, education and training programs, humanitarian assistance projects, and many other activities. In 1988, Taiwan also resumed its role in the ADB and set aside $1 billion annually from its abundant reserves to subsidize developing countries. Moreover, Taiwan set up a fund under the auspices of the European Bank for Reconstruction and Development to assist the East European states in their market reforms.

6.4   Taiwan's transformed regional economic relations

In the process of industrialization, Taiwan's regional economic relations evolved over time, reflecting changing international, regional, and domestic conditions. For quite a long period in the postwar years, Taiwan's regional economic ties almost solely focused on Japan with some limited economic exchanges with other capitalist economies in the region, while the Cold War politics effectively prevented Taiwan from having any economic as well as political and other contact with mainland China and other communist states. In the post-Cold War era, however, whereas Taiwan continued to maintain close economic ties with Japan, its regional economic relations became more diversified and balanced in the context of global, regional, and domestic political and economic transformation.

For geopolitical and economic reasons, Taiwan maintained a very strong economic connection with Japan in the postwar years with its roots dating back to the Japanese colonial period. Furthermore, Taiwan's strong economic ties with Japan were encouraged and nurtured by the United States in the context of the Cold War and reinforced by the island's hostilities with Communist China. As a result of the Korean War, Taiwan was effectively turned into an integral part of the Japan-centered economic and security framework built by Washington in East Asia. As the island did not experience the same degree of suffering under Japanese colonial rule as Korea did, it was much easier for Taiwan to quickly establish such an economic partnership with Japan under the auspices of the United States in the postwar years. While the circumstances had substantially transformed, the postwar Japanese–Taiwanese economic partnership was in many ways very similar to the pattern that had existed during the colonial era, under which Japan was not only Taiwan's most important trading partner in the region but also the major source of capital and technology for Taiwan's economic development.

Within such a pattern of economic relationship, Japan dominated Taiwan's export trade from the 1950s throughout the mid-1960s, when Taiwan's agricultural exports relied heavily on the Japanese market. In 1952, Japan took 52.6% of Taiwan's exports and in 1955 the proportion reached a peak of 59.5%. Although the share declined thereafter, it was still 37.7% in 1960 and 30.6% in 1965.[59] The ratio continued to decline, as Taiwan moved to export-oriented industrialization from the 1960s onward, which led to a transition of the island from primarily exporting agricultural products to Japan to exporting manufactured consumer goods to the United States and Western Europe.

Rather than reducing its dependence on Japan, however, Taiwan, by pursuing a new development strategy, actually switched its dependence on Japan from its agricultural market to its capital, technology, components, and industrial raw materials, which now became the basis of the island's export-oriented industrialization. By the mid-1960s, Taiwan had been firmly entrenched in a division of labor with Japan, in which Japan provided middle-level technology, production equipment, intermediate goods and components that were manufactured, assembled, or processed in Taiwan for re-export to the United States and Western Europe. Many Japanese companies moved to Taiwan in the 1960s–70s to take advantage of lower labor costs on the island as well as the appreciation of the yen against the US dollar. As a result, Japan became Taiwan's largest or second largest supplier of capital goods, precision machinery, electrical equipment, electronic components, metal products, transportation equipment, base metals, chemicals, and metals. Imported Japanese technology became critical for the survival of many of Taiwan's export industries such as electronics, machinery, appliance, information, and computer industries. It is estimated that more than 60% of Taiwan's exports were derived from Japanese technology, spare parts, components, and raw materials, that around 45% of Taiwan's imported technology came from Japan, and that almost two-thirds of all technology cooperation agreements that Taiwan signed were with Japan.[60]

This division of labor put Taiwan in a position of a sub-contractor to Japanese companies like Mitsubishi, Marubeni and Mitsui, Canon,

Sony, and Hitachi, which was very much reminiscent of the old ties between the two economies during the Japanese colonial era. As in the colonial period, the Japanese by no means intended to create a potential competitor in transferring technology to Taiwan. As such, the type of technology that was supplied to Taiwan was well measured, which was usually at the lower end of the scale. Moreover, the Japanese trading companies controlled distribution channels, which were critical to the growth of Taiwanese exports in almost all industries. It is estimated that a range of 50–70% of Taiwan's exports was under Japanese control.[61]

With such a division of labor, it was inevitable that the expansion of Taiwan's exports had to be supported by increased imports from Japan. As a result, Japan became Taiwan's largest source of imports after the mid-1960s. While Japan supplied 31.2% of the island's total imports in 1952, the proportion rose to 39.8% in 1965 and reached a peak of 42.8% in 1970. Although thereafter the proportion of Taiwan's imports from Japan fell to 27.1% in 1980 and remained in the average of 28–29% in the 1980s–90s and the average of 25.5% for the first half decade of the 2000s, it surpassed the United States as Taiwan's second largest source of imports by a wide margin – for example, 25.2% and 22.8% for Japan versus 11.6% and 11.2% for the United States respectively in 2005 and 2006.[62]

On the other hand, while Taiwan was heavily dependent on the Japanese market for its agricultural exports in the 1950s, this dependence gradually weakened over time as Taiwan's export structure transformed from agricultural products to manufactured products. As a result, the share of exports going to Japan was steadily declining from 59.5% of Taiwan's total exports in 1955 to 37.7% in 1960, 14.6% in 1970, and 11.0% in 1980. The figure hanged around 11% in the 1980s–90s and in 2006 it dropped to 7.3%, which put Japan in a distant sixth place as a market for Taiwan's exports behind China (23.1%), Hong Kong (16.7%), the United States (14.4%), ASEAN (13.9%), and the EU (11.7%).[63]

As a result of this trade pattern, while Taiwan was steadily accumulating surplus in its overall trade, particularly in trade with the United States, and more recently with China and Hong Kong, it maintained continuously increasing huge trade deficit with Japan, rising from $43 million in 1960 to $30.9 billion in 2005 and $30.0 billion in 2006.[64] As Taiwan heavily relies on Japan for the import of a range of equipment and capital goods and more recently for a range of high-tech products for its computer and information industries, this import structure indicates that Taiwan will continue to have a high level of imports from Japan, which will continue to produce huge trade deficit with Japan in the coming years.

Reflecting its increasing dependence on the import of Japanese technology, capital goods, and components in the postwar years, Taiwan also increasingly relied on Japanese capital, particularly after the mid-1960s. As a result, Japanese FDI grew from 5.9% of total FDI in Taiwan in terms of value (approved) in 1965 to 39.7% in 1990. Although Japan's proportion declined thereafter, it maintained an average of 25.5% in the 1990s and an average of 14.2% in 2000–06. The rise of Japanese FDI in Taiwan was matching the decline in importance of US investment, which fell from 88.5% in 1965 to 26.0% in 1990, an average of 24.8% in the 1990s and an average of 13.2% in 2000–06. In terms of the number of projects, Japanese performance was even more impressive with a total of 4944 projects (28.8%) over a period of 1952–2006, far ahead the figure for the United States of 2908 (16.9%).[65] It is important to note that the Japanese investment was in smaller enterprises, concentrated in manufacturing, especially electronics, electric appliances, and machinery industries, which directly led Taiwan's export-driven industrialization.

Around the mid-1980s, there had been transformed global, regional, and domestic conditions. While there was weakening Cold War politics and eventual end of the Cold War at the end of the 1980s and early 1990s, there was also the rise of globalization and regionalism in the world economy. Domestically, Taiwan's economy began to undergo massive structural transformation around the same time. With rising domestic wages and land prices, Taiwan's labor-intensive, export-oriented industries were under the pressure to move offshore to those areas where the costs of labor and land were low. On the other hand, increasing concerns with its dependency on Japan had also led to Taiwan's attempt to upgrade technologies and diversify sources of imports so as to reduce their reliance on Japanese equipment, machinery parts, and components. It was under such circumstances that Taiwan began to make major efforts to develop its economic ties with other regional economies, especially with Hong Kong, China, South Korea, and ASEAN countries. As Taiwan had transformed from a cash-poor capital importer to a cash-rich capital source by the end of the 1980s as a result of its successful industrialization, Taiwan's outward investment was playing an increasingly important role in the restructuring of the island's economy and in expanding extensive economic links with the region.

It was within this context that Taiwan rapidly increased its exports to Hong Kong. While Hong Kong remained Taiwan's third largest market from the 1960s onward, the proportion of Taiwan's exports to Hong Kong never went beyond 10% of its total exports until the end of the

1980s. Particularly, after the mid-1980s Taiwan's exports to Hong Kong rose substantially, from 6.9% of the island's total exports in 1984 to 22.7% in 2001, surpassing the United States as the largest market for Taiwan. After China replaced Hong Kong as Taiwan's largest market in 2004, Hong Kong still remained the second largest market, absorbing 18.0% of Taiwan's exports in 2004 and 16.7% in 2006. On the other hand, the imports from Hong Kong were disproportionately small with the share being 4.2% for 1989, which dropped to negligent 0.9% by 2006. It is important to note that Hong Kong as Taiwan's third largest trading partner, which remained until very recently when it was overtaken by China in 2003, was largely the result of Taiwan's huge amount of exports. Consequently, Taiwan maintained continuous huge trade surplus with Hong Kong with the trade surplus jumping from $2.2 billion in 1985 to $35.5 billion in 2006, surpassing the surplus with the United States by a wide margin since 1991.[66]

In the meantime, there was also rapid development of mutual investments between Taiwan and Hong Kong since the late 1980s. While Hong Kong's accumulated investment in Taiwan was $450 million between 1991 and 2006, Taiwan's investment in Hong Kong was 2.5 billion during the same period, making Hong Kong the fifth largest destination of Taiwan's outward FDI after China, British Central America, the United States, and Singapore.[67]

It is important to point out that the increased economic ties between Taiwan and Hong Kong of the past two decades was largely the result of the rapid development of Taiwan's indirect economic exchanges with mainland China since the mid-1980s. Due to political reasons, there had been no economic contact between Taiwan and China for about four decades. Around the mid-1980s, however, with the thawing of tensions, cross-Taiwan Straits relations began to move from alienation and confrontation to gradual engagement. In the late 1970s and early 1980s, Beijing began to substantially modify its Taiwan policy by announcing a series of measures of reconciliation in the context of China's overall policy of economic reform and opening to the outside world. Starting in 1984, Taiwan gradually relaxed its restrictions on indirect trade and investment with the mainland. In 1987, the Taiwanese government lifted the ban on visits to the mainland by its citizens. In 1991, in order to handle increasing cross-Taiwan Straits issues the Taiwanese government formally established the Mainland Affairs Council (MAC) and the Straits-Exchange Foundation. As a result of a series of moves of reconciliation across the Taiwan Straits, there were rapidly increasing economic, cultural, academic, and athletic exchanges between the two sides, although political obstacles still existed. It was under such circumstances that indirect trade and Taiwanese investment on the mainland through Hong Kong grew very rapidly since the mid-1980s in response to market signals and favorable policy measures adopted by the governments on both sides.

The rapid development of economic ties across the Taiwan Straits was most illustratively characterized by the rapid rise of Taiwan's investment on the mainland. As part of the island's economic restructuring, Taiwan's investment in China increased significantly after the lifting of the ban on Taiwan citizens' visit to the mainland. According to Taiwan's statistics, the amount of Taiwan's FDI in China that had been approved by the Taiwanese government increased from $174 million in 1991 to $7.6 billion in 2006 with the accumulated amount reaching $54.9 billion. In a similar fashion, the number of cases increased from 237 to 1090 during the same period with the accumulated total number reaching 35,542. According to the official statistical data of China, the realized amount of Taiwan's FDI on the mainland increased from $844 million in 1991 (including data before 1991) to $2.1 billion in 2006 with the accumulated total amount reaching $43.9 billion. The contracted amount was even higher, which rose from $3.3 billion in 1991 (including the data before 1991) to $10.4 billion in 2005 with the accumulated total being $90.3 billion. The total number of projects was equally impressive, jumping from 3377 in 1991 to 3752 in 2005 with the accumulated number being as high as 71,847.[68] As a result, while China became the largest recipient of Taiwan's outward FDI by accumulatively receiving 54.5% of Taiwan's total FDI outflows in 1991–2006, Taiwan became the fifth largest investor on the mainland after Hong Kong, British Virgin Islands, Japan, and the United States in terms of value and the second largest in terms of the number of projects after Hong Kong.[69]

Most Taiwanese investments in China came from those labor-intensive industries whose competitive edge had eroded as a result of rising labor costs on the island. By investing in China where labor costs were quite low, these Taiwanese industries attempted to remain competitive and retained their market share. The industries that were most favored by Taiwanese businesses for investment in China included electronics and electrical appliances, basic metals and metal products, chemicals, plastic products, precision instruments, and food and beverage processing. As such, the average amount of each of Taiwan's investment projects in China was only $1.5 million, as compared to $2.0 million of Taiwan's investments in South Korea, $2.8 million in Japan, $2.9 million in Hong Kong, and $8.9 million in Singapore.[70] Taiwanese investors took machinery, raw materials, and intermediate inputs mainly from Taiwan but also from other countries for processing on the mainland. The products were then sold overseas through their existing trade networks, mainly to Hong Kong, the United States, Japan, and Europe, although some products were shipped back to Taiwan. A similar process had once occurred between Japan and Taiwan in the 1960s–70s. But with its economy becoming more mature by the 1980s, Taiwan was now upgrading its technologies and moving upward along the ladder of economic development while at the same time moving offshore those labor-intensive and low value-added industries that were no longer profitable on the island. This pattern of economic ties across the Taiwan Straits not only helped bring a huge amount of Taiwanese exports to China through the shipment of raw materials, equipment, and components from Taiwan to the mainland, but also contributed to the decrease of Taiwan's export of traditional products such as footwear, umbrellas, toys, garments, and bicycles to developed country markets, which now became China's exports.

The rapid rise of Taiwan's FDI in China was accompanied by the equally rapid rise of trade across the Straits. According to Taiwan's statistics, the island's exports to the mainland rose from almost nothing in the late 1970s to $51.8 billion in 2006, which, accounting for 23.1% of Taiwan's total exports for the year, made China Taiwan's largest market. On the other hand, the imports from China also rose substantially from nothing to $24.8 billion during the same period, accounting for 12.2% of the island's imports, which made the mainland Taiwan's second largest source of imports. Overall, while China was Taiwan's 33rd trading partner in 1990, it became the island's fourth largest trading partner in 2001 and jumped to the largest in 2005. By 2006, the total trade volume between Taiwan and China reached $76.6 billion. Particularly significant, China trade brought Taiwan huge trade surplus with the surplus reaching $27.0 billion in 2006. Without its trade surplus with China, Taiwan would run huge overall trade deficits.[71] Taiwan's huge trade surplus with China was partly the result of Taiwan's existing restrictions on imports from China, but more importantly the result of a trade pattern under which Taiwan exported to the mainland high value-added products such as sophisticated raw materials, machinery, equipment, and electronic parts while imports from the mainland were relatively low value-added products such as crude raw materials, consumer non-durables, and food products. As the rapid growth of Taiwan's China trade over the past two decades was achieved when direct economic links across the Taiwan Straits were not formally established yet due to difficult political relations, it could well be anticipated that there would be even more rapid development of economic ties across the Taiwan Straits, should the existing political obstacles be eventually removed.

After the mid-1980s, Taiwan also expanded its economic connection with ASEAN countries by pursuing "southward policy." Particularly significant, Taiwanese companies invested heavily in the ASEAN economies as an effort to seek to relocate their labor-intensive operations in cheaper locations. Taiwanese investment in ASEAN's original five members increased especially rapidly. As a result, between 1987 and 1999 Taiwan's approved FDI stock in Indonesia rose from $29 million to $531 million, that in Malaysia from $13 million to $1399 million, that in the Philippines from $13 million to $544 million, that in Singapore from $11 million to $1117 million, and that in Thailand from $21 million to $903 million.[72] Taiwan overtook Japan as the largest foreign investor in Malaysia in 1989. Taiwan also developed economic relations with the new members of ASEAN. Particularly, Taiwan's investment in Vietnam rose very rapidly with the approved FDI stock in Vietnam jumping from $1.4 million in 1987 to $903.4 million in 1999.[73] As a result, while US and Japanese investment in the region was slowing down, Taiwan substantially increased its investment in the region. By 2006, accumulatively, Singapore had been the fourth largest recipient of Taiwan's outward FDI, Vietnam the sixth, Thailand the ninth, and the Philippines the tenth.[74]

Taiwan's investment in Southeast Asia was primarily concentrated in traditional labor-intensive manufacturing industries such as textiles, electronics and electrical appliances, paper products and printing, chemical products, and metal products and nonmetallic products with the exception of Singapore, where most of Taiwan's investment was in services such as trade, banking and insurance, and wholesale and retail. Over time, however, Taiwan's investments in the region moved toward high-tech industries.

Taiwan's trade with ASEAN was also steadily growing after the mid-1980s. As a result, the proportion of Taiwan's exports to ASEAN's original five member countries increased from 5.5% of Taiwan's total exports in 1987 to 11.4% in 2006. If its five new members are included, then ASEAN was Taiwan's fourth largest market by 2006, which absorbed 13.9% of Taiwan's total exports, after China (23.1%), Hong Kong (16.7%), and the United States (14.4%), but ahead of the EU (11.7%) and Japan (7.3%). On the other hand, imports from ASEAN-10 rose from 10.9% of Taiwan's total imports in 1996 to 11.6% in 2006, making ASEAN the third largest source of imports for the island after Japan (22.8%) and China (12.2%), but ahead of the United States (11.2%) and the EU

(10.6%). Total trade between Taiwan and ASEAN reached $54.6 billion by 2006, making ASEAN Taiwan's fourth largest trading partner after China, Japan, and the United States.[75] It is important to point out that much of this increased trade derived from intra-industry trade by Taiwan's companies that invested in these economies, similar to the process that was occurring between Taiwan and China.

Taiwan also rapidly developed its economic ties with South Korea after the mid-1980s, particularly trade relations. The Taiwan–South Korea bilateral trade jumped from $440 million in 1985 to $22.2 billion in 2006, which accounted for 5.2% of the total volume of the island's trade, making South Korea the seventh largest trading partner of Taiwan after China, Japan, the United States, ASEAN, EU, and Hong Kong. While the proportion of Taiwan's exports to South Korea rose from $254 million (0.8% of Taiwan's total exports) to $7.2 billion (3.2%) during the same period, making South Korea the island's seventh largest market, the rise of imports from South Korea was even more impressive with the share jumping from $187 million (0.9% of Taiwan's total imports) to $15.0 billion (7.4%), which made South Korea the island's sixth largest source of imports. However, Taiwan ran continuously growing trade deficits with South Korea since 1989 with the deficit of 2006 reaching $7.8 billion, making South Korea the second largest source of the island's trade deficit after Japan.[76] On the other hand, however, investment flows were far from matching commodity flows between the two economies. For example, the accumulated amount of Taiwan's approved investment in South Korea by 2006 was $240 million, which accounts for only 0.24% of Taiwan's total accumulated outward FDI.[77] South Korea's investment in Taiwan was equally insignificant.

6.5   Taiwan's economy in the 21st century

Whereas Taiwan's economic success over the past five decades was very impressive, what made Taiwan even more highly regarded was that Taiwan managed to withhold the Asian financial crisis of 1997–98. In contrast, its counterpart, South Korea, together with Thailand, Indonesia, and some other economies in the region, could hardly escape the worst consequences of the crisis. What set Taiwan apart from its crisis-hit neighboring economies in managing to come out of the crisis relatively unscathed was Taiwan's healthy economic fundamentals, including abundant foreign exchange reserves, a current account surplus, and a low level of public external debt. As a result, despite speculative attacks against the New Taiwan dollar during the Asian financial crisis, Taiwan enjoyed a high economic growth rate of 4.8% in 1998, as compared to Singapore (0%), Hong Kong (–5.2%), South Korea (–6.0%), Thailand (–7.2%), Malaysia (–6.0%), the Philippines (0.3%), and Indonesia (–13.5%). Moreover, Taiwan had a low inflation rate of 1.7% for the same year, as compared to Singapore (–0.1%), Hong Kong (2.8%), South Korea (7.5%), Thailand (8.1%), Malaysia (5.3%), the Philippines (9.5%), and Indonesia (59.5%).[78]

As the Taiwanese economy enters the 21st century, a more fundamental challenge facing Taiwan is its changing comparative advantage. To encounter this challenge, both the government and the private sector have taken measures to move further from a low-skilled labor-intensive economy to a high-skilled capital-intensive economy. To this end, the government has adopted a national development plan for the 21st century, which is designed to turn Taiwan into a major APROC. The major theme of the APROC idea is that while labor-intensive industries are moved offshore to such locations of low labor costs as China and Southeast Asian economies, Taiwan itself will mainly concentrate on capital-intensive and high-tech industries and remain competitive at the top end of the global market. In this process, Taiwan will enjoy a strategic location that is an ideal regional headquarters for multinational corporations in East and Southeast Asia. According to the APROC plan, Taiwan should possess specialized centers in such key fields as manufacturing, sea and air transportation, financial services, telecommunications, and media enterprises. With these centers, Taiwan will act as a hub that links commercial and business networks involving China and Southeast Asia.[79] To pursue this objective, Taiwan has adopted a number of policies aimed at not only improving infrastructure but also liberalizing the economy, which is seen as being essential for attracting multinational companies to move their regional headquarters to Taiwan. The economic liberalization involves reducing tariffs and facilitating the removal of non-tariff barriers with the exception of import quotas for both automobiles and agriculture. Since its accession to WTO in early 2002, Taiwan has been committed to further liberalization of its economy and therefore is more exposed to international competition. The government also hopes to improve Taiwan's research and development capability and to diffuse high technology throughout the island through a range of initiatives aimed at encouraging commercially orientated public–private partnerships. To this end, the government aims to build 20–30 industrial parks across the island linked to universities, EPZ, and air and port facilities.[80]

In 2002, the government further adopted the Challenge 2008 Six-Year National Development Plan to set out political, financial, and fiscal reforms and ten key individual plans. Political reform aims to transform government into a system of small, lean, and proactive public administration. Fiscal reform seeks to balance government revenues and expenditures within 5–10 years. And financial reform targets cutting the banking sector's NPL ratio to 5% and raising banks' capital adequacy ratio to 8% within 2 years. The ten key individual plans are designed to accelerate development of the economy, improve the living environment, and upgrade the role of culture and the arts in modern life with a view to building Taiwan into a "green silicon island." According to these plans, moving away from low value-added mid-stream processing and contract manufacturing that provided a key source of growth in the past, Taiwan must now invest more heavily in human resources, R&D, innovation, logistics networks, and living environment. In the meantime, the island must strive to lift its industrial value chain to ensure its future economic prosperity.[81] To implement the Challenge 2008 Six-Year National Development Plan, the government has designated key projects as the New Ten Projects, which are designed to enhance Taiwan's competitiveness, maintain its No. 1 competitiveness ranking in Asia, and make Taiwan one of the world's three strongest economies.[82]

To a great extent, the future fortune of Taiwan's economy will be largely related to the Chinese market, which is an enormous opportunity for both sales and investment. However, involving China as part of Taiwan's APROC ambition will be contingent on improving political relations across the Taiwan Straits. This is because if Taiwan is going to be a regional operation center, it has to be able to service the Chinese market with free shipping, air, financial and telecommunication links, which is essential for multinational corporations that would establish their headquarters in Taiwan. However, it seems that at least for the moment there is still a long way to go for Taipei and Beijing to normalize their political relations.

7
The Chinese Political Economy Since 1949

7.1 The Chinese political economy during Mao's era (1949–76)

After the Chinese Communist Party (CCP) took power in 1949, China's economic development was determined by a complex mix of both external and internal factors. First of all, China's economic development was largely defined by world politics in general and the evolution of its relationship with the United States and the Soviet Union in particular. For the first three decades following its establishment in 1949, the People's Republic of China had been cast in a very unfavorable international environment. In the years after the Korean War throughout the 1960s the Sino-American conflict was the most significant feature of Cold War politics in the Far East. Most notably, after the mid-1950s when American–Soviet relations came to be seen as those of "peaceful coexistence," China was regarded by Washington as the principal threat to peace and stability in the region. Hence the United States was pursuing a diplomatic policy of containing and isolating China through economic embargo and a military alliance system that involved Japan, South Korea, Taiwan, Thailand, the Philippines, Australia, and New Zealand. Consequently, China was effectively isolated from the world economy, denied any possibility of obtaining technology, capital, markets, and advice from the West. Starting in the late 1950s and early 1960s, Sino-Soviet relations, after experiencing a honeymoon in the early and mid-1950s, became troubled and the resultant break between the two communist giants deprived the Chinese of Soviet economic assistance. Under the circumstances, China turned inward and adopted a "self-reliance" development policy with foreign economic exchanges minimized.

Domestically, when the Chinese Communists came to power in 1949, they actually inherited in the most populous country in the world a preindustrial economy that by practically all available measures was near the bottom of the world development scale. The primary objective of the new Chinese leadership was therefore to transform the country into a modern economic power in a relatively short period of time. In order to achieve this objective, the CCP chose to adopt an orthodox Stalinist model of economic development. Moreover, the economic development objective in Mao's China was also subordinated to the broader political goals of building a socialist society, breaking the fetters of foreign domination and becoming a world power. To pursue these political goals, China's development policy was largely shaped and guided by its overall political and social philosophy and Mao's thought. The most important values that helped shape China's development policy included self-reliance, egalitarianism, populism, asceticism, and unlimited power of man. Besides, the experience that the Chinese Communists had obtained in the course of more than two decades of guerrilla warfare and the administration of regional bases also exerted profound influence on China's economic policy.[1] As such, China's economic development during Mao's period was primarily defined by the CCP's broader political and economic objectives, China's historical heritage, the communists' own values and experience obtained in the long period of revolutionary war, the country's natural endowment and Leninism–Stalinism. All these elements interacted with, reinforced, transformed, or modified each other.

It was within this context that the Chinese leadership was determined to achieve rapid industrial development and fundamental social transformation for post-revolution China through a series of policies. In the initial years of its rule, the CCP adopted a range of priority policy measures to control hyperinflation and recover the war-torn economy. In the meantime, the land reform eliminated landlords as a class in China and let peasants for the first time become owners of the land they tilled. These early policies were quite successful. As a result, the 3 years from 1949 to 1952 witnessed impressive recovery and growth with the annual industrial growth rate reaching 34.8% while the annual agricultural growth being 14.1%.[2]

Starting in 1953, China initiated a policy of socialist transformation of the economy, which involved the introduction of centralized economic planning and the transfer of ownership from private to public hands. In September 1953, the First Five-Year Plan (1953–57) was introduced. The transfer of the ownership, which occurred in both the rural and the urban areas in late 1955, established a socialist rural and urban economy. In the rural areas, through agricultural collectivization, the majority of rural families were organized into agricultural cooperatives by 1956. By the end of 1958, agricultural cooperatives were further transformed into people's communes. In the urban areas, the nationalization of industry, banking, and commerce was completed by 1956, with which private enterprises were turned into state-owned enterprises and capitalist and merchant classes were eliminated. Thus, by 1956 the Communist government announced that the transition to socialism had basically been accomplished in China. As such, a socialist economy based on the Soviet model of command economy was established in China, characterized by public ownership, central planning, and administrative control of economic activities.

As a result, the Chinese state controlled almost all economic activities and ran the economy through central planning and administrative directives while the role of market was minimized. Under a highly centralized and comprehensive planning system, the State Planning Commission drew up annual and, more importantly, five-year economic plans to direct economic development. These plans, through mandatory directives, embodied decisions on the allocation of national resources. Specifically, they stipulated the amount and destination of investment, the amount of raw materials to be extracted and processed, the amount of energy to be generated, the amount of manufactured goods to be produced, the prices at which products would be exchanged, and the allocation and wages of labor that was required to achieve these goals. In the meantime, agricultural production was also governed by national quotas, which were in turn divided into provincial, county, and, ultimately, commune quotas. The prices at which quota grain was purchased and sold were determined by the government's plan. Moreover, state-owned enterprises conducted the wholesale and retail trade of most agricultural and industrial commodities. Foreign trade was under the government's strict control according to the plan and only a dozen of state-owned specialized trading companies were allowed to undertake import and export activities. Finally, the People's Bank of China, the only significant bank functioning both as a central bank and as a commercial-like bank, was actually a government vehicle in support of various government-controlled economic activities.

Within this economic system, the public ownership of the means of production constituted an institutional foundation for such a large scale of comprehensive state control of economic activities. The public economy included the state sector and the collective sector. The state sector comprised state-owned enterprises, government organizations, social organizations, and so on, while the collective sector involved various enterprises and institutions that were owned and managed by the people who made up those enterprises and institutions, including rural economic units engaged in farming, rural enterprises run by people's communes and production brigades, enterprises run by cities, counties, and so on.

During Mao's period, state-owned enterprises were the backbone of the Chinese economy. State-owned enterprises operated under the direct control of various functional bureaucracies of the government. State coffers were the only source of their input and at a year's end all their profits were submitted to the government. In cases where an enterprise had a deficit rather than a profit, the deficit would be covered by a government subsidy. The type of products, production volume, and prices were all decided by the government according to economic plans. Without real decision-making power, the enterprise manager was simply supposed to fulfill the target as set by the government. Moreover, the manager's authority was frequently eclipsed by that of the Party secretary within the enterprise's management hierarchy. In addition to business activities as set by the government, state-owned enterprises were also fully responsible for their employees' various welfare benefits, including life-long job security, heavily subsidized housing, utilities, health care, primary and secondary education for their children, stipends that helped to offset living costs, and generous retirement packages. Covering the costs of this comprehensive cradle-to-grave benefit package for their employees created a heavy financial burden on state-owned enterprises and pushed many of them into the red.

In the countryside, the public economy was embodied in collective farms, which took the form of the people's commune after 1958. Initially, the people's commune system, an important part of Mao's Great Leap Forward campaign, was used primarily as a framework for mass mobilization of labor for capital construction projects. The people's commune was later streamlined and, from 1962 on, provided an overall structure for the implementation of China's rural development policies and programs. A large, centralized organization that combined government administration with economic production in the rural areas, the people's commune was designed to enable the government to move the rural economy by administrative fiat. It had a three-tiered system of ownership. The production team, which comprised an average of 20–30 households, constituted the basic unit of agricultural production and account for calculating and dividing collective income. It owned the land and served to organize labor under its jurisdiction for farm work. It was also the unit within which costs and incomes were calculated. At successively higher levels of organization, the production brigade and the people's commune were primarily vehicles of accumulation and rural industrialization. Their principal economic functions were to provide overall planning and harmonize production plans of production teams with those of the state; to act as agents of the state organizations involved in supplying inputs and credit to agriculture and in purchasing agricultural products; to provide production teams with large machinery, water resources, and general management; to promote labor accumulation activities wherever such activities involved several production teams; to accumulate funds to be invested in infrastructure and subsidiary undertakings; and to develop small-scale industries. As the lowest level of state administration in the countryside, the people's commune also took most of the responsibility for the provision of welfare services, education, health care, public security, and so forth.[3]

Obviously, such an economic system enabled the state to control a large volume of economic resources and allocate these resources among various industries as desired by the government. As such, this economic model allowed the government to pursue a development strategy that, while providing only basic needs for the population, emphasized a high level of investment and put priority on the development of heavy industry. By pursuing such a development strategy, the Chinese leadership hoped to achieve industrialization within the shortest period of time. The direct consequence of this development strategy was the suppression of people's current consumption and neglect of the development of agriculture, light industry, and other sectors with resources being continuously poured into heavy industry.

It is important to note that such a development strategy also led to special reliance on the power of ideological and institutional transformation, coercive mass mobilizations, and political campaigns to resolve the economic problems confronting the country. In many areas, Mao's obsession with ideology and his neglect of practical conditions severely harmed the Chinese economy, causing high inconsistency and instability in economic development characterized by turbulent expansions and sudden contractions in either capital construction or production. On two occasions – the Great Leap Forward (1958–60) and the Cultural Revolution (1966–76) – Mao pushed the national economy toward the brink of collapse.

In the nation's external economic relations, Mao's obsession with self-reliance for economic development made China essentially isolated from the world economy. Consequently, China's foreign economic exchanges were minimized and there was little chance for China to obtain technology, capital, markets, and advice from the West.

Over time, it became clear that this development model was generally inefficient. Although during the period 1953–78 China achieved an average annual economic growth rate of 6.1%, much of this growth rate was achieved through simple expansion of the economic scale rather than technological improvement of the economy. Moreover, as a result of the neglect of agriculture, while there was a phenomenal average annual growth rate of 11.4% in industry between 1953 and 1978, there was only a moderate average annual growth rate of 2.7% in agriculture during the same period.[4] Consequently, per capital GDP remained low and people's living standard did not improve, far short of the expectations aroused by promises of a bright socialist future.

7.2   China's economic reform since the late 1970s

As the central planning economy proved inefficiency, the post-Mao Chinese leadership initiated economic reform at the end of 1978. The reform was across-the-board, covering all areas of the economy, including ownership of the means of production, agriculture, state-owned enterprises, employment system, social welfare system, price system, commercial sector, foreign trade system, foreign exchange system, finance, taxation, banking, planning, and others. The principal aspects of the reform included establishing a market-oriented institutional framework, diversifying the ownership structure by promoting nonpublic enterprises, deregulating the economy according to the principles of a market system, encouraging competition by breaking up the state monopolies, reforming public enterprises, restructuring the financial sector and the fiscal system, and opening China to the outside world and integrating the country into the world economy.[5] China's economic reform was pursued through an incremental approach to encircle the opposition from the conservative leaders and to avoid causing social instability. The final objective of the reform was to establish the so-called "socialist market economy," in which market forces would play a decisive role in guiding economic activities while the state undertakes macroguidance of the economy through purely economic measures.[6]

Although China's economic reform was closely related to such domestic factors as the demise of Mao and the growing problems of the Soviet development model, it apparently coincided with the general relaxation of world politics and Beijing's improved relations with both the United States and the Soviet Union at that time. In the meantime, it also coincided with the ongoing transformation in the world economy, engendered by rapid technological advances, liberalization of trade and investment, and expansion in movements of capital, technology, goods, and people across national borders. The post-Mao Chinese leaders were particularly shocked by the achievement of economic miracles by neighboring Japan, South Korea, Taiwan, and Hong Kong in the postwar years. All this development convinced the post-Mao Chinese leadership that in order to survive China must build the nation into a modern, economically respectable power through internal restructuring and external opening to the world economy. It was with this imperative sense that China started its economic transformation in late 1978.

China's economic reform started in the rural areas with the introduction of the "household production responsibility system" in the late 1970s. The new system called for leasing the right to use plots of land to individual households according to a contract stipulating the amount of grain to be produced on the plots for the state quotas. Contracts were awarded on the basis of the household's probable ability to fulfill the terms, given its size and the number of able-bodied workers in it. Everything produced on the leased plot over the contractual amount could be disposed of by the household as it liked – sold to the state, sold in the free market, or consumed by the family. Under this system, land was still collectively owned, but the right to use the land belonged to the farmer who was assigned the land. As the right to use the land became on a permanent basis and transferable, the distinction between use rights and ownership rights was blurred and the collective nature of agricultural production became ambiguous in practice. In the meantime, rural markets began to reopen after 1978 and farmers were allowed to raise pigs, chickens, and ducks and to engage in sideline activities. The "household production responsibility system" and opening of rural markets provided huge incentives for farmers to work hard on their assigned land, thus bringing rapid agricultural growth, particularly in the first half of the 1980s. The rural reform finally led to the abolition of the people's commune system by the mid-1980s.

After the success of the rural reform, the government moved to reform in the urban areas. One of the first reform steps in the urban areas was to reestablish a private sector. Through two constitution amendments in 1988 and 1999, private enterprises were eventually granted legal status and were identified as an important component of the country's socialist market economy. These constitutional amendments paved the way for the revival and fast growth of the private sector. As a result, the ownership structure of the Chinese economy was undergoing a substantial transformation after the late 1970s with the state sector and collective sector steadily shrinking while the private sector rapidly burgeoning and developing.[7] According to the 1996 data, between 1978 and 1996, the state sector shrank from 56% to 41% in terms of GDP and the collective sector had dropped from 43% to 35%, while the private sector expanded from 1% to 24%.[8] The transformation of the ownership structure is particularly reflected in industry. Before the reform was initiated in 1978, the state-owned enterprises contributed 77.6% of the nation's total industrial output while the collective-owned enterprises produced the remaining 22.4%. By 1999, however, the state sector's share of industrial output dropped to only 26.1% while the collective sector increased its share to 32.8%. But most significantly, the private sector, which emerged from nothing and developed rapidly, surpassed the state sector by contributing 41.1% of the nation's industrial production.[9]

Despite the rapid growth of the private sector, however, there were still about 300,000 state-owned enterprises, and the state sector was still the most important force in the Chinese economy, firmly controlling various important and crucial industries, including railway transportation, postal service, telecommunication, civil aviation, banking, insurance, electric power, oil, coal metallurgical industry, chemical industry, foreign trade, mechanical industry, and construction.[10] Besides, the state sector also controlled most of China's whole-sale distributors, retail outlets, and all but a few schools and hospitals. The state-owned enterprises were still the single largest source of employment, employing a workforce approaching 112 million workers.[11]

China's state-owned enterprise reform started in the late 1970s and early 1980s. The goal of the state-owned enterprise reform was to establish a so-called "modern enterprise mechanism," which, by government definition, referred to a package of standards including clear ownership, independent rights for business operation, and shrewd management. Through several stages of reform, the responsibilities of the state were limited to appointing managers, levying taxes, extending credit, establishing new enterprises, and consolidating, closing, moving, or transforming those that failed, while state-owned enterprise managers had more power to run enterprises and assumed the responsibility for their own profit and loss. In 1989, the Chinese government took a further step to permit some state-owned enterprises to transform into shareholding companies and issue stocks. The shareholding system enabled state-owned enterprises to absorb investment from nonstate investors. In the meantime, the government also encouraged state-owned companies to merge with other firms to get stronger.

As part of the overall economic reform, China gradually reformed the employment system, promoted the establishment of a social insurance system, and privatized the housing market. The Chinese government initiated employment reform with the introduction of a contractual employment system as part of restructuring of state-owned enterprises in the early 1980s. As a result, the job assignment system for school graduates was abolished. The economic reform also weakened the rigidity of the household registration system. In support of the employment reform, Labor Law was passed in July 1994, which became effective on 1 January 1995. In the meantime, the government established various employment training programs for the unemployed. Consequently, a real labor market was rapidly emerging and developing. Another important supporting measure for state-owned enterprise reform was to establish a society-wide insurance system from the ground up. As a result, a social insurance system emerged and developed over time that involved pension, unemployment insurance, minimum wage system, basic living insurance, health insurance, on-the-job accident insurance, child-bearing insurance, the rural old insurance, and farmers' health insurance. However, given its complexity, the social insurance system was still far from well-established. As part of the reform, housing was also privatized, which not only relieved state-owned enterprises of another major financial burden but also created a consumer demand for private homes as a new source of economic growth.

The price reform played a decisive role in China's overall economic reform. Given its unique important role, the price reform was conducted ahead of many other reform programs. While the price reform was very sensitive in an economy like China that was vulnerable to the effects of inflation, it was relatively successful. Before the economic reform, prices of almost all commodities were set by the state, and the government used the administrative price mechanism to achieve not only its economic objectives but also specific political and social objectives. Through four stages of reform, a new price system was established, within which market forces played a dominant role while the state primarily held a macrocontrol of some key prices. Consequently, by the end of the 1990s, 92.5% of retail prices, 81.1% of capital goods prices, and 79% of agricultural prices became market-determined. Of a few key commodities that were still allocated to state-owned enterprises were steel, coal, oil, and electric power, and even the prices of these products were gradually raised to the world-market level. Moreover, prices in service industries were now all market-determined and prices of imports were decided through an agent-system.[12] Through the price reform, the structure of relative prices among products was streamlined. Relative prices of agricultural products, raw materials, transportation, postal, and communication services improved, which helped promote the production of agriculture, mining, raw materials and semi-finished products and the development of economic infrastructure.

The commercial system was also transformed. While large state-owned commercial enterprises were turned into shareholding companies or enterprise groups, a huge number of state-owned small commercial and service enterprises were turned into collective and private enterprises. In the meantime, foreign commercial enterprises entered China as partners of Chinese enterprises in joint ventures and as wholly foreign-invested enterprises. In the meantime, the old state-centralized wholesale system was replaced by a market-determined wholesale system that involved various specialized trading centers and wholesale markets at various levels across the country. Future markets also emerged, involving agricultural products and some industrial materials. For its part, the government improved its capability of macrocontrol of commodity circulation by streamlining the governmental administration, adopting relevant laws, establishing reserves for some important commodities, forming funds for important agricultural products, and developing various specialized associations.

As part of the opening policy, China gradually liberalized its foreign trade system. Through four stages of reform, the foreign trade system was substantially transformed. Particularly, since the early 1990s major efforts were made to liberalize the trade regime in support of China's bid for WTO membership and, after 2001, its commitment to liberalization of the trade regime as a new WTO member. As a result, the government, moving away from the previous complete administrative control of both imports and exports, now played a role in keeping the overall balance of imports and exports and the balance of international payments through legal, economic, and other universally adopted measures. The monopoly of specialized trading companies in running foreign trade business was abandoned, and more and more enterprises were authorized to run import and export business. In the meantime, the government encouraged the grouping of trading companies and manufacturing enterprises to improve competitiveness in the international market. State-owned trading companies were also reformed in a similar fashion as state-owned enterprises in other industries. Besides, the list of export commodities that were designated for specific trading companies was greatly reduced and most exports were open to all trading companies. Through these reform measures, China's trade regime was gradually coming closer to the international prevailing practices, and the Chinese domestic market was growingly integrated with the international market. Despite this progress, however, China's existing trade system was still far from what WTO required of its members. According to the government's plan, the long-term objective was to establish a free trade system by 2010, in which the government conducts neutral macrocontrol through legal and economic measures and related policies while all enterprises that go through required registration procedures could conduct import and export business. China's accession to WTO at the end of 2001 further committed China to this objective.

The reform of the foreign exchange system started in the late 1970s, which gradually relaxed the government's control of foreign exchanges and allowed more domestic banks and other financial institutions to be involved in foreign exchange business. The significant move came after 1994, when the Chinese government took the following important steps: (1) allowing convertibility of the Chinese yuan under the current account; (2) combining two (official and market) exchange rate systems, which existed before 1994, into a unified one; (3) establishing the nation's unified foreign exchange transaction center in Shanghai as a foreign exchange market; and (4) establishing a new administrative system over foreign exchange reserves. The objective was to improve the functioning of the foreign exchange market up to the international standard, establish a sound foreign exchange rate system with market playing a more important role, and eventually achieve the total convertibility of the Chinese yuan. On 21 July 2005, the Chinese government took a further step in the reform of its foreign exchange system by formally dropping the over-decade-long policy of pegging the Chinese yuan to the US dollar and letting the Chinese currency float against a basket of major foreign currencies, a move that was immediately followed by the official appreciation of the yuan against the US dollar by 2%. This move was seen as an important step toward the liberalization of the Chinese currency.

There was also a sea change in China's policy toward foreign capital. Consequently, China imported a growingly huge amount of foreign capital since 1979 through various channels, including receiving official loans from foreign governments, the World Bank, the IMF, the ADB, and other international financial organizations; borrowing commercial loans from foreign banks; issuing bonds in international financial markets; and issuing stocks of Chinese enterprises in the foreign stock exchange markets. Most importantly, FDI played an extremely important role in China's opening to the outside world. In order to attract foreign investment, the government established four Special Economic Zones (SEZs) on the southeast coast in 1980, in which preferential policies (favorable tax rates, reduced tariffs, ease of entry and exit for personnel, and a relatively free hand in managerial practices) were adopted to attract foreign investment. In May 1984, China further opened 14 coastal cities as economic development areas. In 1985, China enlarged the coastal opening areas to include the Pearl River Delta, the Yangtze River Delta, Fujian province in the south, and Shandong and Liaoning provinces in the northeast. Then in 1986 the Chinese government issued *The Regulations Regarding Encouraging Foreign Investment*, specifying preferential treatments toward foreign investment in various aspects. In the early 1990s, new economic zones with ambitious plans for new infrastructure were designated in Yangpu in Hainan province and the Pudong area in Shanghai. There were many other cities and areas that were opened since then.

Reform of the financial system was an important part of the economic reform. Before 1978, the People's Bank of China was the only significant bank in China, functioning both as a central bank and as a commercial-like bank. The reform of the financial system started with the establishment of various specialized banks. In February 1979, the Agricultural Bank of China was first reestablished, responsible for banking business in the rural areas. In the following month, the Bank of China was separated from the People's Bank of China, responsible for the nation's foreign exchange business. More significantly, the People's Bank of China was officially turned into a central bank in September 1983, while the Industrial and Commercial Bank of China was established to take over the banking business from the People's Bank of China. In November 1985 the Construction Bank of China was formed and in July 1986 the Bank of Communications was reestablished. Thereafter, nine other banks were established together with a large number of urban credit cooperatives. Starting from 1996, urban credit cooperatives in middle and big cities were first turned into urban cooperative banks and then into urban commercial banks. Moreover, a growing number of foreign banks were allowed to operate in China. After 1994, the Chinese government also created three policy banks successively – the National Development Bank, the Import and Export Credit Bank, and the Agricultural Development Bank. As a result of the organizational restructuring, a banking system was basically established in China, involving the central bank, policy banks, state-owned commercial banks, share-holding commercial banks, and foreign banks. Particularly significant, the People's

Bank of China now functioned solely as the nation's central bank, administering the country's financial system and participating in helping reaching the government's macroeconomic objective of achieving the equilibrium of overall supply and demand and the stability of currency and price through various economic measures such as banks' deposit rate, rediscount rate, open monetary market, and so on. Together with the establishment of the banking system, quite a few of nonbanking financial institutions, such as insurance companies, trust and investment corporations, security corporations, leasing companies, and so on, were also established in China.

Of particular significance in the reform of the financial system was the establishment and development of security markets in China, including the bond market and the stock market. China's bond market was established in 1988, which was primarily dominated by treasury bonds, as the total amount of financial bonds and corporate bonds was still very small. The stock exchange market first appeared in Shanghai in 1990, followed by a second stock exchange market established in Shenzhen in 1991. The stock market in China, though still quite rudimentary, functioned as an increasingly important channel for many middle and big enterprises to acquire needed capital for their investment projects.

Government planning was transformed since the late 1970s. As a result, the scope of mandatory elements of the state's economic plans was substantially reduced while macroguidance was becoming a major form in planning. In the meantime, market forces were playing an increasingly dominant role in various economic activities. As a consequence, economic plans, relieved of various mandatory directives on investment of state-owned enterprises, industrial and agricultural production, price, labor, wages, foreign trade, foreign exchanges, and so on, were now focusing on its role in setting strategic objectives of economic and social development, making economic forecast, macroeconomic control, planning of national economic structure and distribution of production, and undertaking major development projects. In playing this new role, the government was increasingly relying on such economic measures as industrial policies, monetary, financing, taxation, and so on. Reflecting the changed role of the government planning, the State Planning Commission was first reorganized into the National Development Planning Commission in 1998 and then transformed into the National Development and Reform Commission in 2003.

The reform of the fiscal system initially involved the transfer of part of fiscal power from the central government to local governments with the latter having both the rights and the responsibilities of balancing income and spending. However, this decentralization of fiscal power caused an abrupt drop of overall fiscal revenue as a share of GDP from 25.7% in 1980 to 10.8% in 1993 and a shrink of central fiscal revenue as a share of national total from 38.4% in 1985 to 22% in 1993.[13] Under the circumstances, the government introduced a revenue-sharing system in 1994, under which the revenues of the central government and local governments were divided according to types and sources of tax. This new revenue-sharing system brought an end to the fiscal plight, creating a firm foundation for a stable increase in state revenues. In the meantime, through several stages of reform, China gradually created a relatively more transparent, manageable, and equalized, though still rudimentary, taxation system based on a more or less unified circulation tax and income tax. The government's objective was to finally unify all relevant taxes for both domestic and foreign companies and individuals under the principle of national treatment.

The government also moved away from the heavy industry-centered development strategy of Mao's era to a more balanced development strategy that paid more attention to consumption. Accordingly, the government shifted its investment emphasis from capital goods industry to consumer goods industry, especially encouraging development of labor-intensive light industries.

Through a series of economic reform programs since the late 1970s, the Chinese economic system was fundamentally transformed. As a result, the command economy was basically replaced by a market economy, although far from fully fledged.

7.3   China rising as an economic power

As a result of the economic reform and the opening policy, China achieved remarkable sustained rapid economic growth with an average annual growth rate of GDP reaching 10.0% between 1980 and 2003, more than three times the world average of 3.1%. In the meantime, while there was an average annual growth rate of 4.7% in agriculture over the same period, the average annual growth rates of industry, manufacturing, and services reached 11.7%, 11.3%, and 11.2%, respectively.[14] Consequently, the absolute size of the Chinese economy of 2003 in terms of GDP was almost 10 times that of 1978.[15]

The rapid economic growth of China was particularly driven by the rapid export growth, which reached an average annual rate of 16.4% in 1978–2003 with the total volume of exports rising from $9.8 billion to

$438.2 billion over the period.[16] The share of exports in China's GDP jumped from 4.6% in 1978 to 30.9% in 2003.[17]

The FDI was responsible for much of the export growth in China since the late 1970s. While FDI in China rose from $1.2 billion in 1979–82 to $53.5 billion in 2003 with accumulated FDI amounting to $499.8 billion,[18] much of it was involved in export industries. As a result, the contribution of foreign affiliates to China's exports rose from 4.4% of China's total exports in 1980 to 54.8% in 2003.[19] More than 90% of exports by foreign affiliates are manufactures, the most prominent of which are machinery, equipment, and other manufactures. Particularly, the proportion of exports by foreign affiliates in technology-intensive industries rose from 59% to 81% between 1996 and 2000. Besides, foreign-invested companies were also involved in labor-intensive exports.[20] On the whole, foreign affiliates were heavily involved in foreign trade with a total amount of $472.2 billion in 2003, which was worth 55.5% of China's total trade for that year.[21]

Besides, FDI inflows also notably contributed to China's gross fixed capital formation, particularly since the early 1990s (Table 7.1), industrial output, tax revenues, and employment. By 2002, foreign-invested enterprises contributed 25% of China's total industrial output and 20% of national tax revenues. Moreover, foreign-invested companies absorbed 23 million workers, about 10% of the urban labor force, whose consumption helped contribute to economic growth.[22] As a whole, FDI in China accounted for 3.8% of GDP in 2003, rising from 0.2% in 1983.[23]

The rapid economic growth of China was accompanied by a steady transformation of the economic structure from a traditional rural economy to an industrial and service economy. As a result, agriculture was declining, industry (manufacturing in particular) was growing, and services were rapidly rising in terms of their relative importance in the national economy. Between 1978 and 2003, the share of agriculture (including farming, forestry, animal husbandry, and fishery) in GDP dropped from 28.1% to 14.6% and that of industry (including manufacturing, mining, utilities, and construction) remained about the same

Table 7.1 Inward FDI Flows as a Percentage of Gross Fixed Capital Formation in China, 1981–2003

1981–85	1986–90	1991	1992	1993	1994	1995	1996	1997	1998	1999	2000	2001	2002	2003
0.9	2.1	3.3	7.4	12.2	17.3	14.7	14.3	14.6	13.6	11.3	10.3	10.5	11.5	12.4

Source: UNCTAD, *World Investment Report*, various years (New York and Geneva: United Nations).

(44.4% in 1978 and 45.6% in 2003), while the proportion of the services sector (including transportation, postal and telecommunications, commerce, banking, insurance, education, and government organizations) jumped from 23.7% to 33.2%.[24] Accordingly, between 1990 and 2003 the contributing rate of agriculture to GDP growth dropped from 41.9% to 4.0% , while those of industry and services jumped respectively from 41.0% to 69.8% and from 17.1% to 26.2%.[25]

It is important to point out that although the proportion of industry in GDP remained largely unchanged, there was rapid development of manufacturing, making rapidly increasing contribution to the nation's economic growth (Figure 7.1). More significant, the structure of manufacturing was steadily upgraded in the process of rapid growth. High-tech industries – computer, telecommunication, and biomedical industries in particular – developed very fast with their contribution to the national economy steadily growing. Between 1991 and 2002, for example, the high-tech industries rose from $56.4 billion to $254.5 billion with an average annual growth rate of 20%, surpassing the average annual growth rate of all industries by over 10%. As a result, the share of high-tech industries in overall industrial production rose from about 1% to near 15% over the same period. The development of high-tech industries substantially contributed to the restructuring of the Chinese traditional economy.[26] Moreover, China was increasing investment in such key industries as energy, machinery, microelectronics, automobiles, petrochemicals, new materials, construction materials, and infrastructure. Consequently, while China still had a major advantage in labor-intensive industries, its industrial strengths in capital-intensive and high-tech industries were steadily growing.

Value added to manufacturing, 1987 $ billions

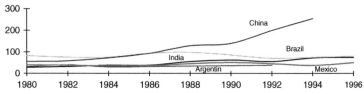

Figure 7.1   Manufacturing Takes Off in China.

Source: The World Bank, *1998 World Development Indicators* (Washington, D.C.: the World Bank, 1998), p. 187.

China's growth as a manufacturing power has paralleled its rise as an exporter of manufactured goods. In contrast, Brazil, which began the 1980s as a leading manufacturer among developing countries, has fallen far behind and is being overtaken by India.

Notably, China had a surprising edge in several narrow areas of technology, such as atomic energy, electronics, computer components, biotechnology, superconductivity, and aerospace. China offered satellite launch services based on simple, low-cost, and reliable technology. The nation's scientists had remarkable success in using gene-splicing techniques to produce a hepatitis B vaccine, high-yield rice strains, virus-resistant tomatoes and potatoes, and genetically engineered tobacco. Chinese research on superconductivity placed it among the world's leaders in this field, and China also led in lasers and optics research and applications with the development of crystal growth and laser surgery technology. Materials science, especially the development of carbon isotopes, was another area in which China made substantial progress.

The transformation of the economic structure was similarly reflected in China's changing export structure, which was moving away from primary and semi-processed products to higher value-added manufactured products. According to the United Nations Conference on Trade and Development (UNCTAD), China's exports of primary products and resource-based manufactures substantially declined from 48.6% of all exports in 1985 to 11.6% in 2000, while the proportion of nonresource-based manufactures jumped from 50.0% to 87.1%. Over the same period, the share of high-tech exports jumped from 2.6% to 22.4%, and medium-technology exports rose from 7.7% to 17.3%. In other words, medium- and high-technology exports combined accounted for about 39.7% of all exports by 2000 (Table 7.2).

Table 7.2   China's Competitiveness in World Trade, 1985–2000

Product	Category	1985	1990	1995	2000
Market shares		*1.6*	*2.8*	*4.8*	*6.1*
Primary products[a]		2.4	2.6	2.5	2.3
Manufactures based on natural resources[b]		1.1	1.3	2.1	2.7
Manufactures not based on natural resources[c]		1.5	3.4	6.1	7.8
Low technology[d]		4.5	9.1	15.5	18.7
Medium technology[e]		0.4	1.4	2.6	3.6
High technology[f]		0.4	1.4	3.6	6.0
Others[g]		0.7	0.7	1.4	1.8
Export structure		*100.0*	*100.0*	*100.0*	*100.0*
Primary products[a]		35.0	14.6	7.0	4.7
Manufactures based on natural resources[b]		13.6	8.2	7.4	6.9

Table 7.2   (Continued)

Product	Category		1985	1990	1995	2000
Manufactures not based on natural resources[c]			50.0	76.2	84.6	87.1
Low technology[d]			39.7	53.6	53.5	47.6
Medium technology[e]			7.7	15.4	16.9	17.3
High technology[f]			2.6	7.3	14.2	22.4
Others[g]			1.4	0.8	1.0	1.1
10 Principal exports (SITC Rev.2)	*A (h)*	*B (i)*	*14.2*	*30.2*	*38.5*	*41.5*
894 Baby carriages, toys, games and sporting goods	*	+	2.5	7.3	8.4	8.5
851 Footwear		+	1.2	4.6	7.2	5.5
764 Telecommunications equipment	*	+	0.4	1.9	3.5	4.9
752 Automatic data units processing machines, units	*	+	–	0.3	1.6	4.1
845 Outer garments, knitted or crocheted	*	+	3.6	4.4	4.1	3.9
759 Parts and accessories of computers, etc.	*	+	0.1	0.3	1.8	3.6
843 Outer garments, women's and girls', textile fabrics	*	+	3.8	5.5	4.8	3.5
831 Travel goods (trunks, suitcases, etc.)	*	+	1.8	3.6	3.6	2.8
893 Articles n.e.s. of plastic materials (div.58)	*	+	0.3	1.4	2.3	2.3
821 Furniture and parts thereof	*	+	0.5	0.8	1.3	2.3

Source: UNCTAD, *World Investment Report 2002: Transnational Corporations and Export Competitiveness* (New York and Geneva: United Nations, 2002), Table VI.5, p. 162.
Notes:
[a] Contains 45 basic products that are simple to process, includes concentrates.
[b] Contains 65 items: 35 agricultural/forestry groups and 30 others (mainly metals, excluding steel, plus petroleum products, cement, glass, etc.).
[c] Contains 120 groups representing the sum of low, medium, and high technology.
[d] Contains 44 items: 20 groups from the textile and garment category, plus 24 others (paper products, glass and steel, jewellery).
[e] Contains 58 items: 5 groups from the automotive industry, 22 from the processing industry, and 31 from the engineering industry.
[f] Contains 18 items: 11 groups from the electronics category, plus another 7 (pharmaceutical products, turbines, aircraft, optical and measuring instruments).
[g] Contains nine unclassified groups.
[h] Groups belonging (*) to the 50 most dynamic in world imports, 1985–2000.
[i] Groups in which China gained (+) world market share, 1985–2000.

In the process of rapid economic growth and economic transformation, China substantially improved its competitiveness in the world economy as reflected in its export performance. According to UNCTAD, China's overall world market share increased from 1.6% to 6.1% between 1985 and 2000. More importantly, the market share of non-natural resource-based exports rose from 1.5% in 1985 and to 7.8% in 2000, of which the market share of low-technology exports increased from 4.5% to 18.7%, medium-technology exports from 0.4% to 3.6%, and high-tech exports from 0.4% to 6.0%. All of China's ten principal export products in 2000, which accounted for 41.5% of total exports, were dynamic products in world trade. Three of them (telecom equipment, automatic data-processing machines, and parts and accessories of computers) were high-tech products, which accounted for 13% of China's total exports (see Table 7.2).

As a result of rapid economic growth and economic transformation, China was reaching the top ranks of many indicators of aggregate economic size and was exerting increasingly powerful influence on the world economy. China became a top producer in an expanding range of industrial and agricultural products. It was the world's largest producer of steel, coal, cement, fertilizer, woven cotton fabrics, sulphuric acid, TV sets, telephones, household refrigerators, and household washing machines. It was the second largest producer of energy, electricity, and chemical fiber. In agriculture, China was the largest producer of cereals, meat, cotton, rapeseeds, peanuts, fruit, and fish in terms of capture production and aquaculture production. China's other significant products included tea, raw silk, sugar beets, and sugarcane.[27]

In the area of trade, China's total volume of trade rose dramatically from about $21 billion in 1978 to $851 billion in 2003.[28] As a result, between 1980 and 2003 China's share of world trade increased from 1.0% to 5.5%. In the meantime, China's share of world exports rose from 1.0% to 5.8%.[29] Consequently, while in 1980 China ranked the 28th exporting country in the world, by 2003 China became the world's fourth largest exporting nation after Germany, the United States, and Japan. In the meantime, China became the world's third largest market (rising from the 22nd place in 1980), only behind the United States and Germany. As a whole, China ranked the fourth largest trading nation in 2003 after the United States, Germany, and Japan.[30]

What is equally significant is that since 1994 China continuously enjoyed an overall trade surplus with the surplus of 1998 reaching a peak of $43.4 billion, although it dropped to $31.8 billion in 2004.[31] It is important to note that China maintained persistent huge trade surplus with the United States since 1993. In 2000, China overtook Japan as the largest source of US trade deficit. In 2004, China's trade surplus with the United States reached $80.4 billion.[32] In recent years, China's huge trade surplus with the United States became one of the sources of economic conflict between the two powers.

In addition to trade, the phenomenal increase in FDI inflows was the symbiotic development in China's opening to the outside world. FDI in China jumped from $1.2 billion in 1979–82 to $53.5 billion in 2003 with the cumulative amount reaching $499.8 billion.[33] As a result, China emerged as one of the largest recipients of FDI in the world. In 2003, China received 9.6% of the total FDI inflows in the world and, more remarkably, 31.1% of total FDI received by developing economies.[34]

China also received substantial multilateral loans from the IMF, the World Bank, the ADB, and other international institutions, as well as bilateral loans from foreign governments to finance the infrastructural projects that China's development required. Besides, China was active in international financial markets, receiving export loans and commercial loans, selling large quantities of treasury bonds and other financial bonds in international financial markets, listing Chinese enterprises in foreign stock markets, and conducting many other activities, such as sale of Chinese B shares, international lease, compensation trade, and so on. In 1979–2003, China borrowed a total of $147.2 billion foreign loans, including loans from international financial organizations and foreign governments, buyers' credits, loans on convertible currency from foreign banks, and bonds issued to foreign countries.[35]

While receiving huge amounts of FDI inflows, China also became a growingly important capital exporting country. Chinese outward FDI began to develop after the Chinese government initiated its open-door policy at the end of the 1970s. However, in the early years of the opening policy, China's outward FDI was insignificant. It was only in the mid-1980s that China's FDI outflows started to experience a first big jump, reaching $628 million in 1985, almost five times that of the previous year. By 2001, China's FDI outflows reached a peak of $6884 (Table 7.3). By 2003, China's accumulated outward FDI amounted to $37.0 billion, making China the fifth largest investors from developing economies after Hong Kong, Singapore, Taiwan, and Brazil.[36] By May 2004, there were a total of 7720 Chinese affiliates spreading over 139 economies in the world.[37]

Largely as a result of continuous huge trade surplus, China's foreign exchange reserves were steadily expanding, increasing from $0.8 billion

Table 7.3   China's FDI Outflows, 1979–2003 (US$ million)

1979	1980	1981	1982	1983	1984	1985	1986	1987	1988	1989	1990	1991
0.5	35	9	44	93	134	628	450	645	850	780	830	913

1992	1993	1994	1995	1996	1997	1998	1999	2000	2001	2002	2003
4000	4400	2000	2000	2114	2563	2634	1775	916	6884	2518	1800

Source: The figures for 1979–87 are from K. G. Cai, "Outward Foreign Direct Investment: A Novel Dimension of China's Integration into the Regional and Global Economy," *The China Quarterly*, 160 (December 1999) p. 860; the other figures are from UNCTAD, *World Investment Report*, various years (New York and Geneva: United Nations).

in 1979 to $609.9 billion in 2004, making China the second largest holder of foreign exchange reserves after Japan. By the end of 2004, China's foreign exchange reserves accounted for 35% of GDP.[38] With such huge foreign exchange reserves, China obtained growing influence on the global economy in general and the international financial market in particular. Such influence was illustrated by China's well-articulated decision on 21 July 2005 to formally drop its over-decade-long policy of pegging the Chinese yuan to the US dollar and subsequent appreciation of the Chinese currency against the US dollar by 2%, which immediately caused global impact.

China's economic power was also reflected in its escalating presence in the American economy in recent years beyond the provision of cheap Chinese products. Like the Japanese who came to purchase US government bonds and properties in the 1980s, the Chinese began to "buy America" with their growing wealth in the 1990s through investing much of its foreign exchange reserves in US government bonds. By the end of 2000, China had become the second largest holder of US government bonds after Japan, indirectly financing US huge trade and budget deficits. More recently, China also moved to the purchase of American companies. In December 2004, a Chinese company, Lenovo Group, purchased the PC division of IBM for $1.75 billion, which was followed by a report that Haier, a Chinese fridge and washing machine maker, bid $1.28 billion for Maytag, a brand name of American appliance manufacturer. A most recent move of the Chinese was a bid for $18.5 billion offered by the China National Offshore Oil Corporation (CNOOC) for takeover of Unocal Corporation, an American oil company with global reach, a bid that beat $16.5 billion offered by Chevron Corporation. All these "buy America" moves by the Chinese not only brought big "shocks" to the Americans, but also caused heated policy debate among American politicians about implications of these Chinese takeovers on US security.

Particularly, CNOOC's bid for Unocal led to the overwhelming passage of a resolution by the US House of Representatives on 30 June 2005, urging the Bush administration to block the proposed transaction as a threat to national security.[39] Although CNOOC later dropped its bid to purchase Unocal in early August 2005 under such strong political opposition from within the United States, the growing prominence of Chinese companies became all the more evident.

The growing weight of the Chinese economy was equally felt in the international oil market. With the rapid economic growth, China dramatically increased its consumption of oil and turned from a net oil exporter to a net importer in the early 1990s. Thereafter, China's oil import was dramatically rising, making China the second largest consumer and importer of oil after the United States. It was widely believed that the economic growth of China, together with that of the United States, was the primary force behind the rapid rise of oil price in the global oil market in recent years.[40] According to *Los Angeles Times*, surging Chinese demand for oil was expected to rise by double-digit growth rates annually throughout the mid-2010s. As such, China was adopting a "go-out" strategy for securing oil supply.[41] China's deepening hunt for oil not only drove the complex global oil politics even more complicated, but also brought a new source of competition and conflict with such major powers as the United States and Japan. In a similar fashion, China's voracious appetite for other materials to feed its rapidly expanding economy – including aluminum, cement, copper, lead, and steel – helped drive up their prices in international markets and created their short-term shortages throughout the world.[42]

The rise of the Chinese economic power was most evidently reflected in its rapidly expanding economic size. According to the World Bank, based on the traditional measurement of current exchange rates, China had the world's fifth largest GNP in 2005 behind the United States, Japan, Germany, and Britain. However, if calculated on a purchasing-power-parity (PPP) basis, China was seen as the second largest economy, well ahead of all other developed economies except the United States.[43] Moreover, in 2002 China was responsible for over 17% of global economic growth, making it second only to the United States.[44]

Since the early 1980s, China became growingly active in participating in multilateral cooperation on economic affairs. China resumed its seat in the IMF and the World Bank in 1980 and obtained the membership in the ADB in 1986. In the meantime, China applied for the membership of the GATT in 1986 and was finally admitted to the WTO (the successor to GATT after 1995) in 2001. Besides, China was also actively involved in regional multilateral cooperation under the framework of the APEC forum, the Asia–Europe Meeting (ASEM), and ASEAN Plus Three (APT). Particularly significant, in the face of the Asian financial crisis, China adopted a responsible policy of keeping its currency stable, a policy that received widespread admiration in the international community. Meanwhile, China also provided over $4 billion through the IMF and other channels to aid the countries hit by the crisis.[45] Consequently, China was increasingly becoming a leading economy in the region.

While China was deepening its integration with the regional and global economy and expanding its involvement in the regional and global economic cooperation and economic affairs, China also became increasingly influential on the regional and global economy with its growing economic power. China's WTO membership not only committed China to WTO principles and disciplines in a multilateral trading system, but also indicated China's growing confidence in participating in the global economic competition according to the rules that had been previously set by Western powers. As a rising economic power, China was obviously creating both new conflicts and new opportunities along with pressures for change in prevailing international structures. Largely because of the dynamism and potential of the Chinese economy, Dwight Perkins describes China as "Asia's next economic giant."[46] According to a report prepared for the Tripartite Commission, unlike the former Soviet Union, which had military power without economic strength, or Japan, which is economically powerful but militarily constrained, China will emerge as a "comprehensive power" with both economic and military strength.[47] This development will inevitably bring substantial impact on the global balance of power in the coming decades.

7.4   China's transformed regional economic relations

During Mao's era, China had minimal economic exchanges with the capitalist economies in East Asia due to Cold War politics as well as Mao's obsession with self-reliance in economic development. Although China maintained some limited barter-based trade relations with Japan, overall Sino-Japanese economic relations were quite limited. In the meantime, while China maintained closer economic ties with Hong Kong, the British colony largely served as a window for China's limited economic exchanges with the outside world.

The dramatic transformation of China's regional economic relations occurred after 1978, when the post-Mao Chinese leadership initiated the economic reform and the opening policy. Since then, China was rapidly expanding economic ties with its neighboring capitalist economies, drawing significant amounts of capital, technology, and entrepreneurial skills from Japan, Hong Kong, Taiwan, and South Korea to support its modernization drive. The established economic ties between China and these economies linked their respective comparative advantages into growing flows of cross-border trade and investment. As a result, the Chinese economy was increasingly integrated with the region.

Sino-Japanese economic relations were formally resumed in 1972 with the normalization of diplomatic relations between the two countries. However, the development of economic relations between China and Japan was quite confined due to the continuing influence of Mao's isolation policy. It was after 1978, when the new Chinese leadership adopted the opening policy and Beijing and Tokyo signed the Treaty of Peace and Friendship that Sino-Japanese economic relations began to develop rapidly. In the meantime, enormous economic complementarities of the two countries provided foundation for such close economic ties. As a result, Japan very soon became China's major economic partner in terms of trade, investment, aid, and technology transfer.

Economic ties between China and Japan were first and foremost linked by bilateral trade. After Beijing started economic reform in the late 1970s, Sino-Japanese trade expanded substantially, jumping from $4.8 billion in 1978 to $133.6 billion in 2003. Consequently, Japan remained China's leading trading partner with the exception of 6 years between 1987 and 1992, during which Hong Kong took the place of China's largest trading partner. In the meantime, Japan also remained the largest source of China's imports during the same period with the exception of 1987–92. On the other hand, while Japan was the second largest market for Chinese exports before 1992, it remained the third largest consumer of Chinese exports after 1993.[48]

The rapid increase in Sino-Japanese trade was accompanied by the transformation of trade structure over time, reflecting changing comparative advantages of the two countries. In the first half of the 1980s, China mainly exported primary products to Japan. Oil and coal made up over half of its total exports to Japan, while manufactured goods accounted for only around 20%, which were almost all low value-added labor-intensive products.[49] Over time, China's exports of primary products were declining while manufactured exports were increasing. As a result, the exports of oil and coal dropped dramatically from 55.5% in 1981 to 3.3% in 2002, while textiles first rose from 10.4% in 1981 to 34.6% in 1995 and then gradually declined to 25.6% in 2002, and foodstuff increased from 10.5% in 1981 to 21.3% in 1986 and then gradually decreased to 9.5% in 2002.

More significantly, China's exports of machinery and equipment rose substantially from negligible 0.8% in 1981 to 33.5% in 2002. The import structure also transformed with the imports of Japanese machinery and transport equipment increasing from 42.2% in 1980 to 57.8% in 2002. In the meantime, iron and steel, which was a major import item in the 1980s, dropped from 27.0 in 1980 to 7.3% in 2002, indicating that China had rapidly developed its own steel industry.[50]

Much of the Sino-Japanese trade since the early 1980s was a direct result of Japanese investment and ODA programs in China. Japanese companies investing in China brought with them equipment together with inputs and components on a continuing basis for their production activities. On the whole, Japanese-invested enterprises imported into China more than they exported to Japan. Moreover, Japanese aid programs in China were frequently tied to the purchase of Japanese equipment and products, especially in the 1980s. Although thereafter the officially tied portion of Japanese aid became negligible, the bulk of Japan's ODA contracts were still awarded to Japanese companies.[51]

Largely as a result of such a bilateral trade structure, China maintained continuously huge trade deficit with Japan for most years, particularly before the 1990s. Although China occasionally enjoyed trade surplus for some individual years (1990–92, 1996–98, and 2000–01), the surplus amount was relatively small and the overall trade balance was still in Japan's favor. During the whole period 1990–2003, China had an overall trade deficit of $24.4 billion with Japan with the annual deficit of 2003 reaching a historic record of $14.7 billion.[52]

Japanese investment in China was another important area of Sino-Japanese economic relations since the late 1970s. However, in the 1980s Japanese FDI in China was relatively small. The turning point came after 1988, when a bilateral investment protection agreement was signed. In March 1990, the Japan–China Investment Promotion Organization (JCIPO) was established. JCIPO and its Chinese counterpart formed a joint governmental commission to promote Japanese FDI in China, a move that signified the commitment of both the governments to the promotion of the investment relationship. In the meantime, China took more measures to liberalize its investment regime after 1989. As a result, following a hiatus caused by the 1989 Tiananmen suppression, there was a surge in Japanese investment in China in the 1990s through the early 2000s with the annual FDI rising from $0.2 billion in 1987 to $5.1 billion in 2003. By the end of 2002, the cumulative Japanese FDI in China had reached $36.3 billion, representing 8.1% of total cumulative FDI in

China, making Japan the third leading source of FDI in China after Hong Kong (45.7%) and the United States (8.9%). In the meantime, Japanese FDI in China involved a total of 25,147 projects at the end of 2002, which made Japan the fourth largest after Hong Kong (210,876), Taiwan (55,691), and the United States (37,280).[53]

The pattern of Japanese FDI in China evolved over time. In the 1980s, Japanese investment in China concentrated on the use of lower production costs in the country for export to other countries. Entering the 1990s, however, many Japanese companies were moving beyond the use of China as a base for export manufacturing to tapping China's large domestic market in the context of slow economic growth and trade protectionism in the West. More significantly, the focus of Japanese investment in China, as elsewhere in East Asia, also moved to integrate China into company-based production networks as part of its regional production strategies.

Although Japanese FDI was relatively small given the size of the Japanese economy, Japan was a major source of FDI that was capable of helping promote China's industrial and technological advances. Despite China's complaints over Japanese reluctance to transfer advanced technology, Japanese FDI was generally seen as helpful in transforming China into a market economy, revitalizing domestic industry, alleviating the shortage of investment funds, importing new industries and technology, bringing in management skills, increasing domestic production, promoting exports, contributing to foreign exchange earnings, increasing tax revenue and employment, and training Chinese employees.[54] Moreover, Japanese FDI contributed to the integration of China into the global and regional economy, and helped strengthen the bilateral relationship and increase mutual interdependence of the two economies through the increased contacts between the two societies.

Japan's ODA to China was an important part of bilateral economic relations since the early 1980s. Although Tokyo offered to provide ODA for China soon after the normalization of Sino-Japanese diplomatic relations in 1972, Beijing rejected Japan's offer several times through the late 1970s due to China's no-foreign-debt doctrine and continuing policy of autarky under Mao's influence. After Deng Xiaoping initiated economic reform in 1978, China's attitude toward ODA from capitalist countries in general and Japan in particular began to change. As a result, talks were held between China and Japan on an aid relationship and in 1979 Beijing formally agreed to accept Japanese ODA under a general policy position that China's sovereignty would not be impaired by foreign aid and the conditions for aid would be appropriate. Thereafter, Japanese ODA to

China increased rapidly and Japan became the single most important source of foreign development assistance for China, representing over half of all ODA that China received from developed countries. China became the largest recipient of Japan's ODA for the first time in 1982 and remained as such through 1986 and in 1993–95, 1997–98, 2002, and 2004 and was the second largest in the years of 1987–90, 1992, 1996, 1999, 2001, and 2003.[55] Although officially denied by both sides, it is widely believed that there was some tacit understanding between Beijing and Tokyo that Japanese ODA to China would serve as some kind of reparations for war damages that Japan had brought to China before 1945, which Beijing had officially surrendered.

The Japanese ODA to China mostly took the form of concessional loans. Besides, under Japan's ODA programs China also received grant aid, technical assistance for projects approved for the loans, and personnel exchange programs for specialists, trainees, and students. In the meantime, China received indirect Japanese aid through Japan's contributions to the assistance programs for China provided by multilateral institutions, including the IMF, the World Bank, the ADB, and UN agencies. Moreover, China also benefited from a variety of other loans from Japan on a nonconcessional basis.

Japanese aid programs to China were initially designed for Japan to secure stable supply of resources from China in the context of the oil crises in the 1970s. By the 1990s, as China became a net importer of oil following its sustained rapid economic growth, the role of Japan's ODA in securing energy supplies from China diminished. Thereafter, Japanese aid programs concentrated on building railways, bridges, airports, and dams and on promoting trade and investment relationship between the two countries. Although representing less than 0.5% of China's GDP, Japan's ODA to China brought positive effects on China's economic growth by providing new employment, constructing infrastructure, supporting exports, facilitating technology transfer, linking up with domestically sourced investment, and stabilizing macroeconomic impacts of capital inflows.

When Sino-Japanese economic relations were resumed in 1972, Japan was an emerging economic superpower while China was a poor developing country. Over time, however, there was changing dynamics between the two countries. Particularly, after the early 1990s while the Japanese economy entered the protracted stagnation, China was rising as a new economic power as a result of its sustained economic expansion since the late 1970s. Consequently, there was escalating rivalry between the two countries over regional economic leadership and increased bilateral disputes over economic issues. Bilateral economic relations also became politicized with rising political tensions regarding wartime accounts in Japanese history textbooks, visits by Japanese leaders to the Yasukuni Shrine paying homage to the country's war dead, the Taiwan question, China's military buildup, the nature of the US–Japan security alliance, territorial disputes, gas disputes, and Japan's quest to gain a permanent seat at the UN Security Council. By the end of 2004, Japanese politicians began to hint the possible termination of Japan's ODA to China as a result of rising tensions in Sino-Japanese relations and growing concern in Japan over the rising Chinese economic power that was challenging Japan's economic dominance in the region.

The Chinese economy was deeply intertwined with Hong Kong's economy for many years. Even during Mao's period, Hong Kong played a unique role in China's limited economic connection with the outside world with a significant proportion of China's foreign trade – especially China's exports – being channeled through Hong Kong. After the late 1970s, Hong Kong played an even more important role in China's new opening policy as an important trading partner, a source of capital and a bridge that linked China with the capitalist world.

The Chinese economy and the Hong Kong economy were first and foremost linked by trade. Largely because of its efficiency in trade, Hong Kong continued to attract the bulk of Chinese trade and function as an *entrepôt* for China. Consequently, China's trade with Hong Kong grew very rapidly from 1978 through the early 1990s with the share of Hong Kong trade jumping from 12.6% of China's total trade in 1978 to 36.6% in 1991. During the period 1988–92, Hong Kong even overtook Japan as the largest trading partner of China. In the meantime, between 1978 and 1991 the share of Chinese exports to Hong Kong rose from 26.0% of China's total exports to 44.7% and the share of imports increased from 0.7% of China's total imports to 27.5%. Although after 1992 the share of Hong Kong trade in China's total trade declined gradually to 10.3% in 2003, Hong Kong remained the second or third largest trading partner of China. It is important to note that the importance of Hong Kong trade for China was particularly reflected in its role in absorbing the bulk of Chinese exports, a large proportion of which were of *entrepôt* nature. Hong Kong took the largest proportion of Chinese exports from 1978 through 1998 and thereafter the second largest, after the United States. By 2003, Hong Kong still absorbed 17.4% of China's total exports, although dropping from the peak of 44.7% in 1991. Consequently, Hong Kong remained the largest source of China's trade surplus except in the year 2000. Over time, the volume of China's trade surplus with Hong

Kong was ever expanding, dramatically rising from $2.5 billion in 1978 to $65.2 billion in 2003.[56]

Hong Kong's growing role in China's trade was not only attributed to the efficiency of Hong Kong as an *entrepôt*, but was also the result of the massive transfer of Hong Kong's manufacturing capacity to China, especially after the mid-1980s. By the early 1980s, Hong Kong had become an NIE that was especially competitive in producing and exporting labor-intensive manufactures. By the mid-1980s, however, there were rising labor costs in Hong Kong, exerting growing pressures on Hong Kong businesses. At about the same time, China opened up its coastal region to foreign investment and trade as part of its economic reform. It was under such circumstances that Hong Kong companies began to take the opportunity to move their labor-intensive manufacturing capacity into China in a huge scale, especially into neighboring Guangdong province, taking advantage of lower labor costs there. As a result, thousands of Hong Kong-invested enterprises were established in China to produce manufactures for export. In the meantime, through a new trade arrangement of "outward processing," Hong Kong companies supplied raw materials and components to Chinese domestic enterprises for processing and re-export. All these exports were primarily directed at the third market but channeled through Hong Kong. This massive relocation of Hong Kong's manufacturing capacity to China together with "outward processing" brought rapid growth of trade between China and Hong Kong, particularly after the mid-1980s through the early 1990s. By the mid-1995, most of labor-intensive manufacturing in Hong Kong had been relocated to China. As a result, Hong Kong was fundamentally transformed from the manufacturing-based economy to a service-based economy, playing a specialized role in providing the Chinese economy with finance, marketing, transport, and communications services.[57]

It was under such circumstances that Hong Kong remained the predominant source of FDI for China since the late 1970s. By 2002, Hong Kong's accumulated FDI in China had amounted to a total of $204.9 billion, which represented 45.7% of total FDI that China had received by the time, almost twice the combined amount of FDI from the United States (8.9%), Japan (8.1%), and Taiwan (7.4%). In the meantime, the number of projects of Hong Kong's FDI was predominant, totaling 210,876 by 2002, which made up 49.7% of all FDI projects in China.[58]

While Hong Kong was the largest investor in China, China was also investing heavily in Hong Kong as the largest destination of Chinese outward FDI. Chinese companies used their affiliates in Hong Kong not only as regional headquarters for their broader strategic objectives of internationalization but also as a vehicle to raise capital by public listing of their shares on the Hong Kong Stock Exchange through either acquisitions or new listings and by the use of various debt instruments. Moreover, as most Chinese-invested companies in Hong Kong were state-owned, they also implicitly assumed a political role of stabilizing the Hong Kong economy. The Chinese-invested companies were playing an increasingly important role in Hong Kong's economy.

After Beijing's resumption of sovereignty over Hong Kong in 1997, Hong Kong remained an independent economy under Beijing's "one country two systems" policy and continued to play an important role in China's connection with other economies. Largely reflecting the deepening integration of the Chinese economy and the Hong Kong economy, and also for political considerations, Beijing moved to sign with Hong Kong the Closer Economic Partnership Arrangement (CEPA) on 29 June 2003, which came into force on 1 January 2004. Under the China–Hong Kong CEPA, tariffs and non-tariff barriers on trade in both goods and services would be phased out and facilitation measures would be adopted to promote trade and investment. As Hong Kong already had a very liberalized trade and investment system, the China–Hong Kong CEPA was in effect designed to make China more opening to Hong Kong.

China–Taiwan economic relations began to develop in the late 1980s as a result of policy changes on both sides of the Taiwan Straits. Since then, the cross-Taiwan Straits economic ties grew and deepened very rapidly in an indirect fashion despite continuing political sour between Beijing and Taipei. Most impressive was the dramatic rise of Taiwan's investment in China. By June 2007, the accumulated FDI from Taiwan amounted to $44.6 billion, ranking the fifth leading source of FDI in China.[59] Moreover, Taiwanese capital was believed to be a significant contributor to the huge increase of FDI inflows in China from the Virgin Islands in recent years. It is therefore estimated that Taiwan's actual total FDI on the mainland through all channels was at least double the official figure and that about 50% of Taiwan's top 1000 companies invested in China. As a result of rapid rise of Taiwan's investment in China, there were now over 1 million Taiwanese living on the mainland, 300,000 of which were in Shanghai alone. Moreover, the rapid rise of Taiwanese FDI in China was accompanied by rapid rise of cross-Taiwan Straits trade, much of which was related to Taiwanese investment on the mainland. As a result, trade between China and Taiwan increased rapidly from nothing before the early 1980s to $58.4 billion in 2003, representing 6.9% of China's total trade, which made Taiwan the fifth largest trading partner of China. Particularly, Taiwan was the second largest source of imports, providing China with 12.0% of total imports in 2003, a figure that was not far behind Japan (13.6%).[60] Consequently, Taiwan enjoyed continuously increasing huge trade surplus with China.[61]

Increasingly closer economic ties with Taiwan were seen by Beijing not only as economically helpful but also strategically and politically important. It is Beijing's belief that closer economic ties would make Taiwan more dependent on the mainland for economic well-being, thus enhancing Beijing's leverage vis-à-vis Taipei in overall relations across the Taiwan Straits and preventing Taiwan from independence.

Although China started to establish limited trade relationship with South Korea as early as the 1980s, Sino-South Korean economic relations began to expand rapidly only after the establishment of diplomatic relations between the two countries in 1992. As a result, China's trade with South Korea rose from 0.6% of its total trade in 1990 to 7.4% in 2003, making South Korea the fourth largest trading partner of China. In the meantime, South Korea was the fourth largest market for Chinese exports, absorbing 4.6% of China's total exports, and the third largest source of Chinese imports, providing 10.4% of China's total imports for 2003. Behind the rapid growth of bilateral trade, however, China maintained continuously increasing trade deficit with South Korea since 1992, which amounted to as high as $23.0 billion in 2003.[62] China's consistent huge trade deficit with South Korea constituted a major source of economic conflict between the two countries in recent years.

Equally impressive was the rapid rise of South Korea as an increasingly important source of FDI for China. Although South Korean companies started to invest in China as late as 1992, South Korean FDI developed very rapidly. By 2002, the accumulative value of South Korea's FDI in China had amounted to $15.2 billion, accounting for 3.4% of total FDI inflows in China, which made South Korea the seventh largest investor in China.[63] South Korean businesses primarily invested in manufacturing, which accounted for 85.6% of all South Korean investment in China in terms of value and 87.2% in terms of the number of projects between 1993 and 2000. South Korean FDI was involved in such labor-intensive industries as textiles, shoes, and furniture, as well as capital-intensive industries like petrochemical and electronic industries. Over 50% of South Korea's investment in China involved South Korean solely invested projects. Moreover, South Korea's FDI mostly came from large companies, which accounted for 61.8% of all South Korean FDI in China between 1993 and 2000. However, the average value of each project was relatively low. Geographically, South Korea's investment concentrated in North and Northeast China, which took over 85% of all South Korean investment in China. While South Korea's FDI was initially motivated by using lower labor costs in China, it later moved to tap the huge Chinese market.[64]

Obviously, while East Asia was so critical to China's economic development, the rise of the Chinese economic power was bringing significant impact on the region as well. For the neighboring economies in the region, as a market, a supplier of raw materials, and a source of inexpensive labor, a rising and opening China could serve as the kingpin of the area and a cushion against creeping protectionism in North America and Western Europe. China's sustained growth became a new engine for the region's growth. Although many of these economic relationships were heavily dependent on good political relations between China and its neighboring states, the ever-growing ties suggest that the growth and deepening of regional economic ties benefited all the parties involved.

7.5　The Chinese economy in the 21st century: major problems and prospect

As a result of the economic reform since the late 1970s, China has achieved remarkable success in economic and social development. Despite the achievements, however, the Chinese economy is still plagued with huge problems when entering the 21st century. While some problems are related to the country's basic economic conditions, the others obviously derive from a transitional economic system that is partly market-driven and partly planned. The problems in both categories are not entirely unrelated.

Of the major problems in the Chinese economy, the continuing lack of infrastructure and growing shortage of energy and resources are most prominent. While the recent years have witnessed an impressive development of many important infrastructure projects in China, the nation's overall infrastructure is still quite insufficient and backward, far from the needs of the country's economic development. There is the backward electric grid, weak telecommunications networks, and poor but over-burdened transportation networks and facilities, especially in the rural areas and in the underdeveloped areas in western and southwestern regions. On the other hand, paradoxically enough, with the country's rapid economic development over the past three decades, the problem of shortage of energy and resources becomes all the more salient. While the shortage of electricity is an old persistent problem in the Chinese economy, there has been in recent years a new problem of growing shortage of some important resources. More significant, China has now become a net resource importing, rather than exporting, country. By 2003, for example, the total volume of minerals that China imported amounted to $37.7 billion while the volume for mineral exports was only $12.7 billion. Particularly, for the single most important item, that is oil, China imported 102.7 million tons in 2002 while exporting only 21.4 million tons with a deficit of 81.3 million tons.[65] Consequently, the insufficiency of infrastructure, energy, and resources is a huge obstacle to further rapid development of the Chinese economy. To overcome this obstacle is one of the challenging tasks facing the Chinese government in the coming decades.

There are awesome problems in agriculture as well. In the first place, China's population is expected to peak at 1.6 billion by 2030, requiring an annual grain supply of 640 million tons. But growth in China's agriculture has been held back by dwindling natural resources, backward agro-technology, and the irrational structure of the rural economy. Per capita arable land has decreased to 0.08 hectare in the past decade, or only one-third of the world's average. To make the matter worse, nearly 20 million hectares of arable land, one-fifth of the total, are affected by pollution.[66] Furthermore, there is continuing loss of farming land to the economic development and erosion of the farming land and rural ecological environment.

On the other hand, although outputs of many major agricultural products have been up sharply since 1978, much of the advance results from increased state-funding and price-supports rather than the improved production skills, and it is somewhat overstated when viewed from the perspective of constant prices and real economic contribution. In the meantime, the small size of the average acreage worked and the average size of the family contract farm unit inhibit the use of efficient large-scale mechanized methods. Consequently, rural productivity remains a problem for the Chinese economy. Furthermore, agricultural infrastructure is highly insufficient. China has serious problems in storage, transportation, and other logistical facilities, which prevent the country from attaining stable self-sufficiency. Particularly, there is a thorny problem of surplus rural labor force, which amounts to 200 million.

China's industry is also plagued with thorny problems despite major progress that has been achieved in the country's industrialization since the late 1970s. In addition to the widespread lack of managerial experience and expertise, the most devastating problem is that the majority of Chinese enterprises are underdeveloped, outdated, and inefficient. As a consequence, many of the industrial products are of poor quality and more expensive than they should be. This may well be explained by Chinese exports, which are still largely those of low value-added products and they primarily depend on low labor costs rather than quality for competitiveness in the international market. Furthermore, many of the Chinese outdated factories still operate in a way that produces much pollution, making China one of the most polluted countries in the world.

Accounting for 33% of GDP, China's services sector is on the whole still relatively weak. Consequently, the services sector is still playing an important role in creating jobs rather than contributing to economic growth. Moreover, many industries in the services sector, such as banking, insurance, commerce, communications, and transportation, are thriving simply because of the government's protectionist policies. It is an open question of whether many of these industries could survive or not after they are opened for foreign investment following China's WTO accession.

The troubled state-owned enterprise sector is the single biggest headache for the Chinese leadership at the turn of the century despite the positive effects of the reform of state-owned enterprises on productivity. It is estimated that between half and two-thirds of the state-owned industrial enterprises are losing money. To avoid putting their workers into the ranks of the jobless, the state continues to subsidize these losses rather than allowing the money-losing enterprises to go bankrupt. Although China is currently restructuring the state-owned enterprises operating at a loss through reform, reorganization, upgrading, and improved management, the prospect is not quite optimistic, given the scope and degree of the problem.

There is also a growing unemployment population in China. According to China's official statistics, by the end of 2003 there was an urban unemployment rate of 4.3% with an unemployed population of 8 million.[67] According to unofficial sources, however, the real unemployment figure could be as high as 8%. Besides, the official figure of unemployment rate does not include the rural unemployed and/or underemployed, those outside the official system, and the urban youth waiting for employment. The above figures even do not include a much larger floating population, estimated over 100 million, from the rural areas who are looking for jobs in urban areas. To make the matter worse, while there is a growing surplus labor, China actually lacks skilled workers.

The unemployment problem could potentially be a very destabilizing and explosive issue for Chinese society and politics, as a well-functioning social insurance system has not yet been fully established in the country.

Despite much progress in establishing a financial system in China, however, the existing financial system is plagued with serious problems. Most importantly, far from real commercial banks, state-owned banks are from time to time still required by the government to grant loans based on public policy criteria rather than economic rationality. Particularly, the government's subsidies continue to flow into money-losing state-owned enterprises through these bank loans because of the government's unwillingness to suffer the political consequences of adding the employees of bankrupt businesses to the ranks of the disgruntled unemployed. As a consequence, there has been an accumulated huge amount of bad loans in the banking system. The existence of these bad loans not only precludes more productive use of capital but also prevents turning state-owned banks into real commercial banks.

On the other hand, the newly emerged treasury bond market and the stock market are rudimentary, far from complete, sophisticated, and well-regulated. In the case of the bond market, for example, commercial banks still play a minimum role in the treasury bond market, thus not only limiting the further development of the treasury bond market but also minimizing the effects of the open market mechanism as adopted by the People's Bank of China. There are major problems with the stock market as well. In the first place, there is still the existence of different types of shares, and some types of shares (say, state-holding shares, company-holding shares, and so on) are not allowed to market. Moreover, there are huge fluctuations of stock prices resulted from speculation, irregularities and lack of a sound supervising mechanism. The dramatic plummeting of stock prices of B shares first and then A shares in the first half of the 2000s is precisely the reflection of these problems. There is now even a talk of the possible collapse of the Chinese stock market.

There are widening gaps between the rich and poor, between the urban and rural areas, and between regions. While the living standards of Chinese people on the whole have improved dramatically over the past three decades as a result of the economic reform, there has been a widening gap between the rich and the poor. On the one hand, a new class of the rich has emerged in China following the economic reform. According to one estimate, this rich class now comprises more than 3 million people. What is more disturbing is that many in this rich group have actually become rich in a short period by abusing their power through various corruptive practices, say, embezzlement of public funds into private account, trading power for huge wealth in various ways, and so on. On the other hand, there has also emerged a growingly large army of the extremely poor, which includes the unemployed resulted from the restructuring of state-owned enterprises, the retired, the floating population in urban areas, and others. While it is difficult to obtain the accurate number of these poor people, some conservative estimation puts this number at about 90 million, 20 million in the urban areas, and 70 million in the rural areas, accounting for 8% of the country's population.

There has been growing discrepancy between urban and rural incomes too. Although rural income has increased threefold since the reform began in 1978, this does not match the fivefold increase in urban incomes during the same period. As a result, while per capita annual net income of urban households was 2.6 times that of rural households in 1978, it increased to 3.2 times in 2003.[68] Consequently, the urban–rural gap becomes more pronounced. The rising discrepancy in income and living standards between the urban and rural areas is a growing concern for the Chinese leadership, as the rural areas, with 70% of the Chinese population, could be a source of potential social unrest.

Furthermore, while the economic reform has witnessed the nation's rapid economic growth on the whole, there is huge difference in growth rate between regions. Consequently, there has been growing gap between regions in terms of GDP and per capita income. Particularly, the coastal provinces have achieved a very rapid average annual growth rate of well above 10% since the early 1980s, largely thanks to their geographical advantage and preferential policies offered to them by the central government, while the average annual growth rate of most inland provinces is quite moderate, ranging from around 6% to below 10%. As a result, there has been a widening gap between regions in terms of per capita GDP. Accordingly, the income gap between regions has also increased over time. The growing disparity between regions would likely bring about serious economic, political, and social consequences and constitute a new significant destabilizing factor in Chinese politics. The widening regional disparity has not only been increasingly aggravating the unfavorable life of two-thirds of the population who live in poor provinces but also is a most important factor that has contributed to growing regionalism within China in recent years. If this regional disparity continues and widens, there might even be growing force for political secession from both poor provinces and rich provinces. This issue increasingly becomes a big concern for the Chinese leadership.

Obviously, the solution to all these major problems in the Chinese economy lies in how the Chinese leadership continues the economic reform and pursues the development strategy in the coming decades. To some extent, it is also defined by the global economic environment and the way that China participates in the world economy in the coming years. While there is no easy prediction on how these problems might be solved, it seems safe to say that it is apparently not an overnight matter to have all these problems solved, if they could finally be solved.

Despite the problems discussed above, however, there is the bright side of the picture as well. According to most observers of the Chinese economy, China's rapid economic growth will be likely to continue for some years to come. For nearly 60 years, the United States has been the economic engine of the Pacific Rim. But that era is drawing to a close and China is growingly becoming a new economic engine of the region. This is well illustrated in the changed trade relationship in the region. In 2003, China overtook the United States as the largest trading partner of South Korea. In 2004, China became Japan's biggest trading partner.[69] It is estimated that if China keeps growing at the current rate, the Chinese economy would even outpace the American economy in terms of GDP by as early as 2039.[70]

8
The Political Economy of Regional Integration in East Asia

8.1 The rising regional economic integration in East Asia since the mid-1980

As a result of Japan's defeat in World War II, the prewar regional political economy of East Asia within the framework of the Japanese empire was substantially transformed. The postwar political economy of East Asia was initially structured under the aegis of the United States, reflecting the political and economic conditions in the region at the time. As part of its postwar strategy in East Asia, Washington encouraged regional economic integration centered on Japan with noncommunist East and Southeast Asia functioning as a market and source of raw materials for the Japanese economy. The development of postwar economic relations between Japan and other capitalist economies in the region basically proceeded along this line. By the mid-1960s, with the normalization of relations between Japan and South Korea, the East Asian political economy had been solidly resumed. Thereafter, the major market economies in East Asia successively achieved economic miracles with Japan emerging as a new economic superpower and South Korea, Taiwan, and Hong Kong becoming newly industrializing economies. In this process, these economies became increasingly interdependent through growing trade and FDI among them. In the late 1970s, China moved away from Mao's policy of self-reliance and began to participate in the regional and international economy. The new orientation of Chinese policy not only changed the political and economic environment in East Asia and opened up new prospects for effective regional cooperation, but also vastly expanded the region's market, natural resources, and industrial potential.

The growing economic ties among East Asian economies were echoing a novel pattern of relations that began to develop in the region during the 1980s. Coupled with growing economic ties, there were increasing political contacts, cultural exchanges, communication, and tourism. Most importantly, there were improved political relations between the former political enemies in the region. These interactions led to a growing web of cooperation, far more extensive than ever before, though it was still a web in the early stages of development, which could be easily disrupted or even destroyed by adverse trends in the region. In the process, a sense of regional consciousness, identity, and mutual interests was formed and increasingly strengthened. Thus, by the 1980s, the improved strategic, economic, and political environment in East Asia had finally set the stage for rapid growth of economic ties in the region.

The process of growing economic ties in East Asia is manifested by the declining importance of the United States both as a market and as a source of investment for East Asian economies and the concurrent deepening economic interdependence among the economies in the region with rising intraregional trade and FDI flows. The relative decline of US economic power and the ensuing intensification of trade frictions between Washington and East Asian states have reduced the importance of the United States as a market for East Asian exports, while the importance of regional markets for the East Asian economies has been steadily growing. The significant change in the direction of East Asian exports and imports is demonstrated by the statistics in Table 8.1. The trend

Table 8.1   Distribution of East Asian Exports and Imports: Intraregional and US, 1985–2003

	Intraregional			United States			World		
	1985	1995	2003	1985	1995	2003	1985	1995	2003
Value of exports ($ billion)	67.6	343.1	576.3	103.9	235.2	312.1	295.7	1,002.6	1,473.0
Share of total exports (%)	22.9	34.2	39.1	35.1	23.5	21.2	100	100	100
Value of imports ($ billion)	67.4	340.4	563.9	45.4	158.1	148.4	253.9	899.7	1,334.5
Share of total imports (%)	26.5	37.8	42.3	17.9	17.6	11.1	100	100	100

Source: Calculated on the basis of data from IMF, *Direction of Trade Statistics Yearbook*, various years, with the exception of the data for Taiwan, which are obtained from Council for Economic Planning and Development (CEPD), ROC, *Taiwan Statistical Data Book, 2004* (Taipei: Council for Economic Planning and Development, ROC, 2004).

Table 8.2 East Asia and the United States: Shares of East Asian Economies' Exports, 1985–2003 (% of Total)

From	Japan			South Korea			Taiwan			Hong Kong			China		
To	1985	1995	2003	1985	1995	2003	1985	1995	2003	1985	1995	2003	1985	1995	2003
East Asia	17.7	24.8	32.4	20.8	32.6	38.4	20.4	37.8	46.0	34.4	43.7	52.5	48.4	49.8	37.6
United States	37.6	27.5	24.8	35.6	19.3	17.8	48.1	23.7	18.0	30.8	21.8	18.7	8.5	16.6	21.1

Source: Calculated on the basis of data from IMF, *Direction of Trade Statistics Yearbook*, various years, with the exception of the data for Taiwan, which are obtained from CEPD, *Taiwan Statistical Data Book, 2004*.

Table 8.3 East Asia and the United States: Shares of East Asian Economies' Imports, 1985–2003 (% of Total)

To	Japan			South Korea			Taiwan			Hong Kong			China		
From	1985	1995	2003	1985	1995	2003	1985	1995	2003	1985	1995	2003	1985	1995	2003
East Asia	11.4	20.9	28.5	26.8	32.1	37.4	30.1	38.2	42.4	61.2	64.6	67.2	46.9	47.4	43.1
United States	20.0	22.6	15.6	21.1	22.5	13.9	23.6	20.1	13.2	9.5	7.7	5.5	12.2	12.2	8.2

Source: Calculated on the basis of data from IMF, *Direction of Trade Statistics Yearbook*, various years, with the exception of the data for Taiwan, which are obtained from CEPD, *Taiwan Statistical Data Book, 2004*.

toward growing intraregional trade is similarly evidenced from the data on individual economies in East Asia (Tables 8.2 and 8.3).

In any analysis of growing intraregional trade in East Asia, it is important to point out that a large proportion of this growth in intraregional trade is directly attributed to the increased manufacturing and intra-industry trade, deriving from the rising FDI flows between the economies in East Asia. The regional FDI in East Asia, accompanied by transfers of technology and management know-how and access to world markets, has been primarily flowing from Japan to other economies in the region and from NIEs to China since the mid-1980s. It is important to note that China has also heavily invested in Hong Kong for political as well as economic reasons.

While US FDI dominated the region during the 1950s–60s, starting in the late 1960s, Japanese corporations were taking an increasingly larger share of regional FDI. Particularly, stimulated by massive trade surplus and the rapid appreciation of the yen, Japanese foreign investment had a big boost in the second half of the 1980s. By the end of 1989, Japan had accumulated a total of $254.4 billion in FDI outflows. In absolute terms, the United States received the largest amount of Japanese overall FDI – $104.4 billion (41.0% of the total) – and the European Community (EC) as a whole received $40.0 billion (15.7%), while the amount going to East Asia was only $16.7 billion (6.6%). However, the East Asian economies received the lion's share of Japanese FDI to non-OECD member economies.[1] Although the Japanese overall FDI lost momentum after 1900, the shift of Japanese investment to East Asia became even more evident, particularly to China (Table 8.4). Significantly, in 2004 Japanese investment in East Asia, which amounted to $6.8 billion and represented 18.4% of Japan's total FDI outflows, surpassed that in the United States for the first time ever, which fell to $4.8 billion and accounted for only 13.2%.[2] On the other hand, however, Japanese FDI to European Union (EU) countries substantially increased as well after the mid-1990s, which was largely intended to take advantage of the EU's single market that had been created by the end of 1992 (see Table 8.4).

Even more important than the Japanese FDI in terms of value is the number of cases of Japanese investment and a high proportion of Japanese investment in the manufacturing sector in East Asia. As the data on East Asia are not available, the data on Asia as a whole can still be illustrative. According to the statistics of Japan's Ministry of Finance, of the total cases of Japanese overseas investment between 1989 and 2004, 27.4% took place in North America, 23.3% in Europe, and 33.7% in Asia. More important, of a total of 16,424 cases of Japanese investment in Asia, 63.4% (10,418 cases) was in the manufacturing sector, as compared to 26.8% (3576 out of 13,356 cases) for North America and 16.9% (1919 out of 11,387 cases) for Europe. In a similar fashion, of the total value of Japanese FDI in Asia between 1989 and 2004, 56.9% was in the manufacturing sector, as compared to 37.6% for North America and 31.6% for Europe.[3] As will be discussed below, the high proportion of Japanese investment in the manufacturing sector in East Asia is of particular significance, because it is the Japanese investment in manufacturing that is of central importance in the growth of economic integration in the region.

Since the mid-1980s, Hong Kong, Taiwan, and South Korea have also become major investors in the region, particularly in China. Hong Kong is the largest investor among East Asian NIEs. Between 1984 and 1989, Hong Kong's total FDI abroad reached $25.9 billion, of which $12.9 billion (49.7%) went to East Asia. Among East Asian economies, China took the lion's share ($11.7 billion or 91.1%) of Hong Kong's FDI in East Asia (or 45.2% of Hong Kong's total FDI abroad), followed by Taiwan ($756 million and 5.9%), Japan ($281 million and 2.2%) and South Korea ($113

Table 8.4　Japan's Direct Investment abroad, 1985–2004

	1985–89	1990–94	1995–99	2000–04
World total				
$ million	182,463	214,111	263,581	191,381
US				
$ million	84,505	91,902	99,207	42,461
% of world total	46.3	42.9	37.6	22.2
EU-15*				
$ million	33,945	43,049	65,486	74,467
% of world total	18.6	20.1	24.8	38.9
East Asia				
$ million	11,495	15,575	20,578	19,658
% of world total	6.3	7.3	7.8	10.3

Source: Data for 1985–89 are based on Japan External Trade Organization (JETRO) various years (cited in Glenn D. Hook, Julie Gilson, Christopher W. Hughes and Hugo Dobson, *Japan's International Relations: Politics, Economics and Security* (London and New York: Routledge, 2001), Table 2, pp. 450–7; data for 1990–2004 are based on Ministry of Finance, Japan, statistics database (http://www.mof.go.jp/english/index.htm, accessed on 5 March 2006), converted from the Japanese yen to the US dollar at the annual average exchange rate with the exception of the data for 2004, which are converted from the Japanese yen to the US dollar on the basis of the monthly average exchange rate of December 2004. The exchange rates for 1990–2003 are taken from Statistics Bureau, Japan, *Japan Statistical Yearbook 2005* (Tokyo: Japan Statistical Association and the *Mainichi Newspapers*, 2005); the exchange rate for 2004 comes from Bank of Japan, Statistics database (http://www.boj.or.jp/en, accessed on 5 March 2006).
* EU-15 refers to 12 countries that signed the Treaty of Maastricht in 1992, which transformed the EC into the EU in 1993 – including France, Belgium, Luxemburg, Netherlands, Italy, Germany, UK, Ireland, Denmark, Greece, Spain and Portugal – plus three new members that joined the EU in 1995, namely, Austria, Sweden and Finland. Regardless of different dates of joining the EU, they are put together for the convenience of comparison. On the other hand, ten new members that joined the EU in 2004 are quite marginal in this comparison, hence not included.

million and 0.9%).[4] By the end of 2003, the stock of Hong Kong's FDI outflows reached $338.6 billion, of which $119.6 billion was in China (35.3%).[5] With huge foreign exchange reserves, Taiwan became a new important source of capital in the world and a growingly important investor in East Asia. According to Taiwan's official statistics, by the end of 2006 Taiwan's total approved investment stock abroad reached $100.7 billion, rising from $375 million in 1987. In the process, the share of Taiwan's total FDI outflow stock to the United States dropped from 62.2% in 1987 to 7.6% in 2006, while that to East Asia increasing rapidly from 4.0% to 64.6% over the same period. Most importantly, Taiwan's dramatic jump in investment in China since the late 1980s is overwhelmingly responsible for the sharp increase in Taiwanese FDI outflows to East Asia. Of Taiwan's total FDI outflow stock by the end of 2006, China alone took 54.5% ($54.9 billion), surpassing British Central America, which received the second largest amount of Taiwanese outward FDI ($18.5 billion or 18.3%), by a wide margin.[6] Although relatively small compared to those of Hong Kong and Taiwan, South Korea's outward FDI has also grown rapidly. Between 1985 and 1990, South Korean total FDI abroad rose 26 times, from $31 million to $821 million.[7] By 1998, the total stock of South Korean FDI outflows had reached $20.3 billion, of which $5.0 billion, accounting for 24.7%, was in East Asia. Notably, like those of Japan, Hong Kong, and Taiwan, South Korean investment in East Asia concentrated in China, which took about $4.0 billion (80%).[8] By the end of 2003, the total stock of South Korea's actual FDI in China had reached $8.0 billion.[9] As the largest recipient of FDI in the region, China has also heavily invested in Hong Kong. By the end of 2003, the stock of China's FDI in Hong Kong had reached $98.9 billion, accounting for 26.0% of total FDI in Hong Kong, which made China the largest source of inward FDI in Hong Kong if tax-haven economies of British Virgin Islands were excluded.[10] As a result of intraregional FDI flows, the FDI that originated in the region itself has become a major source of FDI in East Asia today (excluding FDI in Japan).

Behind the quantitative data of growing economic ties, what is significant is the qualitative nature of the economic relationships that has developed in East Asia since the mid-1980s. Notably, the ongoing economic integration in East Asia differs significantly from that in Western Europe and North America. As two institutionalized regional economic groupings, the EU and NAFTA have sought to create a single common market, designed to enhance the free movement of goods and production factors to the mutual advantage of their members. By contrast, the growing economic ties in East Asia are the result of changing comparative advantages between the economies in the region and are closely related to the economic restructuring in both capital-exporting and -importing economies with FDI serving as a bridge. Through regionalization of manufacturing production, which is accompanied by rapidly increasing flows of capital, trade and technology transfer, a network of multiple division of labor and commodity chains has been established in East Asia, based on comparative advantages among the economies with different resource endowments and levels of development. In this network of economic ties, Japan is playing a leading role as a major supplier of capital, technology, and advanced products as well as a significant market for raw materials and consumer goods; East Asian NIEs are an important base for industry, finance, and trade, an important supplier of intermediate equipment and products, and a major consumer of raw materials; China serves as a major recipient of FDI, a supplier of raw materials, and a growingly important market for manufactured products. This complementarity of economic ties suggests that all stand to benefit from greater economic integration. The result is that national borders in East Asia, though still real and important, are becoming increasingly porous with the movement of capital relatively free of constraints.[11] According to Edward Lincoln, FDI is more significant than foreign trade in terms of the depth of external ties. Merchandise trade, which is conducted primarily through a limited number of general trading companies, requires relatively little economic intimacy between trading nations or societies and minimum knowledge of foreign cultures, political systems, and other social aspects. On the contrary, FDI, through direct management of a subsidiary in a foreign country, requires closer personal contacts and better understanding of local culture, legal, and political systems.[12] As such, FDI involves closer commitment and afford greater influence than generally are involved in and derived from trading relations.[13] It is in this sense that increasing FDI flows among East Asian economies imply much closer economic integration than the simple statistics may suggest.

While multinational corporations of Japan and NIEs are the driving force behind the flow of regional FDI and the region's increasing integration, Japanese FDI is central to this process. Rapid economic growth and location advantages constitute major attractions of the East Asian economies for Japanese companies. The location advantage includes, among other things, the use of local low-cost and skilled labor, higher profitability of FDI in this region compared to the rest of the world, and progressively (South Korea, Taiwan, China) or thoroughly (Hong Kong) liberalized FDI regimes. Unlike Japanese FDI in third world countries during the 1970s and early 1980s that was heavily concentrated in the natural resource sector, the expansion of Japanese FDI in East Asia since the mid-1980s has primarily been in the manufacturing sector. The result is the expansion of regional division of labor and increasing regional economic integration centered on Japan. Hong Kong, Taiwan, and South Korea have also been promoting the process of regional integration through FDI outflows. While facing the challenge of upgrading their economic structures, these economies are not only receiving Japanese FDI in more advanced industries and service sectors but moving their labor- and land-intensive industries offshore to China through FDI, thus creating a new layer of division of labor in East Asia. This development is particularly manifested in the economic integration of Hong Kong, Taiwan, South Korea, and Japan with geographically adjacent coastal areas of China, linking comparative advantages of adjacent territories in these economies into a dynamic network of regional division of labor.

Indeed, economic integration of this kind resembles the historical flying geese pattern that linked Korea and Taiwan to the metropolitan economy of Japan during the Japanese colonial period. In the postwar years, the economic relationship of the flying geese type revived between Japan on the one hand and South Korea and Taiwan on the other, although under transformed regional and global conditions. Since the mid-1980s, this Japan-centered vertical economic integration in East Asia has expanded to involve China (and ASEAN in a broader sense) with South Korea, Taiwan, and Hong Kong playing an intermediate role between Japan and China. The rapid growth of South Korean, Taiwanese, and Hong Kong investments in China is largely the result of the ongoing structural changes in these three economies, required by changing domestic and international economic conditions – that is, the loss of competitiveness of labor-intensive industries due to the rising domestic labor costs and the emergence of new producers in other regions where labor costs were much lower. As part of this restructuring process, South Korea, Taiwan, and Hong Kong have moved labor-intensive as well as heavily polluting industries into China. On the part of China, investments from South Korea, Taiwan, and Hong Kong have provided mid-level technology and management, both of which seem more suited to a large part of the Chinese economy than, say, investments from Japan. More important, FDI inflows have brought China technology, capital, managerial and marketing know-how, employment creation, and trade growth, and this could eventually lead to changes in the comparative advantages of China's own industries.

Obviously, the flying geese integration has placed Japan in a superior position *vis-à-vis* its neighboring economies. Japan clearly dominates the trade and investment structure of East Asia through a pattern of production structures that has vertically integrated other economies with the Japanese economy over time. Consequently, over the postwar years Japan has gradually replaced the United States as No.1 economic hegemon in the region, and became the dominant economic power in almost all economic fields in East Asian economies. While other economies in East Asia enjoy huge trade surpluses with the United States and Western Europe, they all have huge trade deficits with Japan. Accordingly, Japan plays a leading and critical role in the ongoing economic integration in East Asia.

On the other hand, however, unlike many other third world areas that are locked in a permanent subordinate position in their rigid vertical integration with the West, South Korea, Taiwan, and Hong Kong have been able to improve their respective positions in the vertical relationship of flying geese type in East Asia. Consequently, there has been gradually increasing horizontal trade between Japan and these NIEs. In the meantime, South Korea, Taiwan, and Hong Kong are now playing an intermediate role in this triangular network of vertical economic links, having growing investment in China and Southeast Asian countries. Although China is further behind in the flying geese formation, it has much leeway in the regional division of labor, given its economic size, abundant resources, huge domestic market, and comprehensive economic structure. Thus, the newly emerging division of labor in the region could progressively become more horizontal and equitable in the long run. The flying geese integration, at least in the case of East Asia, seems to represent a relatively complementary and dynamic economic relationship, or a relationship of positive interdependence, though somewhat unbalanced. Clearly, the growing economic ties in East Asia have contributed to the region's prosperity and competitiveness in the world economy. All these economies in the region have obtained benefits from such regional economic relationships.

8.2   Regional economic integration in East Asia: dynamics and constraints

The growing economic integration in East Asia, based on the intensifying flow of economic interaction across ideological–political boundaries, is an autonomous economic process primarily driven by market forces and spearheaded by business rather than the creation of government planning. In fact, throughout East Asia the areas of successful growth are those where economics overrides politics, and where the pace of development is more rapid than governments could deal with. With the increasingly evident enormous success and advantages of this growing interdependence, the governments of Japan, South Korea, Taiwan, and China are now facilitating their development. Consequently, multinational corporations in concert with their respective governments are, attendant to the pursuit of their larger economic objectives, systematically promoting expansion of division of labor and integration of production in East Asia. Thus, an autonomous economic process and policy cooperation are mutually reinforcing.

The market forces driving the growing integration in East Asia are from both without and within. In the first place, growing protectionism and a tendency toward trade blocs in North America and Western Europe has raised serious concerns in East Asia about the continued openness of these two major markets, which have absorbed by far a major part of manufacturing products of East Asian economies. As a result, the regional markets, especially the potential huge Chinese market, are becoming increasingly attractive to the economies in the region. It is in this sense that the growing economic integration among East Asian economies, strategically, would provide a secure alternative outlet for their exports and lessen their dependence on increasingly protected North American and Western European markets, and, technically, could provide opportunities for solving East Asia's intractable economic frictions with the United States and Western Europe.

On the other hand, domestic economic conditions in East Asia have substantially changed following the fast economic growth. The rising labor shortage, growing labor costs, escalating land prices, and strict environmental controls have caused growing production costs and an increasingly difficult operating environment first in Japan and then in South Korea, Taiwan, and Hong Kong. Besides, as Japan, South Korea, Taiwan, and Hong Kong are all moving to their respective new levels of sophistication in terms of technology and value-added products, it becomes imperative for the companies in these economies to relocate their labor-intensive and low value-added industries abroad. As a natural process, the economic forces steadily drive the economic activities across national boundaries to areas of less-expensive land and labor to maintain competitiveness and growth. Furthermore, the steadily appreciating currencies of these economies make acquisition of foreign assets both desirable and less expensive, while continued huge trade surpluses allow the funding of foreign investment. In the last analysis, South Korea, Taiwan, and Hong Kong, like other small industrial nations with limited domestic market capacity, share their "small economy problem" and could find solutions only through trade and investment abroad. In a different situation, China, with plentiful land and labor but short of capital and technologically immature, is facing an increasing need for capital for its modernization and reform programs. All these make the economic relationships among East Asian economies overwhelmingly complementary with their different resource endowments and levels of development. Logically, there is a strong economic rationale for growing economic ties among the economies in the region.

Thus, growing economic integration in East Asia can be viewed as a defensive measure against external imperatives as well as an inevitable necessity with their internal economic development. The growing intraregional trade and FDI flows since the mid-1980s have all been subject to these economic forces. Indeed, either as a diplomatic means or as a policy objective, economics is evidently playing an increasingly important role in shaping international relations in East Asia. As political situation in many third world countries is volatile and economic protectionism in Western industrial countries is growing, Japan has learned to appreciate, even more than before, the value of closer economic ties with its neighboring economies. Japan desperately needs markets and resources; the neighboring economies in the region, with growing purchasing power, could make a sizeable and growing market for Japanese products, and increasing exports of Chinese raw materials could meet some of Japan's resource needs. Japanese surplus capital also needs to find profitable outlets, and, again, these economies are considered as ideal places for investment with their cheaper and increasingly sophisticated labor force. Although the political considerations are largely behind the transformed relations between China and Taiwan and between China and South Korea, economic imperatives are obviously an important reason in both cases. Particularly important, the issue of unification between China and Taiwan has always been considered in political and nationalistic terms in the past. However, it is now also increasingly viewed in an economic perspective on both sides. As geoeconomics gains in importance, both China and Taiwan are looking upon each other increasingly in economic terms. In a world of economic warfare, Taiwan might show more positive interest in a closer relationship with the mainland. The island would be at a disadvantage scrambling for Earth's depleting natural resources in competition with other resource-dependent economies and members of closed trading blocs, such as Western Europe and North America. Closer relationship with the mainland would offer Taiwan access to badly needed resources and a vast potential market. Likewise, the normalization of diplomatic relations between China and South Korea was also largely motivated by economic needs on both sides – South Korea's capital and technology needed by China and Chinese cheap labor and land, resources, and market needed by South Korea. No doubt, growing economic ties in East Asia are deeply rooted in this economic necessity.

As the most significant driving force, Japan is both directly and indirectly associated with the process of economic integration in East Asia. Through the flying geese mechanism, the process of Japanese investment and concomitant trade has had a profound influence on the economic development of South Korea, Taiwan, and Hong Kong. This chain of influence is now extending downward to encompass China. Japanese companies have located or relocated manufacturing operations throughout East Asia to reduce costs, further domestic economic restructuring, protect against the vagaries of other countries' market-access policies, deal with fluctuating exchange rates, and hedge against the possible consequences of regionalist tendencies elsewhere. Japanese investment has played a crucial role in linking the Japanese economy and other economies in East Asia. Through the relocation of manufacturing production offshore, Japanese FDI has stimulated a process of industrial restructuring both in Japan and in the recipient economies in the region. More significant, as part of this process, some of the Japanese industries have not only relocated production abroad but also increased sales back to Japan. Traditionally, Japanese foreign investment in manufacturing was intended to supply either local markets or third markets and not to manufacture products for shipment back to Japan. The shift is a further indication of Japan's deepening integration with other economies in the region.

While East Asia is moving toward regional economic integration, it has so far not been organized into a formal regional grouping like the EU or NAFTA. The regional integration in East Asia is still uninstitutionalized, not discriminatory against the economies outside the region. This very nature of regional economic integration in East Asia is the result of the interactions of internal conditions in East Asia and the region's external linkages. There are political, historical, cultural, ideological, and structural factors in play, both pushing and hindering the process toward institutionalized integration in the region. Obviously, the following five major factors function to promote regional integration and even the formation of a regional grouping in East Asia.

First of all, the East Asian states have mutual interests in keeping a stable political environment in the region for continued fast economic growth, as economic development is top on the national agenda for all governments today. Moreover, in the past several decades, extensive economic ties have been established among the economies in East Asia to the extent that no government can afford any disruption of these ties. On the contrary, the force of inertia is working for continuing deepening of these ties.

Secondly, the economies in East Asia are complementary in terms of production factor endowments and economic structures. They can offer the entire gamut of technological layers, ranging from labor-intensive to knowledge-intensive production and processing systems. While Japan possesses capital and the most sophisticated processing technologies, South Korea, Taiwan, and Hong Kong possess capital and mid-level production and processing technologies. With its abundant human and natural resources and huge market potential, China can provide relatively cheap labor and land and serve as important markets for both capital and consumer goods. Thus, East Asian economies are sufficiently complementary and, in the case of a crisis, they could easily secure technology, capital, labor, and resources from each other with an almost total disregard for the rest of the industrialized world.

Thirdly, in the process of growing economic interactions in the region, there have been an increasing number of issues that have to be dealt with effectively on a collective basis. Two such issues of critical importance relating to economic relations in East Asia, for example, are the need for periodic adjustment of exchange rates and additional means of rectifying persistent trade imbalances. The emergence of several integrated economic subregions along the Chinese coast involves issues of jurisdiction and control, which also require collaboration among the governments involved. There are also noneconomic issues that have to be handled at the supranational level, such as environmental protection, energy security, illegal immigration, smuggling and other crimes, and so forth. Most recently, the need to check the rapid spread of SARS and bird flu further indicates the importance of closer cooperation and policy coordination among regional governments.

Fourthly, the geographical proximity among East Asian economies provides tremendous cost advantages in moving goods and services as well as encouraging technological exchange and direct investment in neighboring economies. It is not accidental that the most integrated subregions are precisely adjacent areas between economies, as is seen in Southern China integrated with Hong Kong and Taiwan and in Northern China incorporated with South Korea and Japan.

Finally, the peoples of East Asia have long shared, in varying degrees, the common cultural tradition – Confucianism, Daoism and Buddhism – as a unifying force. In some subregions there are also ethnic ties and linguistic affinities as a stimulus, such as those between Taiwan, Hong Kong, and Southern China, and to a less extent between South Korea and Northern China. These kinship ties are a contributing factor in economic integration in the subregions involved. Moreover, there is a growing sense of regional consciousness, identity, and mutual interests in East Asia, which becomes an increasingly important force to unify the region.

While the unifying forces are strong, however, there are major obstacles that work against more institutionalized regional integration in East Asia. In the first place, despite growing regional economic ties, the role of economics in East Asia is still largely defined within the existing framework of political relationships among the players involved, and *low politics* is still generally subordinated to *high politics*. Because of the diversity in ideology and socio-political and economic system, deep mutual political understanding and trust have not yet been fully built up among East Asian governments. There also remain regional issues of a political-strategic nature, such as the politically sensitive issues of the divided states (two-Korea division and China–Taiwan division), unresolved territorial issues (the Senkaku or Chiaoyutai atolls contested by Japan, China, and Taiwan), and some jurisdictional issues pertaining to the Sea of Japan, a name that the Koreans refuse to accept. Moreover, there are few signs that the East Asian states themselves are reducing their armaments, and the danger of military confrontation still exists on the Korean peninsula (where more than one and a half million troops are under arms with the DMZ remaining as one of the most hostile borders in the world today), and across the Taiwan Straits. With the increasing attention of the United States to domestic concerns in the post-Cold War era and to the war against international terrorism in the post-11 September period, these regional political and security issues have become all the more projective. It is in this sense that expanding economic cooperation and prosperity in the region would have a serious bearing on the maintenance of peace and stability and on the creation of a peaceful political environment in the entire East Asian region. Moreover, strong nationalist sentiments, stemming from attitudes of resistance to foreign powers, also work against institutionalized regional integration dominated by regional powers.

As far as economics is concerned, East Asian economies are still externally oriented as evident in the high ratio of trade in their GDP, and their fast economic growth is closely related to their external ties. East Asia remains heavily dependent on trade outside the region, especially export markets in North America and Western Europe and energy and resource supplies from the Middle East, Australia, and the Americas. As recent as 2003, there was still 40.1% of Japanese exports going to the United States and EU-15 (24.8% to the US and 15.3% to EU-15). For South Korea, Taiwan, Hong Kong, and China, the share of exports destined for the United States and EU-15 for 2003 was still 30.7% (17.8% for the US and 12.9 for EU-15), 30.9% (18.0% for the US and 12.9% for EU-15), 32.0% (18.7% for the US and 13.3% for EU-15), and 37.6% (21.1% for the US and 16.5% for EU-15) respectively. In particular, although the importance of the United States as a market relative to regional markets in East Asia has declined, it was nevertheless still the single most important market for Japan and China and the second largest market for South Korea, Taiwan, and Hong Kong in 2003, and will remain a vital market for the indefinite future.[14] As such, without access to global markets – the US and EU markets in particular – the opportunities for economic dynamism of East

Asian economies would be severely constrained. This linkage of external economic ties is clearly a big constraint on the formation of any closed regional grouping in East Asia.

Furthermore, there are persistent bitter memories in East Asia of wartime Japanese atrocities and exploitation and Japan's disastrous attempt to create a Greater East Asia Co-prosperity Sphere during the 1930s and early 1940s. There is also much concern about a militarily resurgent Japan. In the meantime, Japanese economic hegemony has stimulated region-wide concern about each economy's dependence on Japan for its most important trade and investment relations. This, together with the growing trade deficit with Japan, concerns other economies in the region. Although South Korea, Taiwan, Hong Kong, and China are developing greater economic strength, they are not yet sufficiently strong to cooperate – or compete – on equal terms with Japan in any possible regional grouping. As such, they would be wary of entering into too close association with Japan, for political and psychological as well as economic reasons. Japan and others, however, are concerned about a China that might manage to combine its growing economic power with political cohesion in such a fashion as to reach genuine military power. Largely because of these concerns, continued US strategic presence in the region is still strongly supported by most East Asian states as essential for the region's security and for balancing the regional powers, particularly Japan and China. This is not because the United States is the most loved, but because it is the least feared. With dependence on the United States for security and balance of power in the region, it is therefore unlikely that a closed regional grouping would easily develop in East Asia.

Obviously, competing forces are pushing East Asia in opposite directions. On the one hand, the mounting protectionism and emerging regionalism in Western Europe and North America and the difficulties in the maintenance of multilateralism through the WTO system, together with the increasingly self-confident recognition of an almost limitless potential for intraregional trade and economic cooperation in the region, make it essential and desirable for the region to devise a mechanism (or institution) to increase economic cooperation on a constant basis within East Asia. In the meantime, a kind of interdependent relationship has developed with an extensive network of ties being established in East Asia over the past two decades. East Asian states are therefore more and more motivated to develop close economic ties among them for practical reasons. The relaxed political atmosphere that began to emerge in the 1980s has strengthened this trend. The existence of these conditions has created a favorable environment, and even incentive, for institutionalized regional cooperation in East Asia. On the other hand, however, due to the heterogeneity of interests and motives among the states, it is difficult for East Asian governments to come together in pursuit of some common goals, namely, the formation of a formal regional grouping. For such a regional body to work, it usually requires a political commitment to dilute national sovereignty in favor of broader regional politics (though this commitment can sometimes be weak, as in the case of the European Free Trade Association (EFTA) and NAFTA). In addition, the continuing dependence of East Asian economies on external markets and US military presence further hinder the likelihood of an exclusive regional grouping. The dynamic interactions of both favorable and unfavorable conditions have therefore brought about uninstitutionalized regional integration in East Asia short of establishment of a formal regional grouping.

In a further analysis, largely due to their different stages of economic development and different positions in the world economy, the East Asian economies are pursuing diverse policy objectives. These differences in policy objectives may also explain their respective attitudes toward growing economic ties in the region. The nature of Japan's relations with the United States and Europe is an important factor affecting Japan's choice of foreign policy options. Economic forces and values almost certainly push Japan in the direction of multilateralism. As such, Tokyo always stresses that, despite its major commitment to investment and rapidly growing trade in the region, Japan is playing no favorites. However, the constant fear of being rejected by the West and forced to "change Japanese culture" (pressures from the West to share more burdens in both economics and politics/security) can strengthen the forces of going regional. This scenario is similar to that of London that insisted on its special relationship with Washington when joining the EEC that would build closer ties between Britain and its continental neighbors. Under such circumstances, there is also a growingly strong regionalist sentiment in Japan. On the part of other East Asian economies, while they have strong desire to maintain close economic ties with Japan, they are surely to resist a Japan-dominated regional economic bloc for historical, political, economic, and psychological reasons. As such, it is, ironically, perhaps only a Japan that is closely associated with the West that would be acceptable as a partner to its neighbors in the region.

Difference in policy objectives may also explain why there has been little consensus among economies in East Asia as to the nature and scope of multilateral economic cooperation in the region. Japan seems to envisage regional cooperation in a much broader and longer-term framework of vertical and horizontal division of labor among East Asian economies as a possible means to protect Japan's economic supremacy from economic blocs of Western Europe and North America. By contrast, China tends to view it as the participation of regional economies in regional development projects. South Korea, Taiwan, and Hong Kong tend to view regional cooperation as a way to expand their export market. Although these views might not be mutually exclusive in the longer run with the gradual deepening of economic cooperation in the region, they cannot be easily compromised.

Despite these constraints, however, the Asian financial crisis of 1997–98 forced government and business leaders as well as academics across the region to rethink the issue of institutionalized regional integration.

8.3   Moves toward a regional economic grouping in East Asia in the wake of the Asian financial crisis

The crisis that started in Thailand in July 1997 was originally a financial crisis, characterized by sharp depreciation of currencies, plummeting asset values, dramatic drop of stock prices, and huge capital outflows. However, it soon deteriorated into an overall region-wide economic crisis and rapidly spread to East Asia, hitting the economies in the region severely, South Korea in particular. As the most serious economic crisis in East Asia in terms of scope, depth, and nature ever since the end of World War II, the Asian financial and economic crisis thus became a major milestone in the economic transformation in East Asia. Particularly, the Asian financial crisis stimulated rethinking of the issue of institutionalized regional economic cooperation among political leaders, businesses, and academics in the region.

While the causes of the Asian financial crisis are seen as multidimensional at both domestic and global levels, the lack of a regional mechanism for close economic policy coordination and cooperation among the governments in the region is widely cited as being responsible for so rapid spread of a crisis unchecked across the region in such a magnitude. This bitter experience not only further proves that economies in the region are now so closely interdependent, but also tells how greatly East Asian economies are exposed, vulnerable, and even fragile to an economic crisis that originates in a neighboring economy. As a consequence, there has been a dramatic change in thinking among political and business leaders in East Asia with a growing realization of urgent need for the creation of a formal regional mechanism to deal with a similar crisis in the future and to maintain the economic growth of the region. It is in this sense that the Asian financial crisis has created an imperative that has significantly transformed the political economy of East Asia, thus laying new background for regional economic cooperation in East Asia.[15]

In a further analysis, the nature and magnitude of trade links in the region were probably more significant mechanisms for the region-wide contagion of the Asian financial crisis than "competitive" currency devaluations. According to a 1998 World Bank report, *East Asia: The Road to Recovery*, intraregional exports among East Asian and Southeast Asian countries accounted for almost 40% of total exports in 1996, up from 32% in 1990. If Japan was included, the figure rose to 50%. These high levels of intraregional trade reflect a process of specialization and outsourcing of activities from the more advanced to the lower income countries in the region. About three-fourths of the intraregional trade is in raw materials, intermediate inputs, and capital equipment, which accounts for more than 50% of the total East Asian imports of these products. Such trade complementarity probably increased the speed and directness of the contagion across the region.[16]

Under such circumstances, the Asian financial crisis created an imperative for East Asian governments to establish a more systematic mechanism for regional cooperation and policy coordination. Consequently, government and business leaders in the region were increasingly serious about the issue of regional institution-building in the wake of the Asian financial crisis, a development that dramatically deviated from the past attitudes of both governments and business leaders in the region. While proposals were made in launching a single Asian currency and other regional financial reforms, there was more serious discussion and proposals across the region for the formation of official regional arrangements in the trade area, as this was a relatively simpler area for regional cooperation to start with. In this respect, Japan was most active, in sharp contrast to its past official position regarding regional economic arrangements. The first such move came from Kazuo Ogura, Japanese ambassador to South Korea, in mid-September 1998, when he openly called for the establishment of a trade alliance between Japan and South Korea as opposed to economic blocs in the West. This was the first time ever that a senior Japanese official had made such a proposal in public.[17] On 20 March 1999, during his visit to Seoul, Japanese Prime Minister Keizo Obuchi in his address at Korea University further urged that Japan and South Korea take a leading role in creating a free trade zone in East Asia that stands on par with the EU.[18]

A more significant move came on 21 May 1999, when Japan's famed MITI formally proposed in its annual report on trade that Japan takes the lead to pursue a regional trade bloc in East Asia. The proposed trade bloc would encompass Japan, South Korea, Hong Kong, and Taiwan. The new regional arrangement was envisioned to counteract such economic groupings as the EU and NAFTA. In addition, the MITI asked the government to take a step beyond building an economic bloc. "We should not only pursue a limited economic grouping such as a free trade zone or tariff pact, but also activate human exchanges and promote mutual understanding," the report states. The report also notes that the Japanese economy must break out of the current recession for Asia to stage an export-led recovery and to get back on the road to coherent economic development again.[19]

Although the South Korean government initially responded to Japan's proposal with some hesitation, largely for fear of the Japanese dominance in such a trade bloc due to the huge gap in economic strength and industrial structure between the two countries, Seoul soon started talks with Tokyo on the proposed bilateral free trade agreement (FTA) at both government and private levels. As a concrete step, several government and private research institutes in both Japan and South Korea began research projects concerning various specific aspects of an FTA between the two countries.[20] After 5 years of joint studies on the issue, in October 2003 Japan and South Korea formally decided to launch an official negotiation on a bilateral FTA.

While Beijing was initially quite cautious on any such regional free trade arrangements for political, economic, and psychological reasons, it soon became quite positive in pursuing an FTA with Japan and South Korea.[21] Chinese officials openly called for an FTA with Japan in several occasions. On 18 May 2005, Chinese Vice Premier Wu Yi explicitly called for a Chinese–Japanese FTA in a speech at the 50th anniversary of Japan's East Sea Japanese–Chinese Trade Center in Nagoya, Japan.[22] On the Japanese side, a report prepared by the Economic and Social Research Institute, a think tank affiliated with the Japanese Cabinet, is very positive about a Japanese–Chinese FTA, concluding that an FTA with China, compared to similar FTAs with other countries, would bring Japan the most benefits by raising Japan's GDP by 0.5%.[23] Despite this, however, Tokyo is still quite hesitant about such a move toward a Japanese–Chinese FTA at the moment, wary of rising Chinese influence with its growing economic power.

While the movement toward a Chinese–Japanese FTA remained stagnant, China and South Korea achieved quite some success in moving toward a bilateral FTA. Following several years of preliminary studies of the issue on both sides, Chinese President Hu Jintao and South Korean

President Roh Moo-hyun reached an agreement on joint research on a Chinese–South Korean FTA during the APEC summit held in Santiago, Chile in November 2004. The decision made by the political leaders of the two countries soon materialized when the government think thanks of both countries – the Development Research Center of the State Council of the PRC and the Korea Institute for International Economic Policy–formally launched joint feasibility study of a Chinese–South Korean FTA on 20 March 2005. As this research project is sponsored and financed by both governments, it is widely seen as a prelude of formal government negotiations between the two countries.[24] Obviously, a Chinese–South Korean FTA, if signed, would provide stimulus for a similar arrangement between China and Japan.

While efforts were made at bilateral FTAs in East Asia in the wake of the Asian financial crisis, at Japanese Prime Minister Obuchi's initiative, Japan, China, and South Korea held an unprecedented tripartite summit on 27 November 1999 on the sidelines of the ASEAN Plus Three meeting in Manila. The tripartite agreement reached from this summit committed the three countries to a joint research forum to seek ways of institutionalizing economic cooperation among them. Under the agreement, the three leaders designated their respective think tanks to work out concrete steps to boost trilateral economic cooperation and identify ten target sectors for such cooperation, including commerce, customs, maritime, environmental, and fisheries sectors. In view of the absence of formal regional dialogue or consultative bodies in East Asia, this Manila tripartite summit was therefore seen as historic.[25] In the following year, the tripartite summit was formally institutionalized and became regular. Moreover, as concrete steps of institutionalized trilateral cooperation, seven functional bodies at the ministerial level were formally established to pursue trilateral cooperation and policy coordination in specific areas.

Mostly significantly, at the fifth tripartite summit held in Bali, Indonesia on 7 October 2003, the leaders of the three countries signed a historical document for the promotion of tripartite cooperation in regional and global affairs in the 21st century, "The Joint Declaration on the Promotion of Tripartite Cooperation among the People's Republic of China, Japan and the Republic of Korea." In the meantime, the Three-Party Committee was established, headed by foreign ministers, to study, plan, coordinate, and monitor cooperation activities. The joint study conducted by the think tanks of the three countries submitted to the tripartite summit a report and policy proposal on the feasibility of a trilateral FTA with the conclusion that a trilateral FTA would bring substantial macroeconomic effects favorable to the three countries. In 2004, the joint study group started a sector-oriented study of the economic effect of a tripartite FTA on such specific sectors as agriculture, electric machinery manufacturing, and automobile.

During the sixth tripartite summit in Vientiane, Laos on 29 November 2004, the leaders of the three countries endorsed two important documents that had been adopted by the Three-Party Committee on 27 November 2004, "The Action Strategy on Trilateral Cooperation among the People's Republic of China, Japan and the Republic of Korea" and "The Progress Report of the Trilateral Cooperation among the People's Republic of China, Japan and the Republic of Korea." The Action Strategy outlines the strategic direction of the trilateral cooperation in the future, while the Progress Report summarizes the progress of the trilateral cooperation since the adoption of the Joint Declaration in 2003. During the 2004 tripartite summit, while Japanese Prime Minister Junichiro Koizumi called for deepening discussions of an East Asian trilateral FTA at the academic level, Chinese Premier Wen Jiabao emphasized the need to accelerate the work to realize a trilateral FTA. Moreover, Japan stressed the need to further develop a legal framework of investment among the three countries and construct a stable business environment.[26] By 20 November 2007, eight such tripartite summits had been held.

During the third tripartite meeting of the Three-Party Committee held in Kyoto, Japan on 7 May 2005, the foreign ministers of Japan, China, and South Korea reiterated their commitment to continuing study of creating a trilateral free trade zone and agreed to explore a legal framework for investment, to improve business environment and to strengthen cooperation on the energy area among the three countries.[27]

It is also important to note that the moves of the regional governments in the wake of the Asian financial crisis were soon endorsed and supported by business leaders in East Asia, particularly in Japan and South Korea. At the 15th annual meeting between the Federation of Korean Industries (FKI) and the Japan Federation of Economic Organization (keidanren) held in Tokyo in October 1998, the business leaders of the two countries decided to push to set up the so-called "Korea–Japan–China industrial cooperation committee" in an effort to help ease overcapacity and overinvestment problems among regional firms. According to the joint statement released after the meeting, both Japanese and Korean business leaders shared the view that the time was ripe for Japan, Korea, and China to discuss a trilateral free trade zone to further stimulate trade and industrial cooperation in the region. As an initial move toward the trilateral free trade zone, the business leaders agreed to launch joint research on the economic effects of the proposed Korea–Japan free trade zone. Then they would study the possibility of expanding the free trade zone to include China in the longer term.[28]

Again, in early May 1999 business leaders from Japan, South Korea, China, and other economies in the region participated in a regional forum in Seoul and announced a plan to establish an organization to promote economic cooperation in East Asia and stabilize the region's economy. They agreed that East Asian countries need an organization similar to ASEAN to address issues of common interests and to develop efforts to cope with financial crises, eliminate excess industrial capacity, and boost technology transfer. The envisioned regional body would focus on stabilizing member countries' financial systems and preventing the recurrence of a financial crisis.[29] One month later, business leaders from Japan, South Korea, and China met again in Seoul to finalize the plan of setting up a permanent consultative body among them in the following month. The top agenda for the proposed organization included stabilization of Asian currencies, adoption of measures to prevent recurrence of a financial crisis, setting-up of a free trade zone and capital market within the zone, and elimination of excess production capacity.[30] In June 2002, South Korean business leaders further proposed the formation of a joint economic policy coordination body among South Korea, China, and Japan as a preparatory move toward establishing an East Asian free trade zone.[31]

Obviously, as a direct consequence of the Asian financial crisis, these are the most unequivocal moves that government and business leaders in East Asia have ever taken in pushing the establishment of a regional economic grouping, dramatically deviating from the past attitudes of both governments and business leaders in the region.

While Japan, South Korea, and China have taken concrete steps to move toward the creation of a free trade zone in East Asia in the wake of the Asian financial crisis, some fundamental conditions in the region, especially political conditions, remain largely unchanged. Under such circumstances, successful formation of an East Asian regional grouping would depend on how well the following three major obstacles could be circumvented or even overcome.

The first major obstacle seems to be the lack of political trust between the two major regional powers, China and Japan. As is shown in the integration process of Western Europe, cooperation between regional powers is usually the key to a successful regional grouping. It is true that when Western Europe was first set on the track of regional integration, similar mistrust did exist between France and Germany. However, this

Franco-German mistrust was largely subdued in their common concern over an immediate threat to their national security from the Soviet Union in the context of Cold War politics, and was later gradually diluted in the process of Western European integration. When this common security threat disappeared with the end of the Cold War and the breakup of the Soviet Union in the late 1980s and early 1990s, a well-functioning regional mechanism had already been firmly established in Western Europe, tightly binding the two countries in a new cause of defending their common interests in the face of growing economic competition from other regions. By contrast, the mistrust between China and Japan, which has derived from both bitter historical experience and current regional politics, is always real, and more often than not constitutes a top concern in the formulation of respective foreign policies of both countries, especially in the post-Cold War era. It is in this sense that it would be a challenging and difficult task for China and Japan to establish political trust between them, the trust that is so essential for a regional grouping to be successful. In a similar fashion, there must also be political trust among all the participants with diversified national interests if a regional grouping is going to be successful. This is because any effective institutionalized regional cooperation would inevitably require political commitment to dilute national sovereignty in favor of broader regional goals, although this commitment can sometimes be weak, as in the case of the EFTA and NAFTA.

A second major obstacle is America's opposition to the formation of a regional grouping in East Asia, in contrast to Washington's early strong encouragement of the European integration due to its geopolitical and strategic considerations at the time. Having a huge economic stake in the dynamic East Asian region, Washington has long been suspicious of any regionalist scheme in East Asia that might harm its own economic interests there. As such, the United States has always tried to put economic relations in East Asia within the framework of APEC, through which US influence over economic affairs in the region could be maximized. Washington's strong opposition to Asia's proposal for creation of an Asian Monetary Fund (AMF) is an indication of Washington's attitude toward the issue of an Asian economic grouping.[32] As the United States still has profound influence on political, security, and economic matters in the region, East Asian governments had to compromise Washington's opposition should a regional grouping be successfully formed.

Even regional and international political factors aside, East Asian states are less experienced in multilateral negotiations on regional institution-building, contrary to Western Europe that has historically had comprehensive experience in institution-building in various areas. As institutionalized regional cooperation requires surrender of part of national sovereignty, which is politically very sensitive everywhere, functionalist institution-building skills with spill-over mechanism in full play are therefore highly crucial for a regional grouping to be successful. In this respect, politicians in East Asia particularly lack skills of effective bargaining and compromise in multilateral negotiations, as the political culture in oriental societies is traditionally prone to consensus rather than bargaining and compromise.

Despite these major obstacles, however, there are favorable conditions and strong forces in the context of the Asian financial crisis that might help circumvent or even overcome the obstacles mentioned above, thus pushing forward the creation of a regional grouping in East Asia.

In the first place, political relations in East Asia, although sometimes strained (particularly between Japan and its two neighbors, China and South Korea), are well managed by regional political leaders, who are generally quite rational. As all the states in the region have an immense stake in maintaining a stable and peaceful regional environment for economic growth and prosperity, the governments in East Asia have been making persistent and arduous efforts in improving their mutual understanding and political relations. This is well explained by the very fact that despite the lack of true political trust in the region, regional leaders have maintained multiple bilateral and multilateral dialogue channels for discussion, consultation, and cooperation. Particularly, the political leaders in the region deliberately make efforts to prevent their disagreements in the political area from affecting their policy coordination and cooperation in economic and other low politics areas.

Secondly, by the early 21st century, growing economic regionalism in the world economy has created a general important external imperative for East Asian economies. There are some 250 regional trade agreements that have been formally notified to the GATT/WTO up to December 2002, including 130 that were notified after the GATT was transformed into the WTO in January 1995, of which over 170 are currently in force. On top of that, 70 more that have not yet been notified are estimated to be operational. By the end of 2005, the total number of regional trade agreements approached 300 if those planned or already under negotiation are included.[33] As such, the vast majority of WTO members are affiliated with one or more such regional trade agreements. Consequently, about 97% of total global trade involves countries that are members of at least one regional trade arrangement, compared with 72% in 1990.[34] Particularly, of the three global economic centers, East Asia is the only region that is not yet formally organized into a grouping of any form, while Western Europe has been entrenched in the EU and North America has been formed into the NAFTA. What makes East Asia even more worrisome is the expansion of the EU to involve Eastern European countries in 2004 and the prospect of the enlargement of NAFTA to form a Free Trade Area of the Americas. Given the heavy dependence of East Asian economies on these two major markets and their outward-oriented development strategies, the intensifying regionalism in Europe and North America causes increasing fear among East Asian governments of the diversion of trade and investment flows. On the other hand, an East Asian regional FTA could bring substantial benefits to all the parties involved, as is shown in Table 8.5. Moreover, the EU and NAFTA not only form themselves into increasingly closed markets but also come to the bargaining table in multilateral trade negotiations as blocs. This leaves East Asian states frequently in a much weaker bargaining position in multilateral trade negotiations as individual negotiators. All this brings an unorganized East Asia a strong sense of exclusion and isolation in global economic competition. It is under such circumstances that East Asian governments have become more serious about pursuing an East Asian regional grouping in the wake of the Asian financial crisis.

Thirdly, the immature financial liberalization that the IMF and Washington pushed hard on East and Southeast Asian economies in the early 1990s is now widely believed as precipitating the 1997 Asian crisis.[35] As globalization proceeds, many forms of international capital flows have risen dramatically, including FDI, portfolio investment

Table 8.5 Balance Sheet for FTAs Involving South Korea, Japan, and China: GDP Growth (%) and Economic Gains ($ million)

	South Korea-China-Japan FTA		South Korea-China FTA		South Korea-Japan FTA		China-Japan FTA	
	GDP growth	Economic gains	GDP growth	Economic gains	GDP growth	Economic gains	GDP growth	Economic gains
South Korea	3.2	12,644.5	2.4	10,687.8	1.1	3682.8	−0.2	−1189.6
China	1.3	8,191.2	0.2	917.0	0.0	−358.0	1.1	7335.3
Japan	0.2	12,265.1	0.0	119.9	0.0	2184.7	0.2*	10,289.8

Source: Japanese Cabinet Secretariat, quoted in C. Moon and T. Kim, "South Korea's International Relations: Challenges to Developmental Realism," in S. S. Kim (ed.), *The International Relations of Northeast Asia* (Oxford: Rowman & Littlefield Publishers, Inc., 2004), p. 269.
* This estimated figure was obtained in early 2002. The Economic and Social Research Institute of the Japanese Cabinet raised this figure to 0.5% in early 2005. See the earlier discussion of this section.

through country funds, bank loans, bond lending, derivations (swaps, options, forward transactions), reinsurance, and other financial instruments. These unfettered financial flows from advanced to emerging markets had finally brought profound destabilization in East and Southeast Asia, causing a region-wide financial crisis. Once the Asian financial crisis set in, the IMF quickly interpreted it as a traditional balance of payments crisis brought about by government fiscal excesses and therefore suggested policy prescriptions that involved the usual remedies of fiscal and monetary contraction and high interest rates. Furthermore, to cope with the fundamental structural causes of the crisis, which the IMF ascribed to the Asian model, it recommended further financial liberalization together with far-reaching changes in basic social institutions.[36] All these Washington-backed IMF policy prescriptions, which were required under IMF rescue package, caused catastrophic economic and social consequences in the crisis-hit countries (although some of these policies were later modified somewhat after the serious negative consequences of IMF prescriptions were growingly revealed and criticism of the IMF was mounting). These Western-enforced, particularly US-enforced, policies together with Washington's strong opposition to the creation of the AMF, which was proposed in the early stage of the crisis by East and Southeast Asian countries to help bail out the crisis-hit economies and stop the further spread of the crisis, have strengthened what Richard Higgott calls the region's "resentment" of American dominance and therefore increased willingness of East and Southeast Asian countries to explore regional cooperative relationships that would help to weaken this American dominance in the political economy of the region.[37]

Fourthly, in the current round of efforts to form a formal regional grouping, regional leaders seem to be more pragmatic and creative in pursuing their objective. Both government and business leaders seem to be adopting a pragmatic strategy that is based on the approaches of functionalism and incrementalism. As political issues are still highly sensitive in East Asia, East Asian leaders seem to have started the process of regional grouping in the economic sphere, avoiding sensitive political issues at this initial stage. By this, East Asian governments have obviously followed the APEC formula, under which political issues are put aside so that political rivals, such as China versus Taiwan, can be involved in the same venture. In a similar fashion, this APEC formula may also enable Japan and China to cooperate on regional economic and other functional issues in a common regionalist scheme while keeping their disagreements on political issues for the time being. This is precisely the approach that has been adopted within the framework of the tripartite summit among Japan, China, and South Korea, which is conducted in an informal way with the discussion being purely confined to economic cooperation. Obviously, this pragmatic strategy will likely increase the chance of success in the eventual formation of a formal regional economic grouping in East Asia. Equally significant, it seems to be an effective strategy to start with bilateral FTAs first and then gradually transform them into a region-wide free trade grouping, involving all East Asian economies. This strategy would likely work because it is relatively easier to conclude a bilateral FTA than a multilateral one. Furthermore, once a trilateral FTA is formed among Japan, South Korea, and China, it would be possible to bring in Taiwan and Hong Kong on the basis of the model of the APEC and the WTO, which has well accommodated the membership of the three Chinese constituencies.

Finally, understanding that the official process of creating a regional grouping is usually quite slow, involving lengthy bargains and negotiations, the regional business community has started rolling the ball to find out those areas that are mutually beneficial for cooperation rather than passively wait until their governments have everything settled. By taking their own initiatives, the business community is therefore helping create a more favorable environment for their governments to speed up the process of regional institution-building.

No doubt, it is no easy job to have the existing formidable political and other obstacles in East Asia removed. Nevertheless, what is significant is that at the turn of the century the governments in the region have started the process of forming a formal regional economic grouping in East Asia. It seems that a formal East Asian economic bloc is not as unimaginable as it was in the past.

8.4   East Asia and Asia-pacific cooperation

The East Asian states' ongoing moves toward a regional grouping occur in a much broader context of the accelerating globalization since the 1980s, which has not only made national economies increasingly integrated through trade, finance, production, and a growing web of treaties and institutions, but also brought fundamental impact on economic growth, the distribution of income and wealth, patterns of trade and finance, and political institutions. As East Asian economies all heavily rely on the global economy for market, capital, technology and resources, the region is highly susceptible to the negative as well as positive effects of globalization. Especially, concurrent with the trend of globalization is the rising economic regionalism and protectionism in the world economy, Western Europe and North America in particular, which exerts mounting pressure on East Asia, the only major region that has not yet been organized into an economic grouping. It is within such a context that since the late 1980s East Asian governments have been searching for cross-Pacific economic cooperation within the framework of APEC. Because of political, economic, and historical factors in the region and because of the outward-oriented economic structures of East Asian economies, there is a dual fear that has persistently remained in the region – an internal fear of the region dominated regional powers and an external fear of the closing of the markets in the West in general and the US market in particular. As such, APEC is pursued by East and Southeast Asian governments as a useful umbrella to achieve their dual policy objective to balance the regional powers on the one hand and to serve as a guarantee for the continuation of free access to the North American market on the other. In the meantime, APEC is also viewed as an additional useful mechanism for constructing a more smooth economic relationship across the Pacific and resolving the protracted conflicts in the US–East Asian economic relationship. Moreover, APEC is seen by its members as a safe haven for their global connections in the face of the overbearing EU.[38]

Launched in 1989, APEC started as an informal dialogue group that links East and Southeast Asia with Oceania, North America, and South America. In its initial years, APEC largely focused on exchanges of views and project-based initiatives. The concerns simply were to advance the process of APEC and to promote a positive conclusion to the Uruguay Round of multilateral trade negotiations. A turning point came in 1993, when American President Clinton elevated APEC by inviting heads of state and government for an informal summit meeting in Seattle, during which the leaders envisioned APEC to be a community of Asia-Pacific economies and a flexible forum for promoting economic growth in the region. Since then, the annual APEC summit meetings have set the direction and pace of APEC's development, and APEC has become a primary regional vehicle for facilitating economic growth, cooperation, trade and investment in the Asia-Pacific region. Particularly significant is the annual session of Bogor, Indonesia in 1994, during which APEC leaders set a goal of free and open trade and investment in the Asia-Pacific by 2010 for developed member economies and 2020 for developing members. In the subsequent annual sessions, APEC leaders reiterated this goal of trade and investment liberalization, while at the same time promoting a range of other goals like business facilitation, economic and technological cooperation, human resources development, and sustainable and equitable development.

Most notably, in pursuing its declared objectives, APEC adheres to the principle of the so-called "open regionalism," that is, the promotion of regional economic integration without discrimination against nonmembers. In keeping with its overall philosophy of loose cooperation and open regionalism, APEC has few institutional structures and operates on the basis of nonbinding commitments, open dialogue, and equal respect for the views of all participants. Unlike the WTO or other multilateral trade bodies, APEC has no treaty obligations required of its members. Decisions made within APEC are reached by consensus, and commitments are undertaken on a voluntary basis. This unique structural and functional feature of APEC reflects the organization's effort to accommodate high diversities among its members in terms of economic structure, the level of economic development, political and economic system, ethnicity, culture, society, ideology, history, policy approaches, policy objectives, and views on regional cooperation. This forum is therefore different from such tightly structured regional arrangements as the EU and NAFTA.

Whatever its structural features, APEC is the first regional institution that involves all East Asian economies. With its geographical vastness, APEC involves a far larger and more diversified area than any other "regional" institutions. As such, according to John Ravenhill, APEC could actually be seen as a trans-regional as well as a regional institution, which is more similar to the ASEM than to the free trade areas that exist in the Asia-Pacific region in terms of institutionalization and decision-making procedures.[39] Due to highly diverse interests and policy objectives between its Anglo-American members and East and Southeast Asian members, APEC does not always reflect and represent the interests of East and Southeast Asia. Particularly, by the mid-1990s it became apparent that there was a growing division within APEC between the Anglo-American members and the East and Southeast Asian members over the direction of the organization. While the Anglo-American members pushed hard for the binding nature of APEC and focused on the promotion of trade and investment liberalization in the Asia-Pacific, East and Southeast Asian members insisted on the loose and consultative nature of APEC and emphasized trade facilitation, economic and technical cooperation among Asia-Pacific economies.[40] Moreover, as is shown during the Asian financial crisis of 1997–98, East and Southeast Asian economies were under no protection and assistance of any form under the existing framework of APEC. This raises the question of efficacy of APEC for East and Southeast Asian economies.[41] Last but not least, the principle of "open regionalism" as advocated by APEC does not bring any effective protection of East and Southeast Asian economies from the ongoing protectionism and regionalism elsewhere, although the idea does help promote the universal norm of global trade and investment liberalization. As such, APEC, with all its limitations and weaknesses, is unable to help East and Southeast Asian states pursue their common interests of maintaining regional economic stability and promoting prosperity.

Under such circumstances, East and Southeast Asian governments have been making efforts to promote institutionalized cooperation in the region since the Asian financial crisis. The idea of forming an exclusive East and Southeast Asian regional grouping was first explicitly proposed by Malaysian Prime Minister Mahathir Mohamad in 1990, when he openly called for the formation of the East Asian Economic Group (EAEG). However, Mahathir's proposal not only received strong opposition from the United States, but also met with cold response from other East and Southeast Asian governments, which were not only under the US pressure of not supporting this idea but were themselves wary of Mahathir's plan. Despite the failure of the EAEG plan, the idea of an East Asian grouping was revived in the wake of the Asian financial crisis. As the lack of regional institutionalized policy coordination and cooperation is widely seen as a major cause of the rapid and unchecked spread of such a damaging crisis across the region, East and Southeast Asian leaders realized the urgent need for the creation of a regional mechanism that would allow institutionalized cooperation among the governments in the region to deal with those regional issues of a common stake. This understanding led East and Southeast Asian governments to increase efforts for regional institution-building and formation of an East Asian regional grouping.

The efforts to move toward institutionalized regional cooperation finally led to the creation of the ASEAN Plus Three (APT) forum. According to Douglas Webber, APT, which is seen as the "in effect" EAEG, has even "gone far beyond" Mahathir's original proposal.[42] Initiated by ASEAN, APT first emerged from the need of ASEAN and three East Asian countries – China, Japan, and South Korea – to prepare for the first ASEM meeting to be held in 1996.[43] But very soon, particularly in the wake of the Asian financial crisis, APT evolved into an institutionalized forum of consultation and cooperation between ASEAN and three East Asian powers over a growing range of regional issues. Most publicized of the APT forum is its annual informal summit meeting (which was first held in 1997) that immediately follows the annual

ASEAN summit on top of a range of regular ministerial and other official meetings involving foreign ministers, finance ministers, economic ministers, central bank governors, and senior officials from other ministries and government offices. As concrete steps, the East Asian Vision Group (EAVG) and the East Asian Study Group (EASG) were established within APT respectively in 1998 and 2001 "to explore practical ways and means to deepen and expand the existing cooperation" among ASEAN and three East Asian countries "and prepare concrete measures and, as necessary, action plans for closer cooperation in various areas."[44] It is within this process of growing regional consultation and cooperation that there have been growing calls for APT to be transformed into an East Asian FTA. Most prominent among these calls is the one given by South Korean President Kim Dai-jung at the 2001 APT submit meeting in Brunei.

While the enthusiasm for an East Asian grouping, East Asian FTA in particular, has been mounting in the wake of the Asian financial crisis, there are still obstacles to its realization. Most notable among these obstacles are US opposition, lack of political trust among regional governments, smaller states' fear of an East Asian grouping dominated by Japan and China, Sino-Japanese rivalry, the huge gap in the level of economic development among East Asian countries, and different policy priorities. Largely because of these obstacles, it is interesting to note that regional cooperation in East Asia within the framework of APT contains two important features. The first feature is that regional cooperation has been initiated and led by small players rather than major powers in the region. This proves to be a wise strategy to start an institution-building process in the region, given the complexity of regional politics and distrust of major regional powers. As this process of regional cooperation is initiated by small players in the region, it is therefore possible for all the states in the region, big or small, to be less suspicious of the idea of regional grouping and more comfortable to get involved, which could hardly have happened if the process had been initiated by either regional powers, Japan or China.

However, it is important to point out that ASEAN only plays a "quasi-leadership role" in the process of regional cooperation through APT due to the lack of leadership by regional powers. This role of ASEAN within the framework of APT is made possible only because such an arrangement has received tacit consent from both Japan and China, which feel that this arrangement serves their respective interests quite well for the time being. If APT is to be transformed into a true institutionalized regional grouping of any form, it would be very difficult to imagine how ASEAN, given its limited capacity and internal divisions, could provide needed strong leadership that is usually assumed by major powers. This probably explains in an important way why it is difficult for APT to be transformed into an East Asian grouping within its current framework.

A second important feature of APT process is that while ATP provides a forum of consultation and cooperation for ASEAN and three East Asian powers, specific dialogues for substantial cooperation are conducted largely through three parallel mechanisms of ASEAN Plus One (APO) forums, that is, ASEAN plus China, ASEAN Plus Japan, and ASEAN Plus South Korea. Realizing the constraints that still exist in the region in implementing APT-wide cooperative programs at the current stage, APT leaders therefore adopt this practical strategy of promoting regional cooperation through APO to circumvent the obstacles to APT-wide cooperation. As a result, specific cooperative projects are largely pursued between ASEAN and three East Asian powers on a bilateral basis within the framework of APO. This feature of reliance on bilateral cooperation with the framework of APO is well illustrated in the successful conclusion of the China–ASEAN bilateral FTA on 29 November 2005 and the ongoing process of negotiations on a similar bilateral FTA between Japan and ASEAN and between South Korea and ASEAN.

Although substantial cooperation within the framework of APT is largely conducted on a bilateral basis, APT still shows the increasing consciousness of distinctively regional concerns, identities, and politico-economic practices and represents East Asia's most unequivocal movement toward regional institutionalized cooperation involving all major economies in the region (with the notable exception of Taiwan).[45] Although no consensus has been reached yet within APT on how East Asian institution-building is to be achieved, APT leaders do envision the creation of an East Asian FTA as a long-term policy objective.[46]

9
Conclusion

The development of the East Asian political economy over the past century has followed a unique process that is driven by dynamic forces at both regional and national levels. Through over a century of extensive and substantial interactions with each other, East Asian states have not only achieved industrialization and economic success by following a very similar path of economic development but have also been organized into an integrated regional economy.

Japan has historically played a pivotal role in the development of the East Asian political economy. The regional political economy in East Asia was originally brought into being by imperialist Japan in its pursuing a Japanese empire in East Asia from the late 19th century through World War II. Japanese colonial policy not only substantially transformed the economy of Taiwan and Korea but also helped create a regional economic relationship that subordinated Taiwan and Korea to Japan through a vertical division of labor in East Asia, known as flying geese integration. Under this pattern of regional economic relationship, the Japanese imperialist power coercively connected colonized Taiwan and Korea with the Japanese product-cycle phases with declining industries being continuously moved out of Japan to its colonies in the process of economic development. Both Taiwan and Korea, from very early on, were made to take over economic activities that were no longer found profitable in Japan. This transfer of production activities from Japan into its colonies proceeded throughout the colonial era. It started with agriculture through Japanese-directed modernization of rice and sugar production in Taiwan and Korea destined for the colonial metropolis. In the 1930s, Japan started a new stage of this process by transferring such industries as iron, steel, chemical, and electric generation production from the home island to its colonies within the Japanese empire.

This Japanese-coerced process of flying geese integration in East Asia was interrupted as a result of the dismemberment of the Japanese empire in 1945 following Japan's defeat at the end of World War II. However, the regional division of labor of flying geese nature resumed between Japan on the one hand and Taiwan and South Korea on the other in the postwar years under the auspices of US hegemony in the context of Cold War politics. For strategic considerations, the US not only subordinated its economic interests to geopolitical interests and supported the economic development of its East Asian allies through a range of aid programs and preferential policies but also encouraged the economic integration of its allies in East Asia around Japan. Hence, by the 1960s through the 1970s, both Taiwan and South Korea received declining textile and consumer-electronic industries from Japan. In the 1980s, Japanese companies were transferring cars and steel production to Taiwan and South Korea. Through this process, the capitalist economies in East Asia became increasingly interdependent with Japan at the core of this regional economic relationship in the postwar years.

Since the mid-1980s, this Japan-centered vertical economic integration in East Asia has expanded to involve China (and Southeast Asian countries) with Taiwan, South Korea, and Hong Kong playing an intermediate role between Japan and China. While Japan continues to move its declining industries to not only Taiwan and South Korea but also China, Taiwan and South Korea (together with Hong Kong) have been able to improve their respective positions in the vertical relationship of flying geese type in East Asia and begun to move labor-intensive industries into China and Southeast Asian countries.

Japan has been playing a very important role in not only organizing the regional economy around the Japanese economic power but also influencing the development path of national economies in the region through its developmental state structure. The basic developmental state structure of the modern Japanese political economy had solidly been formed in the 1930s. In the postwar years, it became more comprehensive and sophisticated. The major elements of the developmental state structure of the Japanese political economy included national economic planning that covered most major industries, adoption of deliberately designed industrial policy to promote the desired industries as identified by the state, a major role of the state in capital formation, maintenance of an important public sector, promotion of export-driven industrialization, support of the formation of big business conglomerates and establishment of a close link between government and business, adoption of various monetary, fiscal, tax and foreign exchange policies according to state planning priorities, and an authoritarian political system with the labor movement being excluded. While still a market-based capitalist economy, the developmental state, through various policy measures, attempted to manipulate the market mechanism and have it serve the national goals of development. This structure of the Japanese political economy were first planted by the Japanese colonial authorities in Taiwan and Korea during the colonial period and was in many ways inherited by the postcolonial Taiwanese and South Korean states, which substantially influenced the course of their economic development in the postwar years.

According to developmental state theory, a strong authoritarian developmental state is crucial for developing countries as latecomers to achieve successful economic development in a competitive global economy. Moreover, a strong autonomous state is also essential to overcome conflicting interests of strong domestic interest groups and, through intervention in the market, direct market forces in a way that would strengthen the nation's international economic competitiveness and achieve national development goals. Indeed, the state played a crucial role in the economic success of Japan, South Korea, and Taiwan in the postwar years. The governments of these economies were directly and actively involved in guiding the process of industrialization through channeling resources into particular sectors, protecting domestic and newly emergent industries, providing subsidies and assistance to leading firms, promoting technology imports, inducing high rate of domestic savings, maintaining high rates of investment, promoting education, maintaining a cheap and skilled labor force, and promoting equitable distribution of income and rapid improvement of living standards. Moreover, the strong states in East Asia were also characterized by the existence of an autonomous and competent bureaucracy, which made effective state intervention possible.[1]

This developmental state model is in many ways adopted by post-Mao China. During Mao's era, Communist China relied on the Soviet model of command economy for economic development in which the state directly ran the economy through central planning and administrative commands with the role of the market basically eliminated. As the command economy increasingly proved inefficient and even disastrous, the post-Mao Chinese leaders initiated economic reforms in 1978 to move away from the command economy to embrace a capitalist system that is in many ways very similar to the developmental state capitalism of other East Asian states. Although the transformation has not yet been completed, it is evident that compared with that of Japan,

South Korea, and Taiwan, China's developmental state is characterized by more comprehensive and intensive government intervention, a much higher level of public sector and a political system that is communist in name but authoritarian in substance. Like other capitalist economies in East Asia, the adoption of the developmental state capitalism has helped China achieve sustained rapid economic growth over the past three decades.[2]

In the 1980s and onward, both external and internal conditions of the East Asian political economy substantially transformed. In the first place, as a result of the relative decline of the American hegemonic power and the end of the Cold War, America's role in East Asia's economic development had substantially transformed from that of unconditional political, military, and economic support to its allies of the postwar years to a more complicated one that was less defined by geopolitics and more driven by economic rationality. Consequently, the American factor in the East Asian political economy as had been known during the Cold War era was no longer existent. Instead, East Asia–US economic relationship became that of both competition and cooperation. While there was rising economic disputes over a range of issues ranging from trade and market access to intellectual property rights protection, there was also a high level of economic interdependence between the US and East Asia as reflected in the huge volumes of trade and investment (both direct and portfolio) flows across the Pacific. On the other hand, the global economic climate had also changed by the 1980s as a result of rising economic globalization, deepening institutionalized economic liberalization, and growing economic regionalism in the global economy.

Equally significant, as East Asian economies became mature following decades of rapid economic growth and transformation, the developmental state – a development model that was primarily designed to pursue a narrow objective of rapid economic growth in a context of economic backwardness – became increasingly irrelevant. Under the circumstances, starting in the 1980s East Asian states were compelled to initiate a process of economic liberalization. In the meantime, the political, social, and economic transformation in the East Asian states as a result of rapid economic growth in the postwar years also forced the start of a process of political democratization, which substantially affected the political bases of the East Asian developmental state in many ways. Previously closed and tightly knit policy networks became more institutionally porous and pluralistic; the bureaucracy became delinked from the ruling parties; legislatures became increasingly accountable to voters; and civil society was reinvigorated.[3] Consequently, the East Asian developmental state gradually eroded. The Asian financial crisis of 1997–98 and Japan's bank crisis of the 1990s seemed to signal the final decline of the East Asian developmental state.

While the postwar developmental state model has declined, the East Asian states, with the exception of China that is still focusing on catch-up development, that are still developmentally oriented are not retreating from their role in promoting economic development. Rather, they continue to experiment with industrial policies, R&D policies, social welfare reforms, and economic policy, but in more creative ways, albeit under many more constraints. In continuing to play an important role in economic, social, and political development in the postdevelopmental state era, however, the East Asian states have been, to use Joseph Wong's concept, "adapting" to the plethora of new and more complex challenges of a more liberalized economy, autonomous society, and democratized political system. While East Asia states pursue this adaptation differently due to their different conditions, what is common among them is that the ongoing adaptation in East Asia is a dynamic but long process.[4]

Significantly, the East Asian political economy, which had been primarily defined by the Cold War politics and American hegemony as well as the developmental state in the postwar years, is now driven by a set of totally different forces at both national and regional levels. Most importantly, the economic dynamism of East Asia since the mid-1980s has been closely linked to an autonomous process of intensifying regional economic integration that is primarily driven by market forces rather than government planning, although later endorsed by the governments. Following the fast economic growth in the postwar years, domestic economic conditions had substantially changed first in Japan and then in South Korea, Taiwan, and Hong Kong by the mid-1980s. Consequently, there was rising labor shortage, growing labor costs, escalating land prices, and strict environmental controls, which caused growing production costs and an increasingly difficult operating environment. In the meantime, Japan, South Korea, Taiwan, and Hong Kong were all moving toward their respective new levels of sophistication in terms of technology and value-added products. Under such circumstances, it became imperative for the companies in these economies to relocate their labor-intensive and low value-added industries overseas, particularly into China. As a result, the economic forces steadily drove the economic activities across national boundaries to areas of less expensive land and labor to maintain competitiveness and growth. In this process, East Asian multinational corporations, as a force in systematically promoting expansion of division of labor and integration of production in East Asia, became a strong driving force of the region's continued rapid economic growth. On the other hand, the concerns over the rising economic regionalism in North America and Western Europe – East Asia's two major markets – made the regional markets, especially the potential huge Chinese market, become increasingly important to the economies in the region. This constituted another important factor behind the rising economic integration in East Asia. While economic integration in East Asia is a market-driven process of increased intraregional trade and investment flows but short of a formal grouping like the EU and NAFTA due to complex historical, political, and national psychological factors in the region, it is evident that East Asia has been slowly and gradually moving toward more institutionalized regional cooperation in recent years as exemplified by a growing number of regional initiatives like the institutionalized China–Japan–South Korea tripartite summit, ASEAN Plus Three, East Asia Summit, and so on.

The East Asian political economy was dominated by Japan from its inception at the end of the 19th century to the end of World War II. In the postwar years, the United States as a hegemonic power was a sole dominant force in the political economy of East Asia for about two decades and Japan gradually regained its dominance over East Asian economies after the late 1960s. By the early 21st century, however, there has been the rise of Chinese economic power following its sustained rapid economic growth since the 1980s. In the meantime, there has also been rising influence of regional economic powers like South Korea, Taiwan, and ASEAN. Consequently, the East Asian political economy has now been increasingly influenced jointly by American, Japanese, Chinese, and other national powers and regional players. This will inevitably make the political economy of East Asia much more complex in the 21st century than before.

East Asia has achieved the phenomenal economic growth over the past five decades. The momentum of East Asian dynamism has transformed the region into a global center of large-scale investment, trade, and economic development and has substantially altered the international division of labor and the structure of world trade and investment. With growing economic power, East Asia has formed a political and economic hub of the broader region of the Asia-Pacific today, which has substantially influenced global politics and economics and will continue to influence the trajectory of global politics and economics for decades to come.

Notes

1. Introduction

1. B. M. Russett, *International Regions and International System: A Study in Political Ecology* (Chicago, IL: Rand McNally & Company, 1967), p. 11.
2. J. K. Fairbank, E. O. Reischauer, and A. M. Craig, *East Asia: Tradition & Transformation*, revised edn (Boston, MA: Houghton Mifflin Company, 1989).
3. See, for example, B. Cumings, "The Origin and Development of the Northeast Asian Political Economy: Industrial Sectors, Product Cycle, and Political Consequences," *International Organization*, vol. 38, no. 1 (Winter 1984) 1–40.
4. In this regard, the postwar East Asian political economy was largely defined by Kenneth Waltz's "third" image of the international structure or system. See K. N. Waltz, *Man, the State and War: A Theoretical Analysis* (New York: Columbia University Press, 1954).

2. The historical origin of the East Asian political economy, 1895–1945

1. M. R. Peattie, "Introduction," in R. H. Myers and M. R. Peattie (eds), *The Japanese Colonial Empire, 1895–1945* (Princeton, NJ: Princeton University Press, 1984), p. 24.
2. For a discussion of the relative importance of economic interests in the acquisition of Japan's empire, see H. Conroy, *Japan's Seizure of Korea: 1868–1910: A Study of Realism and Idealism in International Relations* (Philadelphia, PA: University of Pennsylvania Press, 1960), pp. 442–91.
3. For a discussion of this issue, see Peattie, "Introduction," pp. 12–13; W. Lockwood, *The Economic Development of Japan: Growth and Structural Change, 1868–1938* (Princeton, NJ: Princeton University Press, 1954), p. 534.
4. Peattie, "Introduction," pp. 6–8.
5. Ibid., p. 25.
6. Ibid., p. 31.
7. Under the *bao-jia* system, the Taiwanese population was divided into groups of 100 households each with one head of each group accountable for the behavior of those families under his authority. This person in turn held each family head accountable for the conduct of that family.
8. For a discussion of this dual land tenure system in Taiwan on the eve of Japanese colonial rule, see C. Ka, *Japanese Colonialism in Taiwan: Land Tenure, Development, and Dependency, 1895–1945* (Boulder, CO: Westview Press, 1995), pp. 11–41.
9. S. Ho, "Colonialism and Development: Korea, Taiwan, and Kwantung," in R. H. Myers, and M. R. Peattie (eds), *The Japanese Colonial Empire, 1895–1945* (Princeton, NJ: Princeton University Press, 1984), pp. 371–2.

10. S. Ho, *The Economic Development of Taiwan, 1869–1970* (New Haven, CT: Yale University Press, 1978), pp. 27 and 31.
11. Ibid., p. 31.
12. These figures and estimates are taken from Lai T., R. H. Myer, and W. Wou, *A Tragic Beginning: The Taiwan Uprising of February 28, 1947* (Stanford, CA: Stanford University Press, 1991), pp. 38–9.
13. H. J. Lamley, "Taiwan Under Japanes Rule, 1895–1945: The Vicissitudes of Colonialism," in M. A. Rubinstein (ed.), *Taiwan: A New History* (Armonk, NY: M.E. Sharpe, Inc., 1999), p. 238.
14. Ho, *The Economic Development of Taiwan*, p. 82.
15. Lai *et al.*, *A Tragic Beginning*, p. 34.
16. Ho, *The Economic Development of Taiwan*, p. 93.
17. Ibid., p. 31.
18. Lamley, "Taiwan Under Japanese Rule, 1895–1945," pp. 236–48.
19. K. Lee, *A New History of Korea*, translated by E. W. Wagner with E. J. Shultz (Cambridge, MA: Harvard University Press, 1984), p. 319.
20. A. Buzo, *The Making of Modern Korea* (London and New York: Routledge, 2002), p. 19.
21. B. Cumings, "American Policy and Korean Liberation," in F. Baldwin (ed.), *Without Parallel: The American–Korean Relationship Since 1945* (New York: Pantheon Books, 1974), p. 49.
22. Buzo, *The Making of Modern Korea*, p. 26.
23. Lee, *A New History of Korea*, p. 348.
24. M. Hart-Landsberg, *The Rush to Development: Economic Change and Political Struggle in South Korea* (New York: Monthly Review Press, 1993), pp. 105–6.
25. Lee, *A New History of Korea*, p. 351.
26. C. J. Eckert, K. Lee, Y. I. Lew, M. Robinson, and E. W. Wagner, *Korea Old and New: A History* (Cambridge, MA: Korea Institute, Harvard University, 1990), pp. 257–8.
27. Lee, *A New History of Korea*, p. 349.
28. Ibid.
29. Ibid., pp. 354–5.
30. D. Suh, *The Korean Communist Movement, 1918–1948* (Princeton, NJ: Princeton University Press, 1967), p. 202.
31. Lee, *A New History of Korea*, p. 358.
32. Buzo, *The Making of Modern Korea*, p. 38.
33. Ibid., pp. 43–4; Eckert *et al.*, *Korea Old and New*, p. 136.
34. Peattie, "Introduction," p. 23.
35. Ibid., p. 36.
36. R. H. Myers and Y. Saburo, "Agricultural Development in the Empire," in R. H. Myers and M. R. Peattie (eds), *The Japanese Colonial Empire, 1895–1945* (Princeton, NJ: Princeton University Press, 1984).
37. Ho (1984), pp. 355–60.
38. Peattie, "Introduction," pp. 36–7.
39. Ho, "Colonialism and Development: Korea, Taiwan, and Kwantung," pp. 355–7 and 368.
40. Suh, C., *Growth and Structural Changes in the Korean Economy, 1910–1940* (Cambridge, MA: Council on East Asian Studies, Harvard University, 1978), pp. 143–56; S. Ho, "The Development Policy of the Japanese Colonial

Government in Taiwan, 1895–1945," in G. Ranis (ed.), *Government and Economic Development* (New Haven, CT: Yale University Press, 1971), p. 328.

41. Ho, "Colonialism and Development: Korea, Taiwan, and Kwantung," pp. 351–2.
42. Ibid., p. 370.
43. Ibid., pp. 370–1.
44. Several decades after Kaname Akamatsu's "flying geese model," Raymond Vernon developed the product-cycle concept in his influential 1966 essay, "International Investment and International Trade in the Product Cycle," *Quarterly Journal of Economics*, 80 (May 1966) 190–207. See also K. Kiyoshi, *Direct Foreign Investment: A Japanese Model of Multinational Business Operations* (New York: Praeger, 1978), pp. 150–1.
45. Cumings, "Northeast Asian Political Economy," p. 3.
46. Hart-Landsberg, *The Rush to Development*, p. 108.

3.   The external setting and internal dynamics in the post-1945 Era

1. See R. Jervis, "The Impact of the Korean War on the Cold War," *Journal of Conflict Resolution*, vol. 24, no. 4 (December 1980) 563–92.
2. T. Nakamura, *The Postwar Japanese Economy: Its Development and Structure, 1937–1994*, 2nd edn (Tokyo: University of Tokyo Press, 1995), p. 25.
3. Cumings, "Northeast Asian Political Economy," p. 19.
4. J. Halliday, *A Political History of Japanese Capitalism* (New York: Pantheon, 1975), p. 197.
5. M. Schaller, *The American Occupation of Japan – The Origins of the Cold War in Asia* (Oxford: Oxford University Press, 1985), p. 179.
6. J. Halliday, "Capitalism and Socialism in East Asia," *New Left Review*, no. 124 (November–December 1980) 11.
7. Cumings, "Northeast Asian Political Economy," p. 33.
8. Ibid., p. 25.
9. G. Thompson, "Introduction: Contours of Economic Development in the Asia-Pacific," in G. Thompson (ed.), *Economic Dynamism in the Asia-Pacific: The Growth of Integration and Competitiveness* (London and New York: Routledge, 1998), pp. 8–9.
10. For a summary of development state in East and Southeast Asia, see C. Clark, "Political Development, Administrative Capacity, and the Challenge to the Developmental State Model Posed by the 1997–1998 Financial Crisis in East and Southeast Asia," in K. T. Liou (ed.), *Managing Economic Development in Asia: From Economic Miracle to Financial Crisis* (Westport, CT: Praeger Publishers, 2002), pp. 13–31.
11. S. B. Linder, *The Pacific Century: Economic and Political Consequences of Asian-Pacific Dynamism* (Stanford: Stanford University Press, 1986), pp. 39–48.
12. I. M. D. Little, "The Experience and Causes of Rapid Labour-Intensive Development in Korea, Taiwan Province, Hong Kong, and Singapore and the Possibilities of Emulation," in E. Lee (ed.), *Export-Led Industrialisation and Development* (Geneva: International labour Organisation, 1981), pp. 42–3.

13. T. Michell, *From a Developing to a Newly Industrialized Country: The Republic of Korea, 1961–1982* (Geneva: International Labour Office, 1988), p. 14.
14. F. Froebel, J. Heinrichs, and O. Kreye, *The New International Division of Labour: Structural Unemployment in Industrialised Countries and Industrialisation in Developing Countries* (Cambridge and New York: Cambridge University Press, 1980), p. 13.
15. Cumings, "Northeast Asian Political Economy," p. 28.
16. See, for example, R. Wade, "The Asian Debt-and-Development Crisis of 1997–?: Causes and Consequences," *World Development*, vol. 26, no. 8 (August 1998) 1535–53.
17. S. J. Maswood, "Developmental States in Crisis," in M. Beeson (ed.), *Reconfiguring East Asia: Regional Institutions and Organisations After the Crisis* (New York: RoutledgeCurzon, 2002), p. 32.

4. The Japanese political economy since 1945

1. T. Nakamura, *The Postwar Japanese Economy: Its Development and Structure, 1937–1994*, 2nd edn (Tokyo: University of Tokyo Press, 1995), p. 44.
2. M. Schaller, *The US Occupation of Japan: The Origins of the Cold War in Asia* (Oxford and New York: Oxford University Press, 1985), pp. 288–9. See also W. R. Nester, *Japan's Growing Power over East Asia and the World Economy: Ends and Means* (London: Macmillan Press Ltd., 1990), pp. 38–9.
3. H. Patrick and H. Rosovsky (eds), *Asia's New Giant: How the Japanese Economy Works* (Washington, D.C.: Brookings Institution, 1976), p. 45.
4. Nester, *Japan's Growing Power*, p. 43.
5. Nakamura, *The Postwar Japanese Economy*, p. 50.
6. Cumings, "Northeast Asian Political Economy," p. 25.
7. The rates between 1949 and 1985 come from Nihon Ginko, various years [cited in G. D. Hook, J. Gilson, C. W. Hughes, and H. Dobson, *Japan's International Relations: Politics, Economics and Security* (London and New York: Routledge, 2001)], Table 4 Yen-dollar rate 1949–99, p. 459; the rates between 1986 and 2004 are from Statistics Bureau (Japan), *Japan Statistical Yearbook*, various years (Tokyo: Japan Statistical Association and the Mainichi Newspapers).
8. Nakamura, *The Postwar Japanese Economy*, pp. 206–7.
9. D. I. Okimoto, *Between MITI and Market: Japanese Industrial Policy for High Technology* (Stanford, CA: Stanford University Press, 1989), pp. 55–85.
10. M. Tolchin, "Pentagon Says it Lags in Some Technologies," *New York Times* (22 March 1990), cited in T. D. Lairson and D. Skidmore, *International Political Economy: The Struggle for Power and Wealth* (Fort Worth, TX: Holt, Rinehart and Winston, Inc., 1993), p. 133.
11. IMF, *Direction of Trade Statistics Yearbook*, various years (Washington, D.C.: International Monetary Fund).
12. V. Argy and L. Stein, *The Japanese Economy* (New York: New York University Press, 1997), p. 76.
13. W. G. Beasley, *The Rise of Modern Japan*, 2nd edn (New York: St. Martin's Press, 1995), p. 244.

14. Argy and Stein, *The Japanese Economy*, p. 81.
15. Nakamura, *The Postwar Japanese Economy*, pp. 91–5.
16. For a comprehensive discussion of MITI's role in the Japanese miracle in the postwar years, see C. Johnson, *MITI and The Japanese Miracle: The Growth of Industrial Policy, 1925–1975* (Stanford, CA: Stanford University Press, 1982). Also see T. Wakiyama, "The Implementation and Effectiveness of MITI's Administrative Guidance," in S. Wilks and M. Wright (eds), *Comparative Government-Industry Relations: Western Europe, the United States, and Japan* (New York: Oxford University Press, 1987), ch. 9, pp. 209–32.
17. W. Horsley and R. Buckley, *Nippon: New Superpower, Japan since 1945* (London: BBC Books, 1990), p. 63.
18. Argy and Stein, *The Japanese Economy*, pp. 205–13.
19. R. J. Barnet, *The Alliance. America-Europe-Japan. Makers of the Postwar World* (New York: Simon & Schuster, 1983), p. 269.
20. Argy and Stein, *The Japanese Economy*, pp. 82–3.
21. Nakamura, *The Postwar Japanese Economy*, p. 102.
22. *The Economist* (London) (27 May–2 June 1967), Special Report, "The Risen Sun: Japan – Seven Keys to the Sun".
23. The data for the 1950s are obtained from World Bank, *World Tables 1976* (Baltimore and London: The Johns Hopkins University Press, 1976), p. 398; the data for the 1960s come from World Bank, *World Development Report, 1983* (New York and London: Oxford University Press, 1983), p. 151.
24. World Bank, *World Development Report, 1982* (New York and London: Oxford University Press, 1982), p. 113.
25. Ibid., *World Development Report, 1997*, p. 235.
26. Ibid., *World Tables*, various years (Baltimore and London: The John Hopkins University Press), *World Development Report*, various years (Oxford: Oxford University Press), and *World Development Indicators*, various years (Washington, D.C.: World Bank).
27. UN Statistics Division/Department of Economic and Social Affairs, *Industrial Commodity Statistics Yearbook: Production Statistics*, various years (New York: United Nations).
28. Statistics Bureau (Japan), *Japan Statistical Yearbook*, various years.
29. World Bank, *World Development Indicators, 2005*, p. 215.
30. Argy and Stein, *The Japanese Economy*, p. 183.
31. Statistics Bureau (Japan), *Japan Statistical Yearbook*, various years.
32. Data for 1950–80 are based on Hook *et al.*, *Japan's International Relations*, Table 1 Japan's Trade 1950–98, pp. 442–9; data for 1985–2004 are based on IMF, *Direction of Trade Statistics Yearbook*, various years.
33. World Bank, *World Development Indicators, 2005*, pp. 254–6.
34. Ministry of Finance (Japan), on-line statistics database, http://www.mof.go.jp/english/index.htm, accessed on 9 December 2005.
35. Hook *et al.*, *Japan's International Relations*, Table 2, pp. 450–7; Argy and Stein, *The Japanese Economy*, p. 224.
36. Argy and Stein, *The Japanese Economy*, p. 224.
37. Ministry of Finance (Japan), statistics database, http://www.mof.go.jp/english/index.htm, accessed on 6 August 2005; converted from the Japanese yen to the US dollar at the annual average exchange rates.

38. UNCTAD, *World Investment Report: Transnational Corporations and the Internationalization of R&D* (New York and Geneva: United Nations, 2005), Annex tables B.1 and B.2, pp. 303–12.
39. Nakamura, *The Postwar Japanese Economy*, pp. 197–200.
40. Ministry of Finance (Japan), statistics database, http://www.mof.go.jp/english/index.htm, accessed on 14 November 2005.
41. Ibid.
42. Ibid.
43. Ibid.
44. Statistics Bureau (Japan), *Japan Statistical Yearbook*, various years, converted from the Japanese yen to the US dollar at the annual average exchange rates.
45. US Department of the Treasury, "Report on Foreign Portfolio Holdings of US Securities at End-June 2004" (30 June 2005) JS-2622, http://www.ustreas.gov/press/releases/js2622.htm, accessed on 18 November 2005.
46. R. T. Murphy, "Power Without Purpose: The Crisis of Japan's Global Financial Dominance," *Harvard Business Review*, no. 2 (March–April 1989) 73–4.
47. Statistics Bureau (Japan), *Japan Statistical Yearbook*, various years, converted from the Japanese yen to the US dollar at the annual average exchange rates.
48. OECD Development Assistance Committee, online statistic database, http://www.oecd.org, accessed on 4 December 2005.
49. Calculated from OECD Development Assistance Committee, online statistic database, http://www.oecd.org, accessed on 4 December 2005. DAC includes 22 countries, namely Australia, Austria, Belgium, Canada, Denmark, Finland, France, Germany, Greece, Ireland, Italy, Japan, Luxembourg, Netherlands, New Zealand, Norway, Portugal, Spain, Sweden, Switzerland, United Kingdom, and the United States.
50. IMF, http://www.imf.org and World Bank, http//www.worldbank.org both accessed on 8 December 2005.
51. Hook *et al.*, *Japan's International Relations*, p. 18.
52. Asian Development Bank (ADB), online statistics data, http://www.adb.org, accessed on 12 December 2005.
53. D. Arase, *Buying Power: The Political Economy of Japanese Foreign Aid* (Boulder: Lynne Rienner, 1995), p. 203; T. Shiraishi, "Japan and Southeast Asian," in P. J. Katzenstein and T. Shiraishi (eds), *Network Power: Japan and Asia* (Ithaca: Cornell University Press, 1997), pp. 189–90.
54. Hook *et al.*, *Japan's International Relations*, pp. 195–6.
55. Data for 1980 and 1985 are based on JETRO various years (cited in G. D. Hook *et al.*, *Japan's International relations*, Table 2 Japan's FDI 1951–97, pp. 450–7); data for 1990–2004 are based on Ministry of Finance (Japan), online statistics database, http://www.mof.go.jp/english/index.htm, accessed on 2 November 2005, with the Japanese yen converted to the US dollar at the annual average exchange rates.
56. For more detailed discussion on this issue, see Chapter 8 of this book.
57. IMF, *Direction of Trade Statistics Yearbook*, various years.
58. Japan remained China's largest trade partner from 1993 to 2003 and was only marginally surpassed by the United States in 2004, when Japan took 14.5% of China's total trade while the United States took 14.7%.
59. IMF, *Direction of Trade Statistics Yearbook*, various years.

60. JETRO. The figures for 1973 and 1998 are cited in Hook *et al.*, *Japan's International Relations*, p. 197; the figures for 2004 are from JETRO, *Japanese Trade in 2004* (June 2005), http://www.jetro.go.jp, accessed on 15 January 2006.
61. The data for 1960–80 are in Hook *et al.*, *Japan's International Relations*, p. 442; the data for 1995–2003 are from IMF, *Direction of Trade Statistics Yearbook*, various years.
62. World Bank, *World Development Indicators*, various years.
63. Statistics Bureau (Japan), *Japan Statistical Yearbook, 2006*, pp. 93 and 152. The Japanese yen is converted to the US dollar at the annual average exchange rates.
64. Ibid., various years.
65. Ibid.
66. OECD, "Economic Survey of Japan 2005," http://www.oecd.org, accessed on 21 January 2006.
67. Ibid.; Prime Minister of Japan and His Cabinet, "General Policy Speech by Prime Minister Junichiro Koizumi to the 164th Session of the Diet" (20 January 2006), http://www.kantei.go.jp, accessed on 21 January 2006.
68. APEC Economic Committee, *2005 APEC Economic Outlook* (Singapore: APEC Secretariat, 2005), p. 176.
69. OECD, "Economic Survey of Japan 2005".
70. APEC Economic Committee, *2005 APEC Economic Outlook*, pp. 178–9.
71. Ibid.
72. The Special Board of Inquiry, CEFP, *Japan's 21st Century Vision* (April 2005), http://www.keizai-shimon.go.jp/english/index.html, accessed on 21 January 2006.

5. The South Korean political economy since 1945

1. D. S. Macdonald, *US-Korean Relations from Liberation to Self-Reliance: The Twenty-Year Record* (Boulder, CO: Westview Press, 1992), p. 14.
2. Ibid., pp. 14–16.
3. Although the US aid program to Korea started as early as September 1945 under the United States Army Military Government in Korea (USAMGIK), it was basically designed to achieve a set of short-run objectives such as prevention of starvation and disease, boosting of agricultural output and overcoming of shortages of consumer goods. It was only after the end of the Korean War that the United States began to adopt an aid program that would pursue long-term objectives of economic rehabilitation and development. For more discussion of this issue, see E. S. Mason *et al.*, *The Economic and Social Modernization of the Republic of Korea* (Cambridge, MA: Harvard University Press, 1980), pp. 165–208.
4. Ibid., p. 182.
5. Ibid., p. 165.
6. B. Cumings, *Korea's Place in the Sun: A Modern History* (New York: W. W. Norton & Company, 1997), p. 306.
7. Mason *et al.*, *The Economic and Social Modernization of the Republic of Korea*, p. 139.

8. K. Kim, "The Development of Contemporary US-ROK Economic Relations," in T. Kwak, in collaboration with J. Chay, S. Cho and S. McCune (eds), *US-Korean Relations, 1882–1982* (Seoul: Kyungnam University Press, 1982), p. 330.
9. Mason *et al.*, *The Economic and Social Modernization of the Republic of Korea*, p. 200.
10. Ibid., pp. 201–2.
11. Ibid., p. 184.
12. The organizational structure of the EPB remained until 1994 when the EPB merged with the Ministry of Finance to form the Ministry of Finance and Economy (MOFE). In 1998, however, two new bodies were created – the Board of Planning and Budget (BPB) and the Office of National Budget (ONB) – with the former responsible for planning and coordinating national policies, and reforming the public sector, while the latter in charge of compilation of the national budget, which were previously the responsibilities of the MOFE. But this bisected organization structure was very brief. Very soon in 1999 the BPB and ONB merged to create the Ministry of Planning and Budget (MPB), which remained thereafter.
13. K. Choi and Y. S. Lee, "The Role of the Korean Government in Industrialization," in C. H. Lee and I. Yamazawa (eds), *The Economic Development of Japan and Korea: A Parallel With Lessons* (New York: Praeger, 1990), p. 58.
14. J. Cherry, *Business Briefings: Republic of Korea* (London: Cassell, 1993), p. 142.
15. Mason *et al.*, *The Economic and Social Modernization of the Republic of Korea*, p. 93.
16. Cherry, *Business Briefings: Republic of Korea*, p. 138.
17. Kim, "The Development of Contemporary US-ROK Economic Relations," p. 330.
18. Bank of Korea, *The Korean Economy* (Seoul: The Bank of Korea, 2001), p. 6.
19. Ibid.
20. Cherry, *Business Briefings: Republic of Korea*, p. 140; World Bank, *World Development Report 1994: Infrastructure for Development* (Oxford: Oxford University Press, 1994), Table 3, pp. 166–7.
21. Bank of Korea, *The Korean Economy*, p. 6.
22. H. Lee, *The Korean Economy: Perspectives for the Twenty-First Century* (Albany, NY: State University of New York Press, 1996), p. 20
23. Bank of Korea, *The Korean Economy*, pp. 7–10.
24. In 1965 and 1977, current account surpluses of a few million dollars were respectively recorded.
25. Bank of Korea, *The Korean Economy*, pp. 11–14.
26. Ibid., *The Korean Economy* (online version, 2006), http://www.bok.or.kr, accessed on 7 March 2006.
27. World Bank, *World Development Indicators 2002*, Table 4.1, pp. 204–6.
28. IMF, *Direction of Trade Statistics Yearbook*, various years.
29. UNCTAD, *World Investment Report 2002: Transnational Corporations and Export Competitiveness* (New York: United Nations, 2002), pp. 176–7.
30. Ibid., various years.
31. Bank of Korea, cited from National Statistical Office, *GNI-GDP Major Indicators*, http://www.nso.go.kr; Ministry of Finance and Economy, *Statistics –*

Major Economic Indicators, 17 February 2006, http://english.mofe.go.kr, both accessed on 21 February 2006.

32. Calculated from Statistics Division/Department of Economic and Social Affairs, *Statistical Yearbook: Forty-Seventh Issue, 2000* (New York: United Nations, 2003).

33. World Bank, *World Development Report, 1983* and World Bank, *World Development Indicators, 2005*.

34. Calculated from World Bank, *2005 World Development Indicators*.

35. Statistics Division/Department of Economic and Social Affairs, *2001 Industrial Commodity Statistics Yearbook: Production Statistics (1992–2001)* (New York: United Nations, 2003); Statistics Division/Department of Economic and Social Affairs, *Statistical Yearbook: Forty-Seven Issue, 2000* (New York: United Nations, 2003).

36. UNCTAD, *World Investment Report, 2002*, p. 178.

37. Ibid., *World Investment Report, 2005* (New York: United Nations, 2005), Annex Tables A.I.9 and A.I.10, pp. 267–71.

38. Ibid., various years.

39. Ibid., *World Investment Directory: Volume II, Asia and the Pacific* (New York: United Nations, 2000), Tables 14, 15b, 20 and 21b, pp. 442, 444–6, 449 and 451–3.

40. Ibid., *World Investment Report, 2002*, p. 178.

41. B. Bridges, *Japan and Korea in the 1990s: From Antagonism to Adjustment* (Brookfield, Vermont: Edward Elgar Publishing Company, 1993), pp. 101–2.

42. Ibid., p. 106.

43. Ibid., p. 93.

44. IMF, *Direction of Trade Statistics Yearbook*, various years.

45. Ibid.

46. Calculated from ibid.

47. Ibid.

48. Ibid.

49. Lee C., "Economic Relations Between Korea and China," *Korea's Economy 2004*, vol. 20 (Washington, D.C.: The Korea Economic Institute, 2004), p. 70.

50. Ibid., pp. 71–2.

51. Ibid., pp. 72–3; The survey study by KITA is cited in Lee, p. 75.

52. Calculated from IMF, *Direction of Trade Statistics Yearbook*, various years.

53. Bank of Korea, *The Korean Economy* (2006).

54. Ibid., *The Korean Economy* (online version, 2004), http://www.bok.or.kr, accessed on 26 July 2004.

55. Ibid., *The Korean Economy* (2006).

56. *OECD Economic Surveys 1997–1998, Korea* (Paris: Organisation for Economic Co-operation and Development, 1998), p. 2.

57. Kang, S., "Macroeconomic Developments and Restructuring," *Korea's Economy 2003*, vol. 19 (Washington, D.C.: The Korea Economic Institute, 2003), pp. 3–4.

58. Ibid., pp. 4–5.

59. Ministry of Finance and Economy, *Statistics – Major Economic Indicators*.

60. ADB, *Asian Development Outlook, 2003* (New York: Oxford University Press, 2003), p. 51.

61. Ministry of Finance and Economy, *Statistics – Major Economic Indicators*.

62. Kang, "Macroeconomic Developments and Restructuring," p. 5.
63. ADB, *Asian Development Outlook, 2003*, p. 51.

6. The Taiwanese political economy since 1945

1. N. B. Tucker, *Taiwan, Hong Kong, and the United States, 1945–1992: Uncertain Friendships* (New York: Twayne Publishers, 1994), p. 30.
2. N. H. Jacoby, *US Aid to Taiwan: A Study of Foreign Aid, Self-Help, and Development* (New York: Praeger, 1966), pp. 38 and 118.
3. Ibid., pp. 174–6.
4. Ibid., pp. 45–6.
5. Ibid., pp. 38, 85, and 152.
6. Ibid., pp. 118–19.
7. S. P. S. Ho, *Economic Development of Taiwan 1860–1970* (New Haven, CT: Yale University Press, 1978), p. 107.
8. P. T. K. Yen, "Sino-US Relations in the 1980s: An Economic Review," *Sino-US Relations*, vol. XVI, no. 4 (Winter 1990) 9 and 11, cited in G. Klintworth, *New Taiwan, New China: Taiwan's Changing Role in the Asia-Pacific Region* (Melbourne: Longman Australia Pty Ltd, 1995), p. 61.
9. Council for Economic Planning and Development (CEPD), *Taiwan Statistical Data Book, 2007* (Taipei: Council for Economic Planning and Development, ROC, 2007), Table 11-9, pp. 218–26.
10. Klintworth, *New Taiwan, New China*, p. 60.
11. Ibid.
12. Ibid., p. 62.
13. CEPD, *Taiwan Statistical Data Book, 2007*, Tables 11-9, pp. 218–26.
14. Ibid.
15. J. F. Cooper, *Taiwan: Nation-State or Province?* 3rd edn (Boulder, CO: Westview Press, 1999), p. 131.
16. S. Long, *Taiwan: China's Last Frontier* (Basingstoke: Macmillan, 1991), p. 79.
17. *The Republic of China 1998 Yearbook* (Taipei: Government Information Office, 1998), cited in Copper, *Taiwan: Nation-State or Province?*, p. 131.
18. Copper, *Taiwan: Nation-State or Province?*, p. 132.
19. For detailed information on these plans, see CEPD, *Economic Development: R.O.P (Taiwan), 2007* (Taipei: Council for Economic Planning and Development, ROC, 2007), pp. 44–6.
20. Copper, *Taiwan: Nation-State or Province?*, p. 138.
21. CEPD, *Taiwan Statistical Data Book, 2007*, Table 11-9, p. 218.
22. *The Republic of China 1998 Yearbook*, p. 338.
23. A. Kubek, *Modernizing China: A Comparative Analysis of the Two China* (Washington, D.C.: Regency Gateway, 1987), p. 94, cited in Copper, *Taiwan: Nation-State or Province?*, p. 134.
24. A. Syu, *From Economic Miracle to Privatization Success: Initial Stages of the Privatization Process in Two SOEs on Taiwan* (Lanham, MD: University of America Press, 1995), cited in K. Maguire, *The Rise of Modern Taiwan* (Aldershot, England: Ashgate Publishing Limited, 1998), p. 43.
25. See Chen C., "POC Looks to Future with a Vision," *Free China Journal* (10 April 1998) 7, cited in Copper, *Taiwan: Nation-State or Province?*, p. 131.

26. Ho, *Economic Development of Taiwan*, p. 104.
27. A. Y. C. Koo, "Economic Development of Taiwan," in P. K. T. Sih (ed.), *Taiwan in Modern Times* (New York: St. John's University Press, 1973), pp. 402–6.
28. Copper, *Taiwan: Nation-State or Province?*, p. 151.
29. The growth rates for Taiwan are from CEPD, *Taiwan Statistical Data Book, 2007*, Table 1-1a, p. 17; the grow rates for the world and OECD are from the World Bank, *World Development Indicators, 2002*, Table 4.1, pp. 204–6.
30. CEPD, *Economic Development, 2007*, p. 6.
31. CEPD, *Taiwan Statistical Data Book, 2007*, Table 1-1a, p. 17.
32. Ibid., *Economic Development, 2007*, p. 6.
33. Ibid., *Taiwan Statistical Data Book, 2007*, Table 17-10, p. 355.
34. Calculated from ibid., Table 11-4, p. 212.
35. Calculated from ibid., Table 1-1a, p. 17 and Table 11-4, p. 212.
36. Ibid., Table 11-5, p. 213.
37. Calculated from ibid., Table 1-1a, p. 17 and Table 11-4, p. 212.
38. Ibid., Table 1-1a, p. 17.
39. Ibid., Table 1-1b, p. 18.
40. Ibid., Table 13-2, p. 266.
41. Ibid., Tables 2-2, p. 24 and 2-5, p. 27; Table 2-8a, p. 32.
42. Ibid., Table 2-10b, p. 37.
43. Ibid., Table 2-14a, p. 41.
44. Y. Wu, *Becoming an Industrial Nation: ROC's Development on Taiwan* (New York: Praeger, 1985).
45. CEPD, *Taiwan Statistical Data Book, 2007*, Table 1-1b, p. 18.
46. Ibid., Table 2-9b, p. 35.
47. Ibid., Table 11-7, p. 216.
48. Bureau of Foreign Trade (BFT), Ministry of Economic Affairs, *Monthly Report, Year 2006*, http://eweb.trade.gov.tw/mp.asp?mp=2, accessed on 2 November 2007.
49. CEPD, *Taiwan Statistical Data Book, 2007*, Table 11-8, p. 217.
50. Ibid., Table 17-6, pp. 350–1.
51. IMF, *Direction of Trade Statistics Yearbook, 2004*.
52. Calculated from ibid.
53. CEPD, *Taiwan Statistical Data Book, 2007*, Table 11-4, p. 212.
54. Ibid., Table 1c, p. 3.
55. CEPD, *Economic Development, 2007*, p. 16.
56. Ibid., *Taiwan Statistical Data Book, 2007*, Table 4b, p. 12.
57. "Review 200 – Taiwan," *Far Eastern Economic Review* (31 December 1998–7 January 1999) 84–5.
58. UNCTAD, *World Investment Report: The Shift Towards Services, 2004* (New York: United Nations, 2004), pp. 22–3.
59. CEPD, *Taiwan Statistical Data Book, 2007*, Table 11-9f, p. 223.
60. Klintworth, *New Taiwan, New China*, p. 38.
61. Ibid., p. 39.
62. CEPD, *Taiwan Statistical Data Book, 2007*, Table 11-9h, p. 225.
63. Ibid., Table 11-9, pp. 223–4 and CEPD, *Economic Development, 2007*, p. 15.
64. Ibid., *Taiwan Statistical Data Book, 2007*, Table 11-9a, p. 218.
65. Calculated from ibid., Table 13-4, p. 268.
66. CEPD, *Taiwan Statistical Data Book, 2007*, Table 11-9, pp. 218–26.

67. Ibid., Table 13-3, p. 267; Mainland Affairs Council (MAC), *Cross-Strait Economic Statistics Monthly No.175*, Table 13, http://www.mac.gov.tw, accessed on 12 November 2007.
68. MAC, *Cross-Strait Economic Statistics Monthly No.175*, Table 10.
69. Ibid., Tables 13 and 29.
70. Ibid., Table 13.
71. CEPD, *Taiwan Statistical Data Book, 2007*, Table 11-9, pp. 218–26.
72. UNCTAD, *World Investment Directory, Volume VII: Asia and the Pacific*, Table 15, p. 547.
73. Ibid.
74. MAC, *Cross-Strait Economic Statistics Monthly No.175*, Table 13.
75. CEPD, *Economic Development, 2007*, p. 15; CEPD, *Taiwan Statistical Data Book, 2007*, Table 11-9, pp. 218–26.
76. CEPD, *Taiwan Statistical Data Book, 2007*, Table 11-9, pp. 218–26.
77. MAC, *Cross-Strait Economic Statistics Monthly No.175*, Table 13.
78. J. Wang, "Taiwan and the Asian Financial Crisis: Impact and Response," in P. C. Y. Chow and B. Gill (eds), *Weathering the Storm: Taiwan, Its Neighbors, and the Asian Financial Crisis* (Washington, D.C.: Brookings Institution, 2000), p. 149.
79. Maguire, *The Rise of Modern Taiwan*, p. 72.
80. Ibid., p. 73.
81. CEPD, *Economic Development, 2007*, p. 32.
82. Ibid., p. 34.

7. The Chinese political economy since 1949

1. See M. Selden, *The Political Economy of Chinese Development* (Armonk, N.Y.: M. E. Sharpe, 1993), pp. 43–58.
2. R. Shen, *China's Economic Reform: An Experiment in Pragmatic Socialism* (Westport, CT: Praeger Publishers, 2000), p. 28.
3. D. Perkins and S. Yusuf, *Rural Development in China* (Baltimore: Published for the World Bank, by The Johns Hopkins University Press, 1984), pp. 77–9; M. Marshal, *Organizations and Growth in Rural China* (London: The Macmillan Press Ltd., 1985), pp. 46–51.
4. National Bureau of Statistics (NBS), China, *China Statistical Yearbook, 1998* (Beijing: China Statistics Press, 1998), pp. 38–9.
5. UNCTAD, *World Investment Report 1994: Transnational Corporations, Employment and the Workplace* (New York and Geneva: United Nations, 1994), p. 107.
6. For a systematic and comprehensive discussion of China's economic reform, see G. C. Chow, *China's Economic Transformation*, 2nd edn (Malden, MA: Blackwell Publishing, 2007).
7. The private sector includes not only domestic private enterprises but also foreign-invested enterprises and joint ventures.
8. Zhang Z., Huang F., and Li G. (eds), *Twenty Years of Economic Reform: Retrospect and Prospect* (Beijing: China Planning Publishers, 1998), p. 34.
9. Calculated from NBS, *China Statistical Yearbook, 2000*, p. 409.
10. Zhang *et al.* (eds), *Twenty Years of Economic Reform*, p. 29.

11. Ibid., p. 37.
12. Ibid., pp. 118–19.
13. *China Daily* (20 March 1999) 4.
14. World Bank, *2005 World Development Indicators*, pp. 198–200.
15. NBS, *China Statistical Yearbook, 2004*, p. 56.
16. Ibid., pp. 28–9.
17. Calculated from ibid., pp. 24 and 714.
18. Data for 1979–82 are from NBS, *China Foreign Economic Statistical Yearbook, 1999* (Beijing: China Statistics Press, 1999), p. 276; data for 2003 and 1979–2003 are from NBS, *China Statistical Yearbook, 2004*, p. 731.
19. Calculated from Ibid.
20. UNCTAD, *World Investment Report: Transnational Corporations and Export Competitiveness, 2002* (New York and Geneva: United Nations, 2002), pp. 162–6.
21. Calculated from NBS, *China Statistical Yearbook, 2004*, pp. 714 and 730.
22. T. G. Moore, "China's International Relations: The Economic Dimension," in S. S. Kim (ed.), *The International Relations of East Asia* (Lanham, MD: Rowman & Littlefield Publishers, Inc., 2004), p. 106.
23. Calculated from NBS, *China Statistical Yearbook, 2004*, pp. 53, 714 and 731; NBS, *China Foreign Economic Statistical Yearbook, 1999*, pp. 10 and 276.
24. NBS, *China Statistical Yearbook, 2004*, p. 54.
25. Ibid., p. 59.
26. Ministry of Commerce (MOC), China, "Special Study II: The Development and Trade of China's High-technology Industries" (8 December 2004), http://kjs.mofcom.gov.cn, accessed on 10 July 2005.
27. NBS, *China Statistical Yearbook, 2004*; Statistics Division (SD), Department of Economic and Social Affairs, UN, *2001 Industrial Commodity Statistics Yearbook: Production Statistics*; SD, *Statistical Yearbook, Forty-Seventh Issue, 2000*; World Bank, *2005 World Development Indicators*.
28. NBS, *China Statistical Yearbook, 2004*, pp. 28–9.
29. Calculated from World Bank, *1998 World Development Indicators*, pp. 188–5; World Bank, *2005 World Development Indicators*, pp. 214–21.
30. Ibid.
31. IMF, *Direction of Trade Statistics Yearbook*, various years.
32. Ibid.
33. NBS, *China Foreign Economic Statistical Yearbook, 1999*, pp. 275–6; and NBS, *China Statistical Yearbook, 2004*, p. 731.
34. UNCTAD, *World Investment Report*, various years.
35. NBS, *China Statistical Yearbook, 2004*, p. 731.
36. UNCTAD, *World Investment Report: The Shift Towards Services, 2004*, Annex Table B.4, pp. 382–6.
37. Department of Foreign Economic Cooperation (DFEC), MOC, China, online database, http://hzs.mofcom.gov.cn, accessed 14 July 2005.
38. NBS, *China Statistical Yearbook, 2004*, p. 767; WB, *2005 World Development Indicators*, p. 191; "China's Foreign Exchange Reserves Ranking the Second Largest and the Foreign Exchange System on the Verge of Reform," *Beijing Youth* (6 February 2005), http://www.bjyouth.com, accessed on 16 July 2005.
39. P. S. Goodman, "China Tells Congress to Back off Businesses: Tensions Heightened by Bid to Purchase Unocal," *Washington Post* (5 July 2005), www.washingtonpost.com, accessed 5 July 2005.

40. "Analyst: Huge Consumption of Oil by China and the United States is the Primary Cause of Rapid Rise of Oil Price," *Zao Bao* (Singapore) (14 July 2005), http://www.zaobao.com, accessed on 14 July 2005.
41. D. Lee, "China Barrels Ahead in Oil Market," *Los Angeles Times* (14 November 2004) C1 and 4.
42. "Boom Felt Across Globe," *The San Diego Union-Tribune* (21 March 2005) A1.
43. World Bank, *2007 World Development Indicators*, pp. 14–16.
44. Moore, "China's International Relations," p. 114.
45. *Beijing Review* (29 June–5 July 1998), p. 6.
46. D. Perkins, *China: Asia's Next Economic Giant* (Seattle, WA: University of Washington Press, 1986).
47. Y. Funabashi, M. Oksenberg and H. Weiss, *An Emerging China in a World of Interdependence: A Report to the Trilateral Commission* (New York: The Trilateral Commission, 1994), p. 2.
48. IMF, *Direction of Trade Statistics Yearbook*, various years.
49. NBS, *China Trade and Price Statistics, 1989* (New York: Praeger, 1989), p. 164.
50. Calculated from Statistics Bureau, Japan, *Japan Statistical Yearbook*, various years.
51. G. Austinc and S. Harris, *Japan and Greater China: Political Economy and Military Power in the Asian Century* (Honolulu, HI: University of Hawaii's Press, 2001), pp. 158–9.
52. IMF, *Direction of Trade Statistics Yearbook*, various years.
53. Department of Foreign Investment Administration (DFIA), MOC, China, online database, http://wzs.mofcom.gov.cn, accessed on 14 July 2005.
54. Austin and Harris, *Japan and Greater China*, p. 233.
55. OECD, online statistics database, http://www.oecd.org/database/accdstat, accessed on 14 December 2005.
56. Calculated from IMF, *Direction of Trade Statistics Yearbook*, various years.
57. B. Haughton "Between China and the World: Hong Kong's Economy before and after 1997," in G. G. Hamilton (ed.), *Cosmopolitan Capitalists: Hong Kong and the Chinese Diaspora at the End of the 20th Century* (Seattle, WA: University of Washington Press, 1999), pp. 82–5.
58. DFIA, online database.
59. MAC, *Cross-Strait Economic Statistics Monthly No. 175*, Table 29, http://www.mac.gov.tw, accessed on 12 November 2007.
60. Calculated from IMF, *Direction of Trade Statistics Yearbook*, various years.
61. See Section 6.4 of Chapter 6 for more discussion of the rapid development of cross-Taiwan Straits economic ties.
62. Calculated from IMF, *Direction of Trade Statistics Yearbook*, various years.
63. DFIA, online database.
64. Huang F., "An Analysis on Characteristics and Trends of Direct Investments from Korea (*sic*)," *International Economic Cooperation*, no. 9 (2002) 47–9. See Section 5.4 of Chapter 5 for more discussion of the rapid development of economic ties between China and South Korea.
65. NBS, *China Statistical Yearbook, 2004*, pp. 277 and 717.
66. *China Daily* (31 March 1999) 1.
67. NBS, *China Statistical Yearbook, 2004*, p. 119.
68. Ibid., p. 357.

69. "Flexing Power Through Trade," *The San Diego Union-Tribune* (22 March 2005) A1.
70. "The Dragon Awakes," Ibid. (20 March 2005) A1.

8. The political economy of regional integration in East Asia

1. Ministry of Finance (Japan), *Monthly Finance Review*, various issues, cited in OECD, *International Direct Investment Statistics Yearbook 1995* (Paris: Organization for Economic Cooperation and Development), pp. 154–5.
2. Ministry of Finance (Japan), statistics database, http://www.mof.go.jp/ english/index.htm, accessed on 6 August 2005.
3. Calculated from ibid.
4. OECD, *Foreign Direct Investment Relations between the OECD and the Dynamic Asian Economies* (Paris: Organization for Economic Cooperation and Development, 1993), p. 135.
5. Census and Statistics Department (Hong Kong), statistics database, http://www.info.gov.hk/censtatd/eng, accessed on 28 July 2005. The original data are in Hong Kong dollar, which are converted into the US dollar at the 2003 exchange rate.
6. The data for 1987 are from UNCTAD, *World Investment Directory, Volume VII-Part 2: Asia and the Pacific*, pp. 546–7; the data for 2006 are from MAC, *Cross-Strait Economic Statistics Monthly No.175*, Table 13, http://www.mac.gov.tw, accessed on 12 November 2007.
7. OECD, *Foreign Direct Investment Relations*, p. 139.
8. Calculated from UNCTAD, *World Investment Directory, Volume VII-Part 2*, pp. 444–6.
9. Export-Import Bank of Korea, cited in Lee Chang-kyu, "Economic Relations between Korea and China," *2004 Korea's Economy* (Washington, D.C.: Korea Economic Institute), p. 71, http://www.keia.org, accessed on 9 August 2005.
10. Census and Statistics Department (Hong Kong), statistics database. The original data are in Hong Kong dollar, which are converted into the US dollar at the 2003 exchange rate.
11. J. C. Abegglen, *Sea Change: Pacific Asia as the New World Industrial Center* (New York: The Free Press, 1994), p. 83.
12. E. J. Lincoln, "Japanese Trade and Investment Issues," in D. Unger and P. Blackburn (eds), *Japan's Emerging Global Role* (Boulder and London: Lynne Rienner Publishers, Inc., 1993), pp. 134–5.
13. D. Unger, "Japan's Capital Exports: Molding East Asia," in Unger and Blackburn (eds), *Japan's Emerging Global Role*, p. 156.
14. Calculated from IMF, *Direction of Trade Statistics Yearbook 2004*.
15. K. G. Cai, "Is a Free Trade Zone Emerging in East Asia in the Wake of the Asian Financial Crisis?" *Pacific Affairs*, vol. 74, no. 1 (Spring 2001) 10.
16. World Bank, *East Asia: The Road to Recovery* (Washington, D.C.: The World Bank, 1998), p. 11.
17. *The Korea Herald* (17 September 1998) p. 1.
18. "Japanese Prime Minister Lectures at Korea University," Yonhap (20 March 1999), cited from FBIS-EAS-1999-0320.

19. "MITI Proposes Trade Integration in N.E. Asia," Kyodo World Service (21 May 1999).
20. *The Korea Herald* (1 June 1999) p. 12.
21. For a thorough discussion of China's changing attitude and policy toward regional free trade arrangements in East Asia in general and East Asia in particular, see K. G. Cai, "Chinese Changing Perspective on the Development of an East Asian Free Trade Area," *The Review of International Affairs*, vol. 3, no. 4 (Summer 2004) 584–99. This article is reprinted in R. C. Keith (ed.), *China as a Rising World Power and its Response to 'Globalization'* (London and New York: Routledge, 2005), ch. 5, pp. 78–93.
22. "Wu Yi Raises Six Suggestions and Calls for Creating a Chinese-Japanese FTA," Sohu News (China) (19 May 2005), http://news.sohu.com, accessed on 19 May 2005.
23. "Japan's Cabinet: A Japanese–Chinese FTA Brings Huge Benefits," *Zao Bao* (Singapore) (9 January 2005), http://www.zaobao.com, accessed on 9 January 2005.
24. "China and South Korea Start to Negotiate on FTA and Japan's Passive Attitude over Cooperation with China," Sohu News (China) (22 March 2005), http://news.sohu.com, accessed on 22 March 2005.
25. "Japan, China, S. Korea Agree on Joint Research," Kyodo World Service (28 November 1999); "ROK, China, Japan to Conduct Joint Research for Economic Cooperation," *Korea Times* (28 November 1999), website edition.
26. Ministry of Foreign Affairs of PRC, official website, http://www.fmprc. gov.cn/eng; Ministry of Foreign Affairs of Japan, website, http://www.mofa. go.jp, both accessed on 12 August 2005.
27. "China, Japan and South Korea Agreed to Study the Creation of a Free Trade Zone," *Zha Bao* (Singapore) (5 May 2005), http://www.zhobao.com, accessed on 5 May 2005.
28. "ROK, Japan Business Leaders Agree on Increased Exchanges," Yonhap (29 October 1998), cited from FBIS-EAS-98-302; *The Korea Herald* (20 October 1998) p. 1.
29. "Business Leaders Hold Fourth 'Asian Neighbors Forum'," Yonhap (8 May 1999), cited from FBIS-EAS-1999-0508; *The Korea Herald* (10 May 1999) p. 1.
30. "ROK, Japan, PRC Businesses to Form Cooperation Body," Yonhap (3 June 1999), cited from FBIS-EAS-1999-0603; "Private Group to Enhance ROK-Japan-China Economic Ties," Yonhap (17 June 1999), cited from FBIS-EAS-1999-0617.
31. "KCCI Proposes East Asian Economic Council," *The Korea Herald* (7 June 2002), website edition.
32. For a more detailed discussion on the issue of AMF, see R. Higgott, "The Asian Economic Crisis: A Study in the Politics of Resentment," *New Political Economy*, vol. 3, no. 3 (November 1998) 340–6.
33. WTO website, http://www.wto.org, accessed on 11 August 2005.
34. ADB, *Asian Development Outlook 2002* (New York: Oxford University Press, 2002), p. 164.
35. See, for example, N. V. Long, "The East Asian Crisis: Some Historical Roots," *New Political Science*, vol. 21, no. 3 (1999) 395–404.
36. A. Singh and B. A. Weisse, "The Asian Model: A Crisis Foretold?" *International Social Science Journal*, no. 160 (June 1999) 203–15.
37. See Higgott, "The Asian Economic Crisis," pp. 333–55.

38. K. G. Cai, "The Political Economy of Economic Regionalism in East Asia: A Unique and Dynamic Pattern," *East Asia: An International Quarterly*, vol. 17, no. 2 (Summer 1999) 42–3.

39. J. Ravenhill, "Institutional Evolution at the Trans-Regional Level: APEC and the Promotion of Liberalisation," in M. Beeson (ed.), *Reconfiguring East Asia: Regional Institutions and Organisations After the Crisis* (London and New York: RoutledgeCurzon, 2002), p. 227.

40. R. Stubbs, "ASEAN Plus Three: Emerging East Asian Regionalism," *Asian Survey*, vol. 42, no. 3 (May/June 2002) 447.

41. Ravenhill, "Institutional Evolution at the Trans-Regional Level," pp. 239–41.

42. D. Webber, "Two Funerals and a Wedding? The Ups and Downs of Regionalism in East Asia and Asia-Pacific after the Asian Crisis," *The Pacific Review*, vol. 14, no. 3 (2001) 356.

43. For a discussion of ASEM, see C. M. Dent, "ASEM and the 'Cinderella Complex' of EU-East Asia Economic Relations," *Pacific Affairs*, vol. 74, no. 1 (2001) 25–52.

44. EASG, *Final Report of the East Asia Study Group, submitted to ASEAN+3 Summit, Phnom Penh, Cambodia, 4 November 2002*, p. 63, http://www.aseansec.org, accessed on 18 August 2005.

45. M. Beeson, "ASEAN: The Challenges of Organisational Reinvention," in Beeson (ed.) *Reconfiguring East Asia*, p. 197.

46. For more discussion on APT and APO, see K. G. Cai, "The ASEAN-China Free Trade Agreement and East Asian Regional Grouping," *Contemporary Southeast Asia*, vol. 25, no. 3 (2003) 392–5.

9. Conclusion

1. For systematic analyses of how the developmental state led the national economic development and achieved economic success in East Asia, see L. P. Jones and I. SaKong, *Government, Business and Entrepreneurship in Economic Development: The Korean Case* (Cambridge, MA: Harvard University Press, 1980); C. Johnson, *MITI and the Japanese Miracle: The Growth of Industrial Policy, 1925–1975*; A. Amsden, *Asia's Next Giant: South Korean and Late Industrialization* (London: Oxford University, 1989); R. Wade, *Governing the Market: Economic Theory and the Role of the Government in East Asian Industrialization* (Princeton, NJ: Princeton University Press, 1990); S. Haggard, *Pathways From the Periphery: The Politics of Growth in the Newly Industrializing Countries* (Ithaca, NY: Cornell University Press, 1990).

2. For more discussion of the Chinese developmental state, see V. Shih, "Development, the Second Time Around: The Political Logic of Developing Western China," *Journal of East Asian Studies*, vol. 4, no. 3 (2004) 427–51.

3. J. Wong, "The Adaptive Developmental State in East Asia," *Journal of East Asian Studies*, vol. 4, no. 3 (2004) 356.

4. Ibid., 345–62. For analysis of the decline of the East Asian development state, see also Y. T. Kim, "Neolinberalism and the Decline of the Developmental State," *Journal of Contemporary Asia*, vol. 29, no. 4 (1999) 441–61; L. Weiss, "Developmental States in Transition: Adapting, Dismantling, Innovating, not 'Normalizing'," *The Pacific Review*, vol. 13, no. 1 (2000) 21–55.

Bibliography

Publications and Websites of international organizations

ADB, *Asian Development Outlook 2002* (New York: Oxford University Press, 2002).
——, *Asian Development Outlook, 2003* (New York: Oxford University Press, 2003).
——, official website, http://www.adb.org.
APEC Economic Committee, *2005 APEC Economic Outlook* (Singapore: APEC Secretariat, 2005).
APEC's official website, http://www.apecsec.org.sg.
ASEAN EASG, *Final Report of the East Asia Study Group, submitted to ASEAN+3 Summit, Phnom Penh, Cambodia, 4 November 2002.* http://www.aseansec.org.
IMF, *Direction of Trade Statistics Yearbook*, various years (Washington, DC: International Monetary Fund).
——, official website, http://www.imf.org.
OECD, *International Direct Investment Statistics Yearbook*, various years (Paris: Organization for Economic Cooperation and Development).
——, *Foreign Direct Investment Relations Between the OECD and the Dynamic Asian Economies* (Paris: Organization for Economic Cooperation and Development, 1993).
——, *OECD Economic Surveys 1997–1998, Korea* (Paris: Organization for Economic Cooperation and Development, 1998).
——, "Economic Survey of Japan 2005," http://www.oecd.org.
——, official website, http://www.oecd.org.
UNCTAD, *World Investment Report*, various years (New York: United Nations).
——, *World Investment Directory: Volume II, Asia and the Pacific* (New York: United Nations, 2000).
UN Statistics Division/Department of Economic and Social Affairs, *Statistical Yearbook: Forty-Seventh Issue, 2000* (New York: United Nations, 2003).
——, *Industrial Commodity Statistics Yearbook: Production Statistics*, various years (New York: United Nations).
The World Bank, *World Tables*, various years (Baltimore and London: The Johns Hopkins University Press).
——, *World Development Report*, various years (Oxford: Oxford University Press).
——, *World Development Indicators*, various years (Washington, DC: The World Bank).
——, *East Asia: The Road to Recovery* (Washington, DC: The World Bank, 1998).
——, official website, http//www.worldbank.org.
WTO, official website, http://www.wto.org.

Government publications and Websites

China

Department of Foreign Investment Administration, Ministry of Commerce, on-line database, http://wzs.mofcom.gov.cn.

Department of Foreign Economic Cooperation, Ministry of Commerce, online database, http://hzs.mofcom.gov.cn.

Ministry of Commerce, "Special Study II: The Development and Trade of China's High-technology Industries" (8 December 2004), http://kjs.mofcom.gov.cn.

Ministry of Foreign Affairs of PRC, official website, http://www.fmprc.gov.cn/eng.

National Bureau of Statistics, *China Statistical Yearbook*, various years (Beijing: China Statistics Press).

——, *China Trade and Price Statistics, 1989* (New York: Praeger, 1989).

——, *China Foreign Economic Statistical Yearbook, 1999* (Beijing: China Statistics Press, 1999).

Hong Kong

Census and Statistics Department, statistics database, http://www.info.gov.hk/censtatd/eng.

Japan

Ministry of Finance, statistics database, http://www.mof.go.jp/english/index.htm.

Ministry of Foreign Affairs, website, http://www.mofa.go.jp.

Prime Minister of Japan and his Cabinet, "General Policy Speech by Prime Minister Junichiro Koizumi to the 164th Session of the Diet" (20 January 2006), http://www.kantei.go.jp.

The Special Board of Inquiry of the Council on Economic and Fiscal Policy, "Japan's 21st Century Vision" (April 2005), http://www.keizai-shimon.go.jp/english/index.html.

Statistics Bureau, *Japan Statistical Yearbook*, various years (Tokyo: Japan Statistical Association and the Mainichi Newspapers).

South Korea

The Bank of Korea, *The Korean Economy* (Seoul: The Bank of Korea, 2001).

——, *The Korean Economy*, http://www.bok.or.kr.

——, *Key Economic Indicators (1997–2000)*, http://www.bok.or.kr.

The Ministry of Finance and Economy, *Statistics – Major Economic Indicators* (17 February 2006), http://english.mofe.go.kr.

National Statistical Office, *GNI-GDP Major Indicators*, http://www.nso.go.kr.

——, Statistical Database (KOSIS), http://www.nso.go.kr.

Taiwan

Bureau of Foreign Trade, Ministry of Economic Affairs, *Monthly Report*, http://eweb.trade.gov.tw/mp.asp?mp=2.

Council for Economic Planning and Development, *Taiwan Statistical Data Book, 2007* (Taipei: Council for Economic Planning and Development, ROC, 2007).

——, *Economic Development, R.O.C. (Taiwan), 2007* (Taipei: Council for Economic Planning and Development, ROC, 2007).

Government Information Office, *The Republic of China 1998 Yearbook* (Taipei: Government Information Office, 1998).

Mainland Affairs Council, *Cross-Strait Economic Statistics Monthly No. 175*, http://www.mac.gov.tw.

The United States

Department of the Treasury, "Report on Foreign Portfolio Holdings of US Securities At End-June 2004" (30 June 2005), JS-2622, http://www.ustreas.gov/press/releases/js2622.htm.

Books

Abegglen, J. C., *Sea Change: Pacific Asia as the New World Industrial Center* (New York: The Free Press, 1994).
Amsden, A., *Asia's Next Giant: South Korean and Late Industrialization* (London: Oxford University, 1989).
Arase, D., *Buying Power: The Political Economy of Japanese Foreign Aid* (Boulder, CO: Lynne Rienner, 1995).
Argy, V. and L. Stein, *The Japanese Economy* (New York: New York University Press, 1977).
Austin, G. and S. Harris, *Japan and Greater China: Political Economy and Military Power in the Asian Century* (Honolulu, HI: University of Hawaii's Press, 2001).
Barnet, R. J., *The Alliance. America-Europe-Japan. Makers of the Postwar World* (New York: Simon & Schuster, 1983).
Beasley, W. G., *The Rise of Modern Japan*, 2nd edn (New York: St. Martin's Press, 1995).
Bridges, B., *Japan and Korea in the 1990s: From Antagonism to Adjustment* (Brookfield, VT: Edward Elgar Publishing Company, 1993).
Buzo, A., *The Making of Modern Korea* (London and New York: Routledge, 2002).
Cherry, J., *Business Briefings: Republic of Korea* (London: Cassell, 1993).
Chow, G. C., *China's Economic Transformation*, 2nd edn (Malden, MA: Blackwell Publishing, 2007).
Conroy, H., *Japan's Seizure of Korea: 1868–1910: A Study of Realism and Idealism in International Relations* (Philadelphia, PA: University of Pennsylvania Press, 1960).
Cooper, J. F., *Taiwan: Nationa-State or Province?* 3rd edn (Boulder, CO: Westview Press, 1999).
Cumings, B., *Korea's Place in the Sun: A Modern History* (New York: W. W. Norton & Company, 1997).
Eckert, C. J., K. Lee, Y. I. Lew, M. Robinson and E. W. Wagner, *Korea Old and New: A History* (Cambridge, MA: Korea Institute, Harvard University, 1990).
Fairbank, J. K., E. O. Reischauer and A. M. Craig, *East Asia: Tradition & Transformation*, revised edn (Boston, MA: Houghton Mifflin Company, 1989).
Froebel, F., J. Heinrichs and O. Kreye, *The New International Division of Labour: Structural Unemployment in Industrialised Countries and Industrialisation in Developing Countries* (Cambridge and New York: Cambridge University Press, 1980).
Funabashi, Y., M. Oksenberg and H. Weiss, *An Emerging China in a World of Interdependence: A Report to the Trilateral* Commission (New York: The Trilateral Commission, 1994).
Haggard, S., *Pathways from the Periphery: The Politics of Growth in the Newly Industrializing Countries* (Ithaca, NY: Cornell University Press, 1990).
Halliday, J., *A Political History of Japanese Capitalism* (New York: Pantheon, 1975).

Hart-Landsburg, M., *The Rush to Development: Economic Change and Political Struggle in South Korea* (New York: Monthly Review Press, 1993).

Ho, S. P. S., *Economic Development of Taiwan, 1869–1970* (New Haven, CT: Yale University Press, 1978).

Horsley, W. and R. Buckley, *Nippon: New Superpower, Japan Since 1945* (London: BBC Books, 1990).

Jacoby, N. H., *US Aid to Taiwan: A Study of Foreign Aid, Self-Help, and Development* (New York: Praeger, 1966).

Johnson, C., *MITI and the Japanese Miracle: The Growth of Industrial Policy, 1925–1975* (Stanford, CA: Stanford University Press, 1982).

Jones, L. P. and I. SaKong, *Government, Business and Entrepreneurship in Economic Development: The Korean Case* (Cambridge, MA: Harvard University Press, 1980).

Ka, C., *Japanese Colonialism in Taiwan: Land Tenure, Development, and Dependency, 1895–1945* (Boulder, CO: Westview Press, 1995).

Klintworth, G., *New Taiwan, New China: Taiwan's Changing Role in the Asia-Pacific Region* (Melbourne: Longman Australia, 1995).

Kojima, K., *Direct Foreign Investment: A Japanese Model of Multinational Business Operations* (New York: Praeger, 1978).

Lai, T., R. H. Myer and W. Wou, *A Tragic Beginning: The Taiwan Uprising of February 28, 1947* (Stanford, CA: Stanford University Press, 1991).

Lairson, T. D. and D. Skidmore, *International Political Economy: The Struggle for Power and Wealth* (Fort Worth, TX: Holt, Rinehart and Winston, Inc., 1993).

Lee, K., *A New History of Korea*, translated by E. W. Wagner with E. J. Shultz (Cambridge, MA: Harvard University Press, 1984).

Linder, S. B., *The Pacific Century: Economic and Political Consequences of Asian-Pacific Dynamism* (Stanford, CA: Stanford University Press, 1986).

Lockwood, W., *The Economic Development of Japan: Growth and Structural Change, 1868–1938* (Princeton, NJ: Princeton University Press, 1954).

Long, S., *Taiwan: China's Last Frontier* (Basingstoke: Macmillan, 1991).

Macdonald, D. S., *U.S.-Korean Relations from Liberation to Self-Reliance: The Twenty-Year Record* (Boulder, CO: Westview Press, 1992).

Maguire, K., *The Rise of Modern Taiwan* (Aldershot, England: Ashgate Publishing Limited, 1998).

Marshal, M., *Organizations and Growth in Rural China* (London: The Macmillan Press Ltd., 1985).

Mason, E. S., M. J. Kim, D. H. Perkins, K. S. Kim and D. C. Cole with L. Jones, I. Sakong, D. R. Snodgrass and N. F. Meginn, *The Economic and Social Modernization of the Republic of Korea* (Cambridge, MA: Harvard University Press, 1980).

Michell, T., *From a Developing to a Newly Industrialized Country: The Republic of Korea, 1961–1982* (Geneva: International Labour Office, 1988).

Nakamura, T., *The Postwar Japanese Economy: Its Development and Structure, 1937–1994*, 2nd edn (Tokyo: University of Tokyo Press, 1995).

Nester, W. R., *Japan's Growing Power over East Asia and the World Economy: Ends and Means* (London: The Macmillan Press Ltd., 1990).

Okimoto, D. I., *Between MITI and Market: Japanese Industrial Policy for High Technology* (Stanford, CA: Stanford University Press, 1989).

Patrick, H. and H. Rosovsky (eds), *Asia's New Giant: How the Japanese Economy Works* (Washington, DC: Brookings Institution, 1976).

Perkins, D., *China: Asia's Next Economic Giant* (Seattle, WA: University of Washington Press, 1986).

Perkins, D. and S. Yusuf, *Rural Development in China* (Baltimore, MD: The Johns Hopkins University Press, 1984, published for the World Bank).

Russett, B. M., *International Regions and International System: A Study in Political Ecology* (Chicago, IL: Rand McNally & Company, 1967).

Schaller, M., *The American Occupation of Japan: The Origins of the Cold War in Asia* (Oxford and New York: Oxford University Press, 1985).

Selden, M., *The Political Economy of Chinese Development* (Armonk, NY: M. E. Sharpe, 1993).

Shen, R., *China's Economic Reform: An Experiment in Pragmatic Socialism* (Westport, CT: Praeger, 2000).

Simone, V., *The Asian Pacific: Political and Economic Development in a Global Context*, 2nd edn (New York: Addison Wesley Longman, Inc., 2001).

Starr, J. B., *Understanding China: A Guide to China's Economy, History, and Political Structure* (New York: Hill and Wang, 1997).

Suh, C., *Growth and Structural Changes in the Korean Economy, 1910–1940* (Cambridge, MA: Council on East Asian Studies, Harvard University, 1978).

Suh, D., *The Korean Communist Movement, 1918–1948* (Princeton, NJ: Princeton University Press, 1967).

Tucker, N. B., *Taiwan, Hong Kong, and the United States, 1945–1992: Uncertain Friendships* (New York: Twayne Publishers, 1994).

Wade, R., *Governing the Market: Economic Theory and the Role of the Government in East Asian Industrialization* (Princeton, NJ: Princeton University Press, 1990).

Waltz, K. N., *Man, the State and War: A Theoretical Analysis* (New York: Columbia University Press, 1954).

Wu, Y., *Becoming an Industrial Nation: ROC's Development on Taiwan* (New York: Praeger, 1985).

Zhang, Z., Huang F. and Li G. (eds), *Twenty Years of Economic Reform: Retrospect and Prospect* (Beijing: China Planning Publishers, 1998).

Articles

Beeson, M, "ASEAN: The Challenges of Organisational Reinvention," in M. Beeson (ed.), *Reconfiguring East Asia: Regional Institutions and Organisations After the Crisis* (London and New York: RoutledgeCurzon, 2002), ch. 10, pp. 185–204.

Bernard, M. and J. Ravenhill, "Beyond Product Cycles and Flying Geese: Regionalization, Hierarchy and the Industrialization of East Asia," *World Politics*, vol. 47, no. 2 (1995) 171–209.

Cai, K. G., "The Political Economy of Economic Regionalism in Northeast Asia: A Unique and Dynamic Pattern," *East Asia: An International Quarterly*, vol. 17, no. 2 (Summer 1999) 6–46.

——, "Outward Foreign Direct Investment: A Novel Dimension of China's Integration into the Regional and Global Economy," *The China Quarterly*, no. 160 (December 1999) 856–80.

——, "Is a Free Trade Zone Emerging in Northeast Asia in the Wake of the Asian Financial Crisis?" *Pacific Affairs*, vol. 74, no. 1 (Spring 2001) 7–24.

——, "The ASEAN-China Free Trade Agreement and East Asian Regional Grouping," *Contemporary Southeast Asia*, vol. 25, no. 3 (2003) 387–404.

——, "Chinese Changing Perspective on the Development of an East Asian Free Trade Area," *The Review of International Affairs*, vol. 3, no. 4 (Summer 2004) 584–99; reprinted in R. C. Keith (ed.), *China as a Rising World Power and its Response to "Globalization"* (London and New York: Routledge, 2005), ch. 5, pp. 78–93.

Choi, K. and Y. S. Lee, "The Role of the Korean Government in Industrialization," in C. H. Lee and I. Yamazawa (eds), *The Economic Development of Japan and Korea: A Parallel With Lessons* (New York: Praeger, 1990), ch. 4, pp. 53–69.

Clark, C., "Political Development, Administrative Capacity, and the Challenge to the Developmental State Model Posed by the 1997–1998 Financial Crisis in East and Southeast Asia," in K. T. Liou (ed.), *Managing Economic Development in Asia: From Economic Miracle to Financial Crisis* (Westport, CT: Praeger Publishers, 2002), ch. 1, pp. 1–38.

Cumings, B., "American Policy and Korean Liberation," in F. Baldwin (ed.), *Without Parallel: The American-Korean Relationship Since 1945* (New York: Pantheon Books, 1974), pp. 39–108.

——, "The Origin and Development of the Northeast Asian Political Economy: Industrial Sectors, Product Cycle, and Political Consequences," *International Organization*, vol. 38, no. 1 (Winter 1984) 1–40.

Dent, C. M., "ASEM and the 'Cinderella Complex' of EU-East Asia Economic Relations," *Pacific Affairs*, vol. 74, no. 1 (2001) 25–52.

Halliday, J., "Capitalism and Socialism in East Asia," *New Left Review*, no. 124 (November–December 1980) 3–24.

Haughton, B., "Between China and the World: Hong Kong's Economy before and after 1997," in G. G. Hamilton (ed.), *Cosmopolitan Capitalists: Hong Kong and the Chinese Diaspora at the End of the 20th Century* (Seattle, WA: University of Washington Press, 1999), ch. 4, pp. 80–99.

Higgott, R, "The Asian Economic Crisis: A Study in the Politics of Resentment," *New Political Economy*, vol. 3, no. 3 (November 1998) 340–6.

Ho, S. P. S., "The Development Policy of the Japanese Colonial Government in Taiwan, 1895–1945," in G. Ranis (ed.), *Government and Economic Development* (New Haven, CT: Yale University press, 1971), ch. 9, pp. 287–328.

——, "Colonialism and Development: Korea, Taiwan, and Kwantung," in R. H. Myers and M. R. Peattie (eds), *The Japanese Colonial Empire, 1895–1945* (Princeton, NJ: Princeton University Press, 1984), ch. 9, pp. 347–98.

Huang, F., "An Analysis on Characteristics and Trends of Direct Investments from Korea (*sic*)," *International Economic Cooperation*, no. 9 (2002) 47–9.

Jervis, R., "The Impact of the Korean War on the Cold War," *Journal of Conflict Resolution*, vol. 24, no. 4 (December 1980) 563–92.

Kang, S., "Macroeconomic Developments and Restructuring," *Korea's Economy 2003*, vol. 19 (Washington, DC: The Korea Economic Institute, 2003), pp. 1–7.

Kim, Y. T., "Neolinberalism and the Decline of the Developmental State," *Journal of Contemporary Asia*, vol. 29, no. 4 (1999) 441–61.

Koo, A. Y. C., "Economic Development of Taiwan," in P. K. T. Sih (ed.), *Taiwan in Modern Times* (New York: St. John's University Press, 1973), ch. 10, pp. 397–433.

Lamley, H. J., "Taiwan Under Japanese Rule, 1895–1945: The Vicissitudes of Colonialism," in M. A. Rubinstein (ed.), *Taiwan: A New History* (Armonk, NY: M.E. Sharpe, Inc., 1999), ch. 8, pp. 201–60.

Lee, C., "Economic Relations between Korea and China," *Korea's Economy 2004*, vol. 20 (Washington, DC: The Korea Economic Institute, 2004), pp. 69–75.

Lincoln, E. J., "Japanese Trade and Investment Issues," in D. Unger and P. Blackburn (eds), *Japan's Emerging Global Role* (Boulder and London: Lynne Rienner Publishers, Inc., 1993), ch. 9, pp. 133–54.

Little, I. M. D., "The Experience and Causes of Rapid Labour-Intensive Development in Korea, Taiwan Province, Hong Kong, and Singapore and the Possibilities of Emulation," in E. Lee (ed.), *Export-Led Industrialisation and Development* (Geneva: International labour Organisation, 1981), ch. 2, pp. 23–45.

Long, N. V., "The East Asian Crisis: Some Historical Roots," *New Political Science*, vol. 21, no. 3 (1999) 395–404.

Maswood, S. J., "Developmental States in Crisis," in Beeson (ed.), *Reconfiguring East Asia: Regional Institutions and Organisations after the Crisis* (New York: RoutledgeCurzon, 2002), ch. 2, pp. 31–48.

Moon, C. and T. Kim, "South Korea's International Relations: Challenges to Developmental Realism," in S. S. Kim (ed.), *The International Relations of Northeast Asia* (Oxford: Rowman & Littlefield Publishers, Inc., 2004), ch. 8, pp. 251–79.

Moore, T. G., "China's International Relations: The Economic Dimension," In Kim (ed.), *The International Relations of Northeast Asia* (Lanham, MD: Rowman & Littlefield Publishers, Inc., 2004), ch. 3, pp. 101–34.

Murphy, R. T., "Power Without Purpose: The Crisis of Japan's Global Financial Dominance," *Harvard Business Review*, no. 2 (March–April 1989) 71–83.

Myers, R. H. and Y. Saburo, "Agricultural Development in the Empire," in Myers and Peattie (eds), *The Japanese Colonial Empire, 1895–1945* (Princeton, NJ: Princeton University Press, 1984), ch. 11, pp. 420–52.

Okabe, M., "The Japanese Economy in Transition: Introduction and Overview," in M. Okabe (ed.), *The Structure of the Japanese Economy: Changes on the Domestic and International Fronts* (New York: St. Martin's Press, 1995), ch. 1, pp. 1–21.

Peattie, M. R., "Introduction," in Myers and Peattie (eds), *The Japanese Colonial Empire, 1895–1945* (Princeton, NJ: Princeton University Press, 1984), ch. 1, pp. 3–52.

Ravenhill, J., "Institutional Evolution at the Trans-Regional Level: APEC and the Promotion of Liberalisation," in Beeson (ed.), *Reconfiguring East Asia: Regional Institutions and Organisations after the Crisis* (London and New York: RoutledgeCurzon, 2002), ch. 12, pp. 227–46.

Shih, V., "Development, the Second Time Around: The Political Logic of Developing Western China," *Journal of East Asian Studies*, vol. 4, no. 3 (2004) 427–51.

Shiraishi, T., "Japan and Southeast Asian," in P. J. Katzenstein and T. Shiraishi (eds), *Network Power: Japan and Asia* (Ithaca: Cornell University Press, 1997), ch. 5, pp. 169–94.

Singh, A. and B. A. Weisse, "The Asian Model: A Crisis Foretold?" *International Social Science Journal*, no. 160 (June 1999) 203–15.

Stubbs, R., "ASEAN Plus Three: Emerging East Asian Regionalism," *Asian Survey*, vol. 42, no. 3 (May/June 2002) 440–55.

Thompson, G., "Introduction: contours of economic development in the Asia-Pacific," in G. Thompson (ed.), *Economic Dynamism in the Asia-Pacific: The*

Growth of Integration and Competitiveness (London and New York: Routledge, 1998), ch. 1, pp. 1–18.

Unger, D., "Japan's capital exports: molding East Asia," in Unger and Blackburn (eds), *Japan's Emerging Global Role* (Boulder and London: Lynne Rienner Publishers, Inc., 1993), ch. 10, pp. 155–70.

Vernon, R., "International Investment and International Trade in the Product Cycle," *Quarterly Journal of Economics*, no. 80 (May 1966) 190–207.

Wade, R., "The Asian Debt-and-Development Crisis of 1997–?: Causes and Consequences," *World Development*, vol. 26, no. 8 (August 1998) 1535–53.

Wakiyama, T., "The Implementation and Effectiveness of MITI's Administrative Guidance," in S. Wilks and M. Wright (eds), *Comparative Government-Industry Relations: Western Europe, the United States, and Japan* (New York: Oxford University Press, 1987), ch. 9, pp. 209–32.

Wang, J., "Taiwan and the Asian Financial Crisis: Impact and Response," in P. C. Y. Chow and B. Gill (eds), *Weathering the Storm: Taiwan, Its Neighbors, and the Asian Financial Crisis* (Washington, DC: Brookings Institution, 2000), ch. 6, pp. 147–68.

Webber, D., "Two Funerals and a Wedding? The Ups and Downs of Regionalism in East Asia and Asia-Pacific after the Asian Crisis," *The Pacific Review*, vol. 14, no. 3 (2001) 339–72.

Weiss, L., "Developmental States in Transition: Adapting, Dismantling, Innovating, not 'Normalizing' ," *The Pacific Review*, vol. 13, no. 1 (2000) 21–55.

Wong, J., "The Adaptive Developmental State in East Asia," *Journal of East Asian Studies*, vol. 4, no. 3 (2004) 345–62.

Newspapers, news weekly and news Websites

Beijing Review
Beijing Youth, http://www.bjyouth.com
China Daily
Far Eastern Economic Review
The Korea Herald
The Korea Times
Kyodo World Service
Los Angeles Times
The San Diego Union-Tribune
Sohu News, http://news.sohu.com
Washington Post, http://www.washingtonpost.com
World News Connection
Yonhap
Zao Bao, http://www.zaobao.com

Index